To Bill

With very best wishes

Morris

CW00746493

VOTING FOR DEMOCRACY

Voting for Democracy

Watershed Elections in Contemporary Anglophone Africa

Edited by
JOHN DANIEL
University of Durban-Westville
ROGER SOUTHALL
Rhodes University
and
MORRIS SZEFTEL
University of Leeds

Ashgate

Aldershot • Brookfield USA • Singapore • Sydney

© John Daniel, Roger Southall and Morris Szeftel 1999

All rights reserved. No part of this publication may be reproduced, stored in a retrieval system or transmitted in any form or by any means, electronic, mechanical, photocopying, recording or otherwise without the prior permission of the publisher.

Published by
Ashgate Publishing Limited
Gower House
Croft Road
Aldershot
Hampshire GU11 3HR
England

Ashgate Publishing Company
Old Post Road
Brookfield
Vermont 05036
USA

Ashgate website: http://www.ashgate.com

British Library Cataloguing in Publication Data
Voting for democracy : watershed elections in contemporary
    anglophone Africa. - (Centre for democratization studies
    series)
    1.Elections - Africa 2.Africa, English-speaking - Politics
    and government
    I.Daniel, John, 1944- II.Southall, Roger J. III.Szeftel,
    Morris
    324.9'6'0329

Library of Congress Cataloging-in-Publication Data
Voting for democracy : watershed elections in contemporary anglophone
    Africa / edited by John Daniel, Roger Southall, and Morris Szeftel.
        p. cm.
    Includes bibliographical references and index.
    ISBN 1-85521-996-4 (hardbound)
        1. Elections--Africa, English-speaking. 2. Democracy--Africa,
    English-speaking. 3. Democratization--Africa, English-speaking.
    I. Daniel, John. II. Southall, Roger. III. Szeftel, Morris.
    JQ1898.V67 1998
    324.96'0917'521--dc21   98-37431
                                                                    CIP

ISBN 1 85521 996 4

Printed and bound in Great Britain by MPG Books Ltd, Bodmin, Cornwall

Contents

List of Tables

List of Contributors

Rok Ajulu is Senior Lecturer in International Politics in the Department of Political Studies, Rhodes University, Grahamstown.

Carolyn Baylies is Senior Lecturer in Sociology in the School of Social Policy and Sociology, and Director of the Centre for Development Studies, University of Leeds.

Diana Cammack has taught about and researched many aspects of politics in southern Africa, including Malawi's elections and the aftermath of war and the plight of refugees in Mozambique.

Lionel Cliffe is Professor of Political Studies in the Department of Politics, University of Leeds.

John Daniel is Professor and Head of the Department of Political Science, University of Durban-Westville.

Chudi Okoye has worked as a journalist and as an academic researcher on the problems of democratic transition in Nigeria.

Donna Pankhurst is Senior Lecturer in the Department of Peace Studies, University of Bradford.

Roger Southall is Professor and Head of the Department of Political Studies, Rhodes University.

Morris Szeftel is Senior Lecturer in the Department of Politics, University of Leeds.

1 Political Crisis and Democratic Renewal in Africa

MORRIS SZEFTEL

The papers in this book examine the context and conduct of a series of watershed elections held in Anglophone Africa between 1989 and 1994. These elections crystallized a wider process of democratization, underway during the last decade, in which attempts were made to shift from various forms of authoritarian rule (colonial or racial oligarchies, military regimes, one-party states, or presidential rule) to pluralist parliamentary politics. Such attempts at democratic renewal were not confined to Africa's former British colonies. Similar efforts were also made during this period in Francophone Africa and in the war-ravaged states of Ethiopia, Eritrea, Uganda, Angola and Mozambique. Indeed, as Bayart has observed, 'from 1989 most sub-Saharan African countries experienced an unprecedented wave of demands for democracy, which succeeded in bringing about the downfall of several authoritarian regimes and forced others to accept multi-party politics' (1993: x). The essays which follow bring together (for the first time) studies of these events in Anglophone countries of the continent, which share a comparable legacy of British colonialism, an acquaintance with the Westminister constitutional tradition, and even some related historical experiences of decolonization and democratic struggle.

The first in the cycle of elections, for a constituent assembly in Namibia in 1989, brought South Africa's seventy year occupation of that country to an end and so created an independent state out of Africa's 'last colony'. The last, South Africa's 'liberation election' of 1994, allowed South Africans of all races to vote in a democratic election for the first time and formally ended three centuries of racial domination and African exclusion. In the years between these two events, a number of other Anglophone countries held elections, not to end colonial rule or settler domination, but to restore competitive, multi-party politics - in some instances twenty or more years after such systems had been abandoned. In the vast majority of these countries the pluralist constitutions established at the end of British colonial rule were progressively undermined by factional conflict and political instability and

1

ultimately abrogated in favour of military rule or one-party regimes. Now, with the restoration of competitive elections and the re-establishment of the right to organize political parties, there was a return to this earlier legacy.

Precisely because they were linked to this wider process of democratization, and gave formal political expression to it, these elections constitute one of the most important political developments in the last quarter-century in Africa (Bratton and van de Walle, 1997: 3). Not all of them produced a successful transition to a democratic order, as the essays that follow demonstrate. Democratic elections and democratic reform proved neither inevitable nor unproblematic. Yet, if anything, in a continent devastated by international debt, war and violence, famine and disease, corruption and political instability, the attempt at reform was all the more significant where it occured and its achievements, however modest, the more noteworthy. Not surprisingly, therefore, it was initially universally welcomed by all but those whose control of office it threatened. Observers from most parts of the ideological spectrum hoped it might open up constitutional space for democratic forces and pressures for equitable development. Radical Africanists emphasised the opportunities that democratic struggles created for greater equality and social justice in Africa (*The Review of African Political Economy*, numbers 45/46, 1989 and 54, 1992; Gibbon, Bangura and Ofstad, 1992). Mainstream liberals explored the prospects for the development of multi-party systems and liberal institutions, the influence of external actors and the role of civil society (Healey and Robinson, 1992). And African scholars (encouraged by research organizations such as Codesria and OSSREA) focused particularly on questions of development, class, human rights and security (Anyang 'Nyong'o, 1992; Imam, 1992). Democratization produced a new, if temporary, optimism and a justified pride in achievement among those on the continent who fought so hard for it.

The process was far from even and - by the end of the 1990s - generally incomplete. As the century moved to its end, many difficult struggles still lay ahead and many of the gains made proved temporary or modest in their impact. Not all these elections successfully established democratic parliamentary systems. In Nigeria, the process was aborted while the votes were still being counted. In Lesotho, the settling of old scores, between the parties and between the military and the parties, undermined the transition. In Kenya, the elections were won by the old order and new democratic forces finished in disarray - as was to happen in subsequent elections five years later. Even where elections did change the government and where political systems based on ideas of freedom of association and electoral competition were successfully introduced, reform often became mired in the problems of economic underdevelopment. Moreover, the circumstances in which democratization occured, of economic and social crisis, and of state instability, remain capable of undermining every gain. Perhaps most worryingly, there was little evidence that the nature of African politics, rooted in clientelism and the manipulation of communal identities, had changed enough to sustain the momentum of democratization. Thus the prospects for democratization raised wider issues than could be resolved by any single election, however important. As Nelson Mandela put it, after the 1994 elections in South Africa: 'We have not taken the final step of our journey, but the first step on a longer and even more difficult road.' (1994:751).

Democratization and its Alternatives

Democratic elections in Anglophone countries were largely confined to the southern and eastern sub-continent, in states occupying a crescent stretching from the south-western Atlantic coast (Namibia and South Africa) to the eastern equatorial coast (Kenya). Anglophone states in West African fared far less well: in Nigeria, elections were aborted; in Ghana, economic liberalization measures were carried out by a decidedly illiberal regime; and in Sierra Leone, the state collapsed into chaos and civil war. Yet, despite these geographic limits, democratization and democratizing elections affected most regimes, even those who most strenuously resisted it: first, by exciting mass hopes for change; and, then, by imposing pressures on regimes to promise (and appear to) change even where they worked to undermine it. Thus, the Nigerian military, after setting aside the presidential election of 1993 and imprisoning its victor, still felt impelled to promise that it would restore democracy. Thus, too, where 'in 1989, 29 African countries were governed under some kind of single-party constitution, and one-party rule seemed entrenched as the modal form of governance', by 1994 'not a single de jure one-party state remained in Africa' (Bratton and van de Walle, 1997: 8).

Whether there was a genuine processes of democratization, or whether it was merely a smokescreen behind which the old order continued, depended on the specific nature of the process, the political forces involved in it and the role played by the government and ruling party. In Benin, for instance, students and public sector workers forced the single-party regime to cede power at a national conference of representative groups (Allen, 1992). While, the President remained in office, most of his old powers were transferred to a Prime Minister (chosen by the conference) and an interim government. Subsequently Benin developed a multi-party system, the ruling party was dissolved, and none of its surviving fragments participated in the 1991 elections. The use of a national conference to effect constitutional change was a feature of some Francophone states. A rather different sequence can be seen in the Anglophone countries which are the subject of this volume. In Zambia and Kenya, the conference stage was by-passed by the emergence of a loose coalition (the MMD in Zambia, FORD in Kenya) which quickly came to act as the dominant opposition party. In Zambia, the MMD easily defeated the former ruling party in an election; in Kenya, by contrast, the ruling party retained power after an electoral contest against a fragmented opposition (Ajulu, 1993; Baylies and Szeftel, 1992; chapters 5 and 6, below).

Across the continent, in fact, a full transfer of power to the opposition was rare. Opposition boycotts and divisions often ensured victory for the ruling party by default and, where these were absent, electoral manipulation often did so instead. In the Ivory Coast and Gabon, for example, after demonstrations had forced concessions, elections were called before opposition groups could become fully organized and the state's legal and financial resources were used to ensure a victory by the ruling party. And finally, where all else failed, there were cases of the military acting to protect its own interests and those of the ruling establishment. In Togo, as in Lesotho and Nigeria, the army sought to force a reversal of elections, restore some or all of the governing party's powers and legal status, and exclude certain groups from power (Allen, Baylies and Szeftel, 1992: 6-7).

The uneven nature of this process of political transformation makes it possible to group African states in one of four main categories according to their experience of political change in the last quarter century. The first would include those states which underwent some form of liberal democratization process, involving a shift towards a more pluralistic, less authoritarian political order and some overt commitment to increasing human rights and strengthening the rule of law (Allen, Baylies and Szeftel, 1992: 3-10). A second, residual, group would include the dwindling number of states largely untouched by the process, either because long standing multi-party states had previously been established (as in Botswana) or because demands for democratic change were not yet powerful enough to force reform (as in Zimbabwe and Swaziland) or because the process had yet to begin (as in Libya and Morocco).

The third group comprised states where armed rebellions engineered the violent overthrow of corrupt and repressive regimes with the promise to begin building representative institutions and effective government. The group includes Uganda, the most successful so far, and Ethiopia and Eritrea (where significant democratic gains were challenged in the late nineties by territorial conflict between the two states). In Rwanda, Burundi and the former Zaire (renamed the Democratic Republic of Congo) efforts to undertake similar post-bellum reform was blocked by continuing communal violence and the ambitions of predatory elites. These three countries demonstrate some of the characteristics of the fourth group, those states where central institutions disintegrated, or were disintegrating, under the weight of rampant corruption and open looting of public resources, communal violence and civil war. In such cases, the central state either became merely one faction in a murderous struggle for power (as in Sudan, Liberia, Sierra Leone and Congo-Brazzaville) or gave way entirely to the sway of competing warlords (as in Chad and Somalia). The four categories were not entirely exclusive of each other: Rwanda, Burundi and Zaire demonstrated the fine line between renewal through insurrection and collapse into warlordism and communal violence, just as Nigeria teetered between the democratic transition its citizens demanded (and voted for) and violent military repression.

The narrowness of the divide between democratic reform and state 'collapse' further underlines the importance of these watershed elections. However limited the democratic reforms to which they gave expression proved to be in some instances, the elections represented a progressive and positive step away from the political crises which affected so much of the continent. That they were undertaken at all, against the tide of crisis and disintegration, made their achievements all the more noteworthy.

The International Dimensions of Crisis and Democratization

Because the democratic reforms which affected Africa in the early nineties coincided with (and were influenced by) wider international events, there was a tendency to perceive them as local manifestations of a 'global democratic resurgence' which signalled the historic triumph of liberal democracy. The fall of the Berlin Wall in 1989, after all, preceded by only a few weeks the speech by President De Klerk in February 1990 which signalled the end of apartheid and the beginning of a democratic transition in South Africa. Indeed, De Klerk's initiative was quite clearly timed to take advantage of the universal optimism about the prospects for reform which flowed from the events in Berlin. Zambia's 1991 elections, which produced the first change of ruling party and president since independence in 1964, and one of the first occasions in which power changed hands without violence in post-colonial Africa, came less than two months after the collapse of the Soviet Union. For Huntington, these events were part of 'democracy's third wave', a democratic tide starting around 1974, comparable to two earlier 'waves' (the first running from the 1820s to 1926, the second from 1945 to 1962). The 'third wave', argued Huntington (1996: 4), was the result of a number of related factors, including: unprecedented global economic growth in the 1960s which increased wealth, education and the size of the urban middle classes; the 'anti-authoritarian' stance of the Catholic Church in the sixties; decreasing support for authoritarianism among the major powers; the loss of legitimacy of authoritarian regimes as a result of performance failures and the increasing universality of democratic values; and the contagion of early democratic transitions which encouraged others to follow. Above all, the changes of the nineties could be seen to represent

> the utter 'self-discrediting' of communist systems and of such other dictatorial regimes as 'African socialism' and 'bureaucratic authoritarianism'. As a result, antidemocratic forces ... have been weakened throughout the world, democracy has been left 'with no serious geopolitical or ideological rivals', and democrats have regained their self confidence. In fact, as Plattner argues, liberal democracies today are widely regarded as 'the only truly and fully modern societies' (Diamond and Plattner,1996:ix).

Yet, if a few celebrated liberalism's triumph as 'the end of history' (Fukuyama, 1989), most were less sanguine about its prospects. In 1992, Jowitt, for example, warned of the need to 'think of a "long march" rather than a simple transition to democracy' (1996: 35). Similarly, Huntington noted that both the first and second 'waves' had each been followed by a 'reverse wave' which had reduced the number of functioning democracies. Similarly, he considered that a new reverse wave had begun to check the momentum of democratic reform from 1990 (1996: 8-11). Bratton and van de Walle, too, considered that

> the entire wave of regime transition in Africa passed its zenith during 1993, as the emergence of fragile democracies in a few countries began to be offset by a rehardening of political regimes elsewhere (1997: 6).

Political reform, and the problems which confronted it, in turn promoted concern with the needs of the reform process itself, particularly with the kind of institutional changes which might best advance democratization. Some focused on problems of promoting economic development capable of supporting democratic reform (Diamond, 1992). Some were concerned with the impact on democratization of economic liberalization (O'Donnell, 1996).

Others debated the relative merits of parliamentary and presidential political systems (see the essays by Linz and Horowitz, in Diamond and Plattner, 1996). Many were concerned with the need to develop the network of associational activity generally regarded as constituting the 'civil society' necessary to promote active citizenship and limit state authoritarianism (Diamond, 1996a: 230-4). If there was little unanimity about the specific nature of the measures that needed to be taken, there was, nevertheless, a general underlying sense that it was necessary to support political reform if it was to be consolidated and sustained.

In this respect, academic observers anticipated and then reflected the mood among policy-makers in Western capitals and multilateral financial institutions, particularly the World Bank. Initially, these officials were not always consistent in their support for democratic change in Africa. In some countries, they supported ruling groups (as in Benin, Algeria or Zaire) or pressed them to undertake more or less cosmetic reforms (as in South Africa). In others, they actively promoted or assisted democratic pressures. In Kenya, the US ambassador actually held press conferences condemning the government's poor democratic record and demanding multi-party elections. In Zambia, donors pressed the incumbent regime to hold elections, and even forced it to implement unpopular economic measures during the election campaign. They then welcomed the new government's willingness to implement economic restructuring and debt servicing 'conditionalities'. It is perhaps this identification of economic with political reform that explains greater Western enthusiasm for certain regime changes. Alongside 'economic conditionalities', requiring African states to restructure their economies by implementing 'structural adjustment', introducing market reforms, and reducing the proportion of national wealth controlled by the state (Szeftel, 1987), there developed, from the mid-eighties, a set of parallel 'political conditionalities', requiring democratic reforms to promote 'good governance' (Baylies, 1995). These 'conditionalities' had, by the mid-nineties, become a major feature of relations between indebted African governments and their creditors, or 'donor community' as they had come to be called.

At the same time, academic prescriptions and international interventions to promote liberal democratization attracted criticism from scholars who considered that the undertaking was less concerned to promote African democracy than to further Western interests. The bulk of this radical criticism was concerned with the strategy and socio-economic effects of structural adjustment and economic liberalization (see, for instance, Loxley and Seddon, 1994; Leys, 1994; Bush and Szeftel, 1994; Campbell and Parfitt, 1995; Bromley, 1995). Increasingly it was augmented by a critique of liberal democratic reforms as being inappropriate or inadequate instruments for democratization in developing countries. Some questioned the usefulness of imposing liberal conceptual labels, such as 'civil society', on African circumstances (Mamdani, 1996; Allen, 1997). Others questioned the purpose and objectives of the entire project. Contrasting earlier attempts to forge a theory of political development with recent work on democratization, Cammack, for instance, argued that liberal scholars too often abandoned academic detachment in favour of missionary zeal in the 1990s:

> where the theorists of the 1960s found themselves in an impasse in which they could formulate a model of stable liberal democracy but felt unable to recommend its implementation, those of today are avid exponents of the dissemination of democracy. The result has been the proliferation of frankly programmatic procedural guides to the installation of pro-Western liberal democracies in the Third World ... (Cammack, 1997: 224).

For Cammack, this doctrine was less a means of supporting local efforts to build democracy than 'a transitional programme for the installation and consolidation of capitalist regimes in the Third World' (ibid: 1). In order to promote this liberal model, he wrote, the concept of democracy was reduced to procedural issues, notably periodic competitive elections held under universal adult suffrage; thus, Huntington, for one, rejected 'the automatic association of democracy with other values such as social justice, equality, liberty, fulfilment and progress' (ibid: 224).

These objections were echoed by the late Claude Ake's dismissal of recent democratization efforts in Africa as 'largely a matter of form rather than content' (1995: 70). Accusing the IMF and World Bank of 'effectively redefining democratization as economic liberalization' (ibid: 82), Ake asserted that, despite his belief that it was 'the lack of democratic politics ... which is at the root of the African crisis',

> the ascendancy of form over content results in a significant blockage to democratization. For the people of Africa, instead of emancipating them, democratization is becoming a legitimation of their disempowerment. They are effectively worse off than they were before democratization, for their alienation from power and their oppression are no longer visible as problems inviting solutions (ibid: 70).

Ake's sense that democratization actually 'disempowered' the vast majority of Africans, spoke specifically to the fears of many that international sponsorship of democracy was concerned with achieving the form of state most conducive to debt repayment and closer integration of Africa into global markets than with mass empowerment and expansion of citizenship. It also directed attention to the less benign ways in which international influences had shaped Africa's history over three centuries. It reflected not only the uncertain nature of democratization in Africa but also, and more importantly, the differences and conflicts between, on the one hand, international efforts to promote democracy on the continent as part of wider global reforms and, on the other, African efforts to produce democratic reform consonant with indigenous aspirations.

Despite the undoubted importance of processes of globalization and of related international developments which encouraged and supported demands for reform, recent struggles to democratize - and African politics in general - cannot be reduced to a reflection of what unfolded in Eastern Europe or an imitation of the recent success of market liberalism in the West. The case studies in this volume demonstrate clearly how any understanding of the watershed elections of the nineties must be based on an examination of the struggles between key local interests: students, trade unionists, professionals, intellectuals, certain business interests, the media, women, the urban poor, small farmers and the churches among those challenging the government; and, resisting them, the ruling group, their business associates and their external allies. As the case studies demonstrate, 'the specifically African dynamics were perhaps more decisive' and the 'influence of the events of Eastern Europe [and elsewhere] more limited' than is often believed (Bayart, 1993: x-xi). We need to look beyond events in Eastern Europe when we ask why pluralism was so easily and quickly discarded a generation earlier and why demands for multi-party democracy became so difficult to resist in the nineties.

The Roots of Political Crisis and Authoritarianism

Starting with Ghana's independence in 1957, British colonialism rapidly withdrew from Africa. Its legacy was universal adult suffrage, competitive elections for a unicameral legislature, a multi-party political system and - the one departure from the Westminster model - a powerful executive presidency.[1] By the late sixties, the colonial state survived only in its settler form, in Rhodesia until 1980, in South Africa and, indirectly, in South West Africa, where white settlers controlled government and resisted democratic demands by force. For all its ubiquity, however, post-colonial democracy was a fragile construct. In almost all former British colonies, the multi-party state was in reality a dominant-party state. One party, enjoying overwhelming support at independence (further consolidated with the resources provided by office) confronted a small, often divided, often regionalised opposition lacking resources and any real prospect of power. Botswana apart, this seldom endured for long. In Tanzania, the predominance of TANU created a *de facto* one-party state from the start. In Malawi, Kenya, Zambia, Ghana and Sierra Leone, the dominant party, under a powerful executive president, ensured some degree of political stability for a time before giving way to one-party or military authoritarianism. In Ghana, it was replaced by a one-party state and then a military junta in less than a decade. In Sierra Leone the dominant party was replaced by the opposition after elections before the latter was consumed by corruption, military intervention and, finally, state collapse. In Malawi, Kenya and Zambia, it was replaced by one-party states, characterised by increasing authoritarianism, economic stagnation and corruption. Where this dominant party was absent from the outset, as in Lesotho, or where the excluded political interests constituted a large and strategic proportion of the population, as in Nigeria and Uganda, conflict and instability characterised the state from its inception and military rule (rather than one-party civilian regimes) quickly overwhelmed the civil political order. Save for Botswana, multi-partyism had essentially disappeared in Anglophone Africa by the early seventies. Moreover, few one-party or military regimes ruled without the use of emergency powers, preventive detention, draconian labour regulations and the suspension of civil liberties or the rule of law.

There are many reasons for the failure of liberal democratic politics but the complex inter-relationship of three factors were of particular importance: economic underdevelopment, the nature of the inherited state, and the pattern of political mobilization in post-colonial Africa. The first of these has been explored in numerous places so that it is enough here merely to recall the legacy of slavery, colonialism, export cash cropping, plantation production, mineral extraction and migrant labour regimes, all of which entrenched the economies of individual African countries in a wider, international division of labour within which each acted as a specialized supplier of primary export commodities. These economies were characteristically highly skewed and vulnerable to international economic changes and fluctuations. This extreme *dependence* on the expansion and contraction of the global economy (Dos Santos, 1970) was complemented by the level of *unevenness* in their economic and social development. Uneven development took many forms, among them: the combination of declining peasant subsistence economies with multinational export production; extreme inequalities of income; the *differential incorporation* of different regions and ethnic groups into different roles in the economy and the state; and the exclusion of vast numbers of the indigenous population from ownership of property, capital, skills and market opportunities through institutionalized racism (Szeftel, 1987).

The problems confronting the African post-colonial state were rooted in these economic circumstances. Historical experience suggested that it was unlikely that the market forces which had produced these conditions would, once independence was attained, mysteriously reverse themselves without the state actively forcing a change of direction. Moreover, the association of the market and private property with racial discrimination meant that the state was central to African aspirations; political power was regarded as the mechanism by which development and individual opportunities for jobs and upward mobility would be achieved. The state was seen by many as the means to redress past discrimination and promote private wealth.

> Nationalist movements awakened and played on popular dreams of transformation and justice. They mobilized people in the name of democracy and parliamentarism ... and committed their future programmes to economic growth and development (Szeftel, 1987: 118).

This placed a huge burden on the African state:

> It is the state to which nationalist aspirations were directed, the state which thus became the locus of struggles to redefine the relationship of particular societies with international capitalism, and the state to which various groups and interests looked for redress ... (ibid.).

The peculiar conjuncture of colonial exclusion, nationalist promises and political independence thus produced almost limitless expectations of government, both to intervene in the economy to redistribute entitlements and to provide jobs, loans, contracts and favours through political patronage.

Unfortunately, the state was not equipped to bear this burden. Economic underdevelopment and heavy dependence on primary exports gave it an uncertain revenue base which constantly undermined development strategies. More importantly, the nature of the post-colonial state, and specifically the institutions inherited from its colonial predecessor, were entirely inappropriate for the project of social renewal. Lacking established democratic institutions, and run by an alien bureaucracy, the colonial state was designed to ensure order and facilitate the production of export commodities, not to respond to the democratic demands grafted onto it or to expand the content of citizenship.

The order that it represented was based on patterns of differentiation and exclusion which did not transfer positively to pluralist democratic politics. Mamdani identifies the colonial state as a 'bifurcated' system of power, dividing Africans between those who experienced urban racial discrimination and those subjected to rural 'Native Authorities':

> The African colonial experience came to be crystallized in the nature of the state ... Organized differently in rural areas from urban ones, that state was Janus-faced, bifurcated. It contained a duality: two forms of power under a single hegemonic authority. Urban power spoke the language of civil society and civil rights, rural power of community and culture. Civil power claimed to protect rights, customary power pledged to enforce tradition (Mamdani, 1996: 18).

One form, *direct rule*, involved the 'comprehensive sway of market institutions' alongside the exclusion of Africans from civil rights. The other, *indirect rule*, in which 'land remained a communal possession' and the 'market was restricted to the products of labour' exercised power through 'Native Authorities':

> direct and indirect rule actually evolved into complementary ways of native control. Direct rule was the form of urban civil power. It was about the exclusion of natives from civil freedoms guaranteed to citizens in civil society. Indirect rule, however, signified a rural tribal authority. It was about incorporating natives into a state-enforced customary order. Reformulated, direct and indirect rule are better understood as variants of despotism: the former centralized, the latter decentralized (ibid.: 18).

Political independence reinforced both the authoritarian character of the state and the duality of African incorporation into civil and political life. By creating powerful central executives, the independence constitutions ensured that presidential authority would dominate post-colonial legislatures (despite them being chosen by universal suffrage in competitive elections), restrain popular demands for welfare spending and control radical pressures for fundamental changes in economic direction. Despite the tendency by some to see the post-colonial state as reflecting traditional African deference to 'The Big Man' or as an expression of 'neo-patrimonialism' (Bayart, 1993: 70-83; Bratton and van de Walle, 1997: 63-5), presidentialism was, in fact, primarily rooted in the nature of the post-colonial transition.

The tendency towards authoritarianism was underpinned also by the way in which independence incorporated the urban-rural dichotomy into the politics of electoral competition. Drawing on the contrasting experiences of Uganda and South Africa, Mamdani argued that nationalist politicians addressed themselves to the problem of 'deracializing' urban civil society without tackling the question of 'detribalizing' the rural areas. By failing to free rural 'subjects' from the yoke of 'tribal' Native Authorities, nationalist politicians ensured the continued domination of the rural population by traditional communal authorities and denied it the opportunity to take their place in the post-colonial order as individual 'citizens'. This omission, he suggests, not only disadvantaged the peasantry but also, fundamentally, 'contaminated' the process of democratization itself (Mamdani, 1996: 289 and passim). By incorporating the peasantry into party politics without first freeing them from the 'decentralized despotism' of tribal authorities, Mamdani suggests that African politics was 'tribalized' rather than 'democratized'.

This formulation helps to explain why 'civil society' has so singularly lacked autonomy in post-colonial Africa and why ethnic forms of political organization have been so ubiquitous and powerful. LeVine (1993: 276) identifies 'civil society' as an intermediate layer of associational structures occupying the space between the state, on the one hand, and ethnic and kinship networks, on the other. In this conception, 'civil society' refers to the organizations and interests which act to influence public policy and moderate the authoritarian tendencies of community and state. The development of a network of such associations serves to underpin a fundamental feature of liberal democracies, namely the distinction between the public and private domains. Mamdani's argument, in contrast, highlights the failure to incorporate rural voters into the political realm through anything resembling the active, organized citizenship of 'civil society'. Instead, the franchise meant that ethnic identity was catapulted directly into the electoral arena and into the considerations driving state policy. The test of public performance became how well it served particularistic interests.

In a landmark contribution, and working from a different perspective, Allen has examined this process in the transition to independence and beyond, arguing that Britain and France organized a rapid process of decolonization so as to ensure that radical elements lacked the time and resources to develop a strong grassroots base. This permitted the transfer of power to conservative nationalist leaders prepared to guarantee key economic interests. Moreover, 'independence elections' were called at short notice,

> requiring nationalist organizations to mobilize huge new electorates in a very short time. Those that succeeded had combined two strategies for party building and creation of electoral support: a reliance on individuals who

already had considerable local followings, and the use of clientelist ('patronage') politics to bind local notables to the party and local voters to the candidates. In essence, voters were offered collective material benefits (roads, schools, clinics, water, etc) for their votes, while candidates and notables were offered individual benefits (cash, access to licences, credit or land, etc) ... . This combination produced a set of locally-based MPs ... responsive to local demands, and loosely organized into parties whose leaders had access to private or public resources (Allen, 1995: 304).

Political mobilization thus rested on clientelist politics in which local power brokers were incorporated into national political movements and electoral support was exchanged for access to state resources. Moreover, communal land tenure ensured that African clientelism did not rest on the traditional patron-client relationship between landlord and tenant, in the way it had in South Asia, southern Europe or Latin America. Instead it was mobilized through the politicization of identity, using traditional authorities and local notables. Political factions, speaking for ethnic or regional interests, articulated demands and measured entitlements in what came to be called the politics of 'tribalism'. Even in the cities, where rapid inward migration ensured the rise of 'political machines' and local 'bosses', patterns of migrant labour recruitment established in the colonial economy tended to integrate these urban networks into ethnic and regional factions.

Clientelism in this form was extremely unstable. Underdevelopment of the economy meant that governments could not deliver the 'development goods' necessary to satisfy mass expectations. Popular disappointment put pressure on faction leaders to intensify their demands on the centre for an increased share of resources for their region or group, or face being replaced by those who would. Nor was it possible for the central leadership to satisfy all factions when distributing offices and resources. Thus post-colonial politics was characterized by intense factional competition for patronage and by conflicts between factions which frequently became public and acrimonious, producing governmental crises and intensifying communal rivalries. Disappointed leaders could represent their personal frustrations as a snub for an entire region or ethnic group. In these circumstances, multi-party politics allowed dissatisfied factions to threaten the centre with withdrawal to join the opposition, taking with them their regional or ethnic support. Thus, even the largest government majorities were fragile, vulnerable to wholesale defections. It is instructive that, amongst the earliest legislation enacted in Kenya and Zambia, were statutes that tied parliamentary seats to the party that had won them in an election. MPs crossing the floor were required to vacate their seat and fight a by-election if they wished to continue to represent the constituency. While such measures may have moderated the competition for 'spoils' between warring factions, they were unable to control it or to check the corruption that inevitably arose as a result.

Over time, African governments became preoccupied with the need to manage patronage, a need which made them intolerant of debate within their own ranks and increasingly inclined to use presidential power to impose a centrally-determined distribution of patronage on all factions. Attempts to manage patronage had varying degrees of success, depending on the nature of the state and central authority (Allen, Baylies and Szeftel, 1992) but all involved the growth of authoritarianism and the abandonment of the pluralist constitutions inherited at independence. Two particular outcomes are worth noting here. The first, and commonest, we can call *bureaucratic centralism* (Allen, 1995: 305-7). In typical cases (such as Zambia, Tanzania and Kenya) this had four main elements: the continuation of clientelism under central control; the centralization of power in an executive presidency standing above factional competition; the subordination of party politics to a bureaucracy answerable to the presidency, particularly with regard to the distribution of patronage; and the downgrading of representative institutions relative to presidential appointments, including the absorption of much of civil society by the state. The one-party state was the ultimate expression of a process of 'government' replacing 'politics'. The strategy worked well for a time but became increasingly ineffective in the 1980s and finally collapsed almost everywhere. The economic crisis which affected Africa from the mid-seventies, and the rising burden of international debt and increasing austerity which followed in its wake, produced mounting opposition to one-party rule and centralized authoritarianism among a growing middle class of intellectual, professional, trade union, business and other urban groups, all demanding political rights.

The second category, in sharp contrast, involved a smaller number of states in which there was no resolution (however temporary) of clientelist crisis, a process of political restructuring did not occur and competition for resources created a *spoils system*. In some cases, Nigeria and Zaire being examples, political competition was controlled by force and spoils politics briefly institutionalized to allow ruling 'kleptocracies' to plunder state resources for their personal benefit and that of the dominant regional or ethnic interests in the country. More often such states lacked the requisite repressive capacity to achieve even this temporary degree of control, or were unable to consolidate one-party rule, with the result that a 'winner takes all' struggle for spoils ensued, producing intensified corruption, political repression and violence, and tribalism and factionalism in extreme forms in many or all institutions (Allen, 1995: 307-10). In the majority of such cases, the integrity of the state itself came to be threatened, state institutions became consumed by looting of their resources and the state itself began to disintegrate (as in Uganda or Sierra Leone). In such cases, populist revolt (as in Ghana and Uganda) was occasionally an alternative to uncontrolled political violence, civil war and state collapse (Sierra Leone, Sudan, Somalia and Liberia).

Once African economies began to contract from the mid 1970s, clientelist politics could not be sustained. Populations suffering the hardships imposed by debt and structural adjustment became increasingly critical of the shrinking patronage dispensed by an authoritarian state and of the ageing leaders who managed its dispersal while enriching themselves. Moreover, such arrangements could no longer be defended in meetings with international creditors insistent on fundamental economic and political reform as a pre-condition for further assistance. By the end of the 1980s, with the Cold War over, the collapse of these regimes was inevitable. Such pressures tended either to hasten the disintegration of those states consumed by spoils politics (Sierra Leone and Liberia, for example) or to attempt rigidly controlled and unsuccessful experiments in democratization (as in Nigeria). In contrast, the bureaucratic centralist systems were generally better able to undertake reform and begin a process of democratization. The majority of the case studies that follow in this volume began their democratic transitions and organized their watershed elections from this bureaucratic centralist base.

The Prospects for Democratization

The preceding analysis indicates the fundamental nature of the problems which confronted African states at independence and thus permits an understanding of the difficulties that confronted reformers before and after the democratic elections of the 1990s. In the enthusiasm for 'good governance' and multi-party elections, it is important to recall that many African states became independent with pluralist political systems and constitutions in place. Yet few of these survived the first decade of independence. The African leaders who imposed one-party regimes were not all charlatans or despots by inclination. Some considered one-party systems as necessary for development and stability; some even saw in them the possibilities for *increasing* grass-roots democracy and safeguarding the mass of citizens from the corruption of elites. While such structures became instruments for consolidating power and prohibiting opposition, they also undoubtedly reflected an attempt to wrestle with political and economic crisis, as we have seen. In this sense they were products of historical circumstance. It is appropriate to ask if these circumstances have now changed and if new conditions exist which will better support democracy in the new millennium than in the 1960s.

On the positive side, the indications are that there was greater support for liberal democratic values at the end of the century than there had been a generation earlier. The growth of 'civil society' over thirty years fostered the middle class groups which placed a high value on democratic institutions. As the authoritarian state ceased to be able to ensure growth or patronage, these groups increasingly asserted their autonomy from the state and demanded democratization. The institutional level of development of churches, trade unions, business interests, students and the urban intelligentsia became a fundamental factor in the late 1980s and early 1990s in driving the process of democratic renewal.

Nor had this momentum run its course once the democratizing elections were over. Even where successful multi-party elections were held, popular pressures to extend and strengthen democratic institutions and procedures continued and ruling groups (including those brought to power by democratic demands) resisted any further extension. Demands for electoral reform, for a reduction of presidential power and expansion of parliamentary sovereignty, for effective anti-corruption measures, for stronger human rights safeguards, for a more equal resourcing of political parties, have all continued to dominate debate in Africa as they did at the time of the elections. Such debates further underline the important role of these elections in legitimating the democratic agenda.

Yet the problems which undermined both the first generation of multi-party states and the one-party regimes that followed them remain and endanger the gains of the 1990s. Firstly, the elections left the structures of the old politics largely untouched. Politics continued to be concerned with access to state office and resources rather than with ideology and programme. Clientelism and the scramble for spoils even intensified after the elections. In turn, this reduced the early enthusiasm of new governments for constitutional reform, particularly for the dilution of presidential power. It also provoked instances of government repression of civic organizations pressing for further change. Secondly, the democratic reforms of the 1990s were undertaken in the context of continuing debt and economic restructuring which imposed severe hardship on the mass of the population. This had potentially damaging consequences both for the prospects of extending democratic rights beyond a small middle class, and for legitimating democracy in the eyes of workers and peasants (Mamdani, 1996; Rueschemeyer, Stephens, and Stephens, 1992).

Thus, if democracy is to be consolidated in Africa, it will have to be done under hostile conditions. The weakness of civil society makes democratization vulnerable to the destructive effects of what Bayart called 'the politics of the belly' which, in turn, confines democratic politics to a narrow, elite circle and so weakens its relevance to the wider African society. Fundamental to prospects for consolidating the legacy of the multi-party elections will be the development of institutional forms capable of extending meaningful participation to the rural population and the urban poor. There thus remains a long and difficult road towards democracy which has yet to be travelled. As Allen puts it (1995: 319):

> If African states are to regain some of their autonomy, then there will have to be a second and more radical wave of innovation, this time directed ... towards stable, decentralized and democratic systems, at regional, national and subnational levels. Western agencies and African leaders, who have been so thoroughly implicated in past failures, can provide neither guidance nor initiative in this process. Those are far more likely to come from within civil society, which already has experience of coping with the breakdown of centralized-bureaucratic systems, and of the far more difficult task of the reconstruction of civil and political life in the aftermath of terminal spoils politics.

The elections examined in this volume were thus but a first step on the path of democratic reform. Nevertheless, they were an important, even essential, first step, away from 'terminal spoils politics' and state collapse. Even where the elections produced limited democratic progress, even where they were aborted, as in Nigeria, they nevertheless put democracy and pluralist competition on the political agenda and provided African voters with a rare opportunity to express their opinions on the matter. Their verdict was unequivocal: in every case, they voted for democracy.

Note

1. The blending of an executive presidency into the post-colonial settlement served to strengthen the power of the central state against possible challenge by centrifugal regional forces and radical elements within the nationalist movements. It thus suited the outgoing colonial administration, the nationalist leadership and foreign and settler economic interests.

2 Electoral Systems and Democratization in Africa

ROGER SOUTHALL

This discussion of electoral systems and democratization will build upon a reviving interest in constitutions and constitutionalism in Africa. Such concerns rather fell away under the rule of political economy, as scholars sought the causes of political decay in Africa in underdevelopment, imperialism, class struggles, parasitic statism, militarism and so on. However, a renewed focus upon political structures, and the impact they have on political behaviour, has been an inevitable and necessary accompaniment of the study and processes of democratization in Africa, and of a new round of constitution-making. Even so, such debates have entailed only a rather limited focus upon the possibilities opened up by alternative electoral systems.

This is not to overlook the fact that it was common for early works on African politics to cite the differential impact of French and British metropolitan constitutional models upon their ex-colonies. Nonetheless, serious comparative discussion of electoral systems was rare - despite Arthur Lewis's famous dictum about the inappropriateness of the British electoral system in African conditions (Lewis, 1965:71). Nor is it to deny that there was overwhelming agreement about the importance of the evolution of electoral institutions for the development of nationalism and the emergence of political parties. Yet it is to argue that the principal thrust of electoral analysis in Africa has been two-fold. First, as elaborated most comprehensively by Chazan (1979), it has distinguished between categories of elections, whether they have been competitive (providing for the possibility of change of both office-holders and the regime in power), semi-competitive (providing for competition for legislative offices but not for control of government or the regime) or non-competitive (designed to secure the return of officeholders without competition for either offices or control of government). Second, it has sought to identify the various functions performed by elections, whether these have been competitive or otherwise (Hayward, 1987).

In so far as the regular abuse of the electoral process in Africa directed scholarly attention towards study of the one-party state, or to the military and so on, this was wholly understandable. However, the recent wave of democracy in Africa provides an important opportunity for isolating the impact of alternative electoral systems upon political outcomes and the prospects for democracy. In short, with the recent addition to their ranks of Namibia and South Africa, the Anglophone African countries whose elections are studied in this book now include amongst their ranks exemplars of both plurality and proportional electoral systems.

Reynolds (1995) has already capitalised upon this development to argue that:

> The evidence from the emerging democracies of southern Africa strongly suggests that divided societies need proportional representation (PR) rather than plurality elections, and a parliamentary rather than a presidential form of government. A simple parliamentary-PR system, however, is not enough: these fragile democracies are better served by a type of PR that maximizes the geographic representativeness of MPs, as well as their accountability to the voters.

Such a proposal clearly recognises that there is much more to democratization than competitive elections and multi-partyism. As Beetham (1994) argues, an undue concentration upon the electoral process leaves out much else that is important to democracy, such as the control by those elected over the executive and non-elected powers. Nonetheless, so long as it is appreciated that democracy is about the realisation of basic principles of 'popular control and political equality', and hence is always a matter of degree, a focus upon the limits and possibilities of electoral choice remains fundamental to any understanding of the prospects for democratic consolidation.

Upon this understanding of the necessity (but not sufficiency) of electoral choice for democracy, Beetham proceeds to elaborate not only the problems that democracy poses for ethnically or culturally divided societies if it is constructed in a 'winner-take-all' manner, but to endorse Reynolds' further propositions about the superiority of parliamentarianism over presidentialism, and of proportional over plurality electoral systems. He further proposes the merits of regional over centralist forms of government, particularly (again) in ethnically or regionally divided countries. The foundations of these arguments will be subject to a brief review, before their general applicability to Africa is demonstrated by reference to the recent round of competitive elections, as demonstrated by those case studies featured in this book.

Constitutional and Electoral Alternatives for Democracy in Africa

Beetham (1994: 169) is at one with those scholars, such as Lijphart (1984) and Horowitz (1993), who in recent years have reiterated arguments that for democracy to survive, a measure of national unity is one of the most essential conditions. In other words, democracy is dependent upon the consent of people to co-exist. In contrast, if they are so divided along lines of ethnicity, language, religion, historical memory or other sense of identity that they cannot agree to live with each other, the only alternatives are secession, civil war or authoritarian rule. Yet even in less extreme situations, democracy as electoral competition for power will exacerbate divisions as politicians seek to mobilise popular support along those lines that will most readily deliver them the maximum number of votes. Only if electoral and constitutional arrangements are put in place which provide incentives for political parties to appeal across ethnic or other crucial divisions is democracy likely to rise above otherwise fundamentally disintegrative boundaries. Consequently, consideration of electoral systems as alternatives for democratization cannot be divorced from the constitutional context in which they are embedded.

From this perspective, parliamentary systems are today widely viewed as providing a more durable foundation for democracy than presidential ones. According to Stepan and Skach (1993: 10), of 53 non-OECD countries that experimented with democracy for at least one year between 1973 and 1989, parliamentary democracies had a rate of survival more than three times higher than that of presidential democracies. The reason, they argue, is that whereas under parliamentar systems, executives and legislative majorities are mutually dependent, under presidentialism, democracy is a system of mutual independence, with legislatures and chief executives drawing their legitimacy from separate, often fixed, electoral mandates. Parliamentarianism, they conclude, offers a more supportive framework for democracy because of

> its greater propensity for governments to have majorities to implement their programs; its greater ability to rule in a multiparty setting; its lower propensity for executives to rule at the edge of the constitutution and its greater facility at removing a chief executive who does so; its lower susceptibility to military coup; and its greater tendency to provide long party-government careers, which add loyalty and experience to political society (Stepan and Skach 1993: 22).

Having agreed that presidents are too often prone to sidestep or coerce an obstructive legislature, Beetham (1994: 170) adds that the sheer prestige and durability of US presidential democracy may have given it an image of exportability that is seriously misleading.

PR is widely associated with parliamentarianism as providing a firmer base for democracy than plurality electoral systems because it encourages minority representation, voter participation and mutual accommodation, even in divided societies.

The fundamental problem with the plurality or first-past-the-post system, found overwhelmingly in countries influenced in the British electoral tradition, is that more often than not parties are elected to govern on a minority of the vote, and minority parties are systematically under-represented in parliament.[1] The party with the largest minority of the votes is normally transformed into one with an overall majority of the seats, hence becoming the government of the day. (Only one party, the Conservatives in 1935, received a majority of the votes cast in any of the twenty British elections held between 1922 and 1992, yet there were only three governments in that period which took office with a minority of seats, Reynolds, 1993: 21.) This is quite simply because the plurality system is based upon the election of those candidates who receive more votes than any other candidate in single-seat constituencies, supposedly of approximately the same size. As a result of this disproportional system of representation, an adversarial winner-takes-all approach to politics is encouraged, in which the object of the electoral contest is power untrammelled except by the constraining conventions of Westminster parliamentarianism (which have proved far less easily exportable than its mechanics).

In contrast, PR systems, which seek to allocate seats proportional to the votes cast, are said to produce only rarely majorities for individual parties. Proportionality is most accurately achieved if the entire country serves as a single constituency, although it can also be largely attained by use of the system in multi-member, sub-national constituencies. However, whatever the variation used, PR often results in coalition governments, and encourages cross-party compromise and bargaining as normal behaviour. To be sure, as its detractors point out, the dependence of PR systems upon the provision of party lists may give undue muscle to party officials who rank candidates, and post-election horse-trading by minority parties to secure parliamentary majorities may mean that voters only indirectly select governments. Nonetheless, the virtue of PR in guaranteeing and simultaneously legitimating the representation of minorities can simply not be denied. This logic can similarly be extended to voting in presidential systems, when the election of presidents by a mere plurality can be avoided by such devices as run-offs, preference voting or a requirement that winning candidates secure a minimum level of support throughout different regions in a country.

PR, by encouraging coalition and compromise, is proposed as more likely to dispose political actors to a sharing of power. Similarly, regionalism offers a version of power sharing which operates at the parliamentary or executive levels. As Beetham (1994: 171) notes, it may enhance prospects for democratic sustainability, especially in countries which are divided along ethnic lines, by enabling a party which is defeated electorally at the centre to win and exercise power at the level of the region.

This condensation of convergent wisdom concerning the optimum conditions for the consolidation of democracy omits much and must enter serious caveats. For a start, it has concentrated only upon the broadest differences of principle between PR and plurality electoral systems, and has ignored the countless variations upon both (notably the Single Transferable Vote and the Alternative Vote systems) which some scholars feel to be rather more attuned to healing the breaches of divided societies. Equally, as Beetham (1994: 171) further points out, apart from there being a host of other factors (such as whether or not there is a market economy and the level of economic development) which influence prospects, the historical and political circumstances of individual countries are by definition unique, and in consequence there cannot be a single recipe for democratization. Nonetheless, so long as it is recognized that the above discussion is dealing with propensities and not absolutes, and so long as it is similarly accepted that electoral systems must of necessity be located in broader context, it is possible to move forward to an elaboration of the relative virtues in Africa of plurality systems and PR.

Electoral Systems and Recent Elections in Africa

As elaborated by Szeftel in the previous chapter, the wave of democratization that swept Africa since 1989-90 was influenced by the collapse of the communist regimes of Eastern Europe and propelled by both externally-imposed conditionalities and internally-generated discontents with the political and economic failures of authoritarian regimes. Africa has as a result seen a widespread move away from one-party and/or personalistic and military governance back to the multi-party democratic forms which it inherited at independence, this shift latterly underpinned by the remarkable transition from apartheid in South Africa.

Yet, as also noted above, the staging of multi-party elections cannot be a sufficient criterion of democratization. For a start, as is made clear by the following chapter, not only must elections be fairly conducted, but they are by definition devalued unless they despatch contenders to offices of significant influence and power. Second, for all its greater virtuosity, PR can be as subject as the plurality system to corruption, and unless it is operated under conditions that allow for free competition, the multi-partyism that results can co-exist with the authoritarian hegemony of a ruling party without offering the latter any serious challenge. Third, the shift to presidentialism in many African countries has been associated with a wider erosion of the authority and effectiveness of parliaments, and with a decline in the accountability of elected power-holders to those who have elected them. Elections, in other words, will have little virtue unless they are associated with a proper respect for constitutions and constitutionalism. Finally, external pressure for elections in inappropriate circumstances (such as when power-sharing arrangements between warring opponents might provide a firmer basis for a successful transition), or at inappropriate moments (such as when newly-legalised opposition parties are too disorganized to dislodge a long incumbent government), can serve to impede, rather than speed, democratization.

In practice, the recent return to multi-partyism in Africa has been associated with something of a recasting of the constitutional order of the states concerned. The most celebrated case has been South Africa, whose complicated and difficult negotiation process, which lasted from February 1990 through to the election in April 1994, resulted in the installation of a brand new (interim) constitution, based upon the extension of full citizenship to all people of whatever colour. In other cases, however, such as in Zambia and Kenya, there has been a fairly straightforward reversion to adjusted, post-independence forms which, whilst entailing a re-legalization of political opposition, has retained elective presidencies. In Lesotho, meanwhile, the return to civilian from military rule has been based upon the re-adoption, in its essentials, of the Westminster-style arrangements, replete with a bicameral parliament and constitutional monarchy, entrenched in 1966. Yet in all cases, whatever the extent of constitutional re-ordering and debate, the principal test of the democratization exercise has always been the holding of an election between competing political parties, under conditions deemed to be free and fair. The results of elections during this era have been highly variable. This can be demonstrated by reference to the countries which we subject to special review in this book. Thus, apart from the rather special cases of Namibia and South Africa, which saw transitions from white-minority to democratic rule, electoral outcomes have ranged from the defeat and replacement of previously ruling parties in Zambia in 1991 and in Malawi in 1994; the installation of a popularly-elected government in place of an unpopular military in Lesotho in 1993; the re-election of a ruling party, albeit under extremely dubious conditions, in Kenya in 1992; and the outright rejection by power-holders of popular preferences which were unacceptable to them in Nigeria in 1993.

The prospects for democracy in these seven countries varies considerably, yet overall, the contrasting electoral outcomes lend themselves remarkably well to support the thesis that PR provides a firmer basis for democratic consolidation than plurality electoral systems, more especially when it is linked to parliamentarianism rather than presidentialism. To argue this, the following brief overview of the elections held in these countries will move from what are regarded as the least democratic outcomes through to the most democratic. It does not seem coincidental that this will simultaneously move us from plurality systems to PR, and away from presidentialism towards parliamentarianism.

Nigeria 1993 Paradoxically, the Nigerian presidential election of 1993, which was supposed to clear the path for a return to civilian rule but whose result was nullified by the country's military leadership, can serve to demonstrate some of the benefits which can derive from ameliorating the winner-take-all logic of the plurality system.

The election was subject to such heavy official restrictions and interventions that it can scarcely be characterized as free. Most importantly, the military President, General Babangida, had in 1989 rejected some thirteen parties listed by the Electoral Commission, and substituted two new ones of his own making: a slightly left-leaning Social Democratic Party (SDP) and a slightly right-leaning National Republican Convention (NRC). Subsequently, in 1992, Babangida cancelled presidential primaries of both parties on the grounds of massive vote-buying and banned all 23 candidates involved (not a few of whom were awkwardly critical of the military). The contest that eventuated was therefore between two further candidates, Chief Moshood Abiola for the SDP and Alhaji Bashir Tofa for the NRC, who secured their nominations only after the heavyweights had been eliminated. Babangida's cancellation of the former's victory - which official international observers judged to have been fairly won within the restrictive official framework - was consequently only the worst of a host of interventions by a military regime which, when it came to the crunch, was too obsessed with state power to hand over even to a carefully processed successor. Human rights abuses since the election, including the detention of Abiola, have underlined the military's overbearing domination and the problem of securing a lasting transition to civilian rule.

Nonetheless, the 1993 presidential election, and elections for state governors in 1991 and for state legislatures and the bicameral National

Assembly which preceded it in 1992, pointed some way towards the making of democracy in this immense and hugely varied country. First, the parties were reasonably matched. Whilst the NRC emerged with more state governorships, the SDP won majorities in most state assemblies and both houses of the National Assembly. Second, both the parties proved capable of winning support across the traditional regional and ethnic divides which had proved the downfall of previous attempts at democracy. For the first time a southerner won an election for president, and (as was required under the rules for candidates to be elected) both obtained at least one-third of their votes from two-thirds of the states. Third, compared with previous elections, religious polarization was reduced by both candidates being Moslem, and thereby being required to compete for the Christian vote (Campbell 1994).

Consequently, the disastrous aftermath of the election should not be allowed to obscure two major factors which could have contributed favourably to a democratic outcome. The first is that the winner-takes-all principle was in theory heavily diluted by the US-style separation of plurality elections for state and national assemblies, and for governorships and the presidency. The second is that the legally enforced two-party system automatically transformed the plurality into a majority voting system. The two competing parties may have been highly artificial constructs, yet both constituted coalitions which cut across regional, ethnic and religious lines in a manner which might conceivably have helped pull the country together had Babangida not cancelled the result.

In practice, however, such democratic potential was cut short by the transfer from military to civilian rule being centred upon the highly charged contestation for a prospectively immensely powerful presidency. Its all-or-nothing structure made it easier than it otherwise would have been for the military to annul the election, as the banned candidates and diverse political factions readily acquiesced in hope of themselves being able to contest again (Reynolds 1995: 95).

Kenya 1992 The general election of 1992 marked the end of one-partyism and saw the re-birth of multi-partyism. The result saw the authoritarian President Moi returned in the presidential election and KANU winning 93 seats to 82 gathered by three opposition parties. Two minor parties also acquired one seat each. In this case, however, the election campaign was to see the re-appearance of many of the abuses which have characterized numerous African elections.

Commonwealth observers concluded that, overall, the result reflected 'the expression of the will of the people'. However, this was in spite of the numerous imperfections: the registration process saw more than one million young Kenyans denied a vote because of the late arrival of identity cards, the nomination process was flawed, intimidation of opposition parties and voters was rife, and the state-owned media and the governmental machinery unambiguously backed the ruling party. Despite all this, KANU was judged by commentators to have won, not because Moi rigged the election but because of the failure of his opponents to maintain unity (*The Economist*, 9 January 1993).

Even if this judgement is correct, it manifestly ignores the limitations of the plurality system, which amplified the victory of the ruling party in four major ways. First, Moi won the presidential election on a 36.8% minority vote against three other candidates who split the remainder of the vote between them. There was no provision either for Alternative Voting or for a run-off election to secure a majority winner. Second, KANU won sixteen seats unopposed. Third, the one-member constituency system inspired campaigning and voting by ethnic blocs for ethnic candidates, and 'wasted' the votes of minorities. Fourth, and most importantly, it can be demonstrated that the election process was based upon a delimitation of constituencies which systematically, and overwhelmingly disproportionately, favoured KANU: the average number of registered voters in seats won by KANU was 32,699 compared to 51,256 in seats won by the opposition. In short, whereas KANU won 77 out of the 161 contested seats for some 26.6% of the parliamentary vote, the three major opposition parties won their 84 for 73.4%.[2] Whatever the failures of the opposition, and whatever the outright manipulations of the electoral process, it is difficult to avoid the conclusion that a PR-based electoral system would have rendered the defeat of the government in at least the parliamentary elections. In contrast, rather than fostering a culture of tolerance, the plurality system has promoted an adversarial system which, since the election, has seen KANU reacting strongly to the legitimacy of articulate and threatening opposition.

Lesotho 1993 The election of 1993 - which saw a 75 seat to nil victory by the BCP over the BNP - constitutes a classic example of how the plurality system may work to disadvantage minorities. In this case, the BNP secured 22.6% of the vote (against 74.7% for the BCP) but no representation at all in parliament. The return to multi-partyism in Lesotho resulted in a de facto legislative one-partyism in an election which had been preceded by a thorough and balanced delimitation exercise, and an electoral process which independent monitoring organizations all agreed was free and fair. Nonetheless, the one-sidedness of the result left the BNP convinced it had been unfairly robbed, and denied parliament the legitimacy it would have enjoyed had it featured an opposition in the National Assembly. The outcome was that the formerly ruling BNP was soon conspiring with the Royal House and discontented elements in the security forces to remove forcefully the democratically-elected government in August 1994. Democracy was thereafter restored only by virtue of external pressure from Botswana, South Africa and Zimbabwe (Southall and Petlane, 1995).

Zambia 1991 The election of 1991 successfully restored multi-partyism and provided for the peaceful transfer of power. Doubts were expressed about aspects of the voter registration and vote-counting process, and about media bias in favour of the government, but all this came to nothing as the opposition MMD rode to a 125 out of 150 seat landslide victory over UNIP in the legislative election and Chiluba polled just over 76 per cent against Kaunda's near 24 per cent in the two-way presidential race. However, whilst UNIP obtained just over 24 per cent of the parliamentary vote overall, virtually all its 25 seats came from the Eastern Province area.

Baylies and Szeftel (1992) record that the 1991 elections marked 'a major achievement in Zambia's struggle for democracy', with the new political openness facilitating the lodging of a whole string of demands for government to be 'efficient, honest, representative and accountable'. However, they also comment that whilst the shift from a one-party state has provided for the freedom to form political parties, presidentialism remains at the core of the system, executive power has not been institutionally circumscribed, and the overwhelming victory of the MMD and the post-election weakness of UNIP has meant that the multi-party system is formal rather than real.

Recent developments, with criticism mounting over Chiluba's inept and neo-patrimonial style of government, indicate that the MMD has worked to reproduce rather than replace UNIP, and has failed to forge more durable institutions. Meanwhile, the subordination of parliament to the executive renders it of little utility in calling the government to account.

Malawi 1994 Like the Zambian election of 1991, the Malawian presidential and legislative contests of 1994, run on plurality lines, facilitated a return to multi-partyism from the one-party rule of the Malawi Congress Party (MCP). As Cammack argues in this volume, a return to democracy was forced upon a highly reluctant MCP, and the electoral process and campaign was to be marred by numerous abuses intended by the ruling party to swing the outcome its own way. However, the result was a three-way split in the vote between the three major presidential contestants and their parties. As a consequence,

Bakili Muluzi acceded to the presidency on a minority vote (47%, compared to 33% for Banda and 19% for Chakufwa Chihana), and Muluzi's United Democratic Front (UDF) captured 85 seats to 56 for the MCP and 36 for the Alliance for Democracy (AFORD). Muluzi's lack of a parliamentary majority eventually propelled him into offering Chihana a vice-presidency (which had to be invented) and bringing in AFORD as junior parties in a coalition.

It is difficult to imagine that Muluzi would have failed to secure the presidency under either an Alternative Vote system or a run-off election. In this case, too, the correspondence between votes cast for parties and the number of seats they obtained was remarkably close for a plurality election: 46% of the vote for the UDF and 48% of the seats, compared to similar ratios of 33%:32% for the MCP and 19%:20% for AFORD. Superficially, PR could scarcely have done better. This result was obtained only because each major party and presidential contender drew overwhelming support from one of three ethnic groups, each of which dominated one of the country's three regions. However, as Reynolds (1995: 88) observes, the distribution of seats which resulted creates a false picture of homogeneous regional bastions, as significant minority votes were registered against the dominant parties in all three regions (although rather less so in the North, where minority parties garnered 15% of the vote as against in the Central and Southern regions where they gained 36% and 23% respectively). Whereas a PR system might have encouraged parties to have looked to maximise support beyond their regional bases, the plurality electoral system would seem to have amplified, rather than diminished, political mobilization along ethnic lines.

Van Donge (1995: 236) argues that politicians were well aware before the election that regionalism was an entrenched force and that no party would likely secure a parliamentary majority. Consequently, a President elected on a plurality basis could be expected to face a potentially hostile parliament in which his party enjoyed only a minority status. The result was that during the constitutional debate and negotiation which preceded the election, the parties were already pre-disposed to the idea of the formation of a coalition. Indeed, to this end, a constitutional provision was enacted which would require MPs to stand for re-election in a by-election if they chose to switch parties, thereby preventing a president from in effect being able to purchase a post-election majority in parliament.

Cammack[3] vigorously rejects this view, proposing instead that rather than writing a constitution and creating post-election pacts because of the potential dangers of ethnic polarization, the UDF and AFORD were motivated primarily by their determination to prevent the MCP retaining any access to power. She argues, in addition, that after the election party leaders came under immense pressure from western donors to find a compromise that would work. Coalition, she implies, came about in spite of the electoral system, and in no way because of it, except in so far as no party could command a legislative majority.

In short, rather than encouraging links and alliances across boundaries of support, the plurality system identifies regions as either for or against the government. If coalition and consensus between parties exists, it is a product of political arithmetic, and is not inherent to the nature of electoral system itself.

Namibia 1989 and 1994 The 1989 election, whose purpose was to elect a constituent assembly to devise a constitution for an independent Namibia, was conducted under the dual authority of the South African administration as the de facto rulers, and the UN Technical Assistance Group (UNTAG) as representative of the international community. In essence, the electoral process was implemented and administered by the South Africans, subject to the supervision, monitoring and ultimate legitimation of UNTAG.

Having conceded the loss of its historic struggle for control over Namibia to the United Nations, South Africa's objective in the election of 1989, which heralded the transition to democracy, was damage limitation: restricting SWAPO to less than the two-thirds majority in the National Assembly which, under the settlement, would have enabled it to write a constitution without the agreement of any other parties. Its chosen method was by the manipulation of ethnicity, notably via its presentation of SWAPO as a vehicle of the Ovambo (who constituted some 50% of the estimated population), and its encouragement of the remaining numerous minority ethnic groupings to form their own political parties and to fall in under the umbrella of the Democratic Turnhalle Alliance (DTA). PR had been proposed by Pretoria as early as 1985 as the best method for guaranteeing that minorities would secure representation, and for ensuring that an exaggerated victory would not accrue to SWAPO under the plurality system. It was regarded as serving as a counter to the expected victory of SWAPO leader Sam Nujoma in the parallel election for the presidency.

The National Assembly election was conducted in twenty-three polling districts under the national list system and, in essence, was a contest between a majority party (SWAPO) and nine minority parties and alliances of parties, of which by far the most significant was the DTA. Perhaps, inevitably, the electoral process was flawed, with numerous allegations in particular that the South African authorities were less than neutral. Nonetheless, the international forces involved in implementation of Resolution 435 were so

strengthen
power.

eager to secure the transition that numerous abuses were overlooked in the interests of endorsing the result. The electoral system adopted guaranteed proportionality of representation in the National Assembly. This saw SWAPO gaining 57% of the vote and 41 seats, to the DTA's 29% and 21 seats, and 9 seats being allocated proportionately among five other alliances.

Potgieter (1991: 35-6) observes that SWAPO was the leading party in only nine of the polling districts, compared to the DTA leading in 15. SWAPO, he argues, drew support largely from districts containing large numbers of Ovambo (who together accounted for just short of 50% of Namibians) and its support amongst other population groups was rather thin. He therefore concludes that had the single-member constituency system been employed, the configuration of parties in the Constituent Assembly might have been much less favourable to SWAPO. However, other commentators suggest that as the size of the polling districts varied substantially (from 1,990 voters in Bethanie to over 200,000 in Ovambo), this merely goes to indicate the potential for gerrymandering that might have existed under the plurality system (Lindeke, Wanzala and Tonchi 1992: 128-9). Furthermore, it is important to note that both the leading parties drew support from around the entire country. SWAPO obtained between 10% and 20% support in 6 and the DTA in 2 districts, between 20% and 40% in 11 and the DTA in 6 districts, and over 40% in 6 and the DTA in 15 districts.

SWAPO performed substantially less well than it hoped and had predicted. Undoubtedly, this reflected the proliferation of parties encouraged by the South African emphasis upon multiple ethnicity. However, apart from SWAPO going out of its way after the election to forge a national consensus, its lack of a two-thirds majority encouraged a search for compromise which resulted in substantial agreement among all parties in the later adoption of a constitution.

SWAPO's status as a truly national party was confirmed in the election of 1994 when it obtained 73% of the total vote and 53 seats, under an electoral process which international observers unambiguously confirmed as free and fair. In contrast, the DTA obtained 20% and 15 seats, thereby confirming itself as the only credible political force apart from SWAPO. With South African encouragement of ethnic multiplicity out of the way, the number of smaller parties was reduced to just six, who between them obtained just 5.25% of the vote and a mere 4 seats. In the Namibian case, therefore, PR would seem to be leading to the consolidation of a two-party system, albeit one which remains representative of minority interests (Simon, 1995: 114).

Nonetheless, many of the gains of proportionality would seem to be imperilled by the retention of the executive presidency, as in both elections

Nujoma rode to victory upon the back of a national vote (57% in 1989 and 72% in 1994) which was drawn extremely disproportionately (70% in 1989 and 72% in 1994) from the Ovambo vote. The politics of accommodation fostered by PR for the National Assembly may well come to be challenged by the effective monopoly control which SWAPO has come to exercise over the presidency.

South Africa 1994 This was the big one. How (even following President De Klerk's lifting of the long-established prohibitions upon the African National Congress (ANC) and other liberation forces) was a transition from apartheid to democracy and majority rule to be accomplished in this racially diverse and complex country without it descending into violence, even civil war? There was no easy answer, but the fact that (a rather violent) transition was eventually managed, and power transferred from the ruling National Party (NP) to a Government of National Unity dominated by the ANC, reflected the early acceptance by the ANC of PR in response to NP demands.

The NP was desperate to abandon the plurality system because it knew well how its deliberate loading of urban constituencies had sustained its own hold on central power. PR was therefore seen as a way of guaranteeing representation of the White, Coloured and Indian minorities (as well as of conservative Africans) which the NP fully intended to gather to its bosom, and for ensuring a place in the sun for the Inkatha Freedom Party (IFP), whose principal strategy lay in the ethnic mobilization of Zulus to counter the allegedly 'Xhosa-dominated' ANC. Perhaps, too (or so it would seem to have been fantasized in some NP minds) an alliance between itself and the IFP might even summon up a popular majority.

PR was also viewed as instrumental to the forging of an all-inclusive settlement. First, it was linked to diminution of central-state power by the creation of nine provinces, each of which would have their own legislatures, each similarly elected by PR, and each of which would elect ten representatives to a national Senate according to the proportionate strength of parties within them. Second, it was seen as offering a prospect of inclusion in the new central parliament and provincial legislatures to all groupings which could summon up a mere one per cent of the popular vote. Third, it was stipulated in the interim constitution (which would come into operation following the election) that parties obtaining more than ten per cent of the vote would be guaranteed proportionate representation (if they so wished) in national and regional governments of national unity. Fourth, subject to a series of methods for overcoming deadlocks, approval of a final constitution by a post-election parliament (sitting as a Constituent Assembly) would require a two-thirds majority. Finally, the avoidance of a directly-elected presidency in favour of a chief executive, chosen by the National Assembly and whose powers were severely circumscribed by parliament under the constitution, underlined the effort to compromise. Even on these terms, it proved immensely difficult to secure participation by potential losers from democracy. In Kwazulu-Natal, in particular, the level of violence and intimidation by the IFP and its supporters was so great as to deny a free poll and an unhindered count. The outcome was a pragmatic decision by the ANC to concede majority domination of the government of that province to its rival. Nationally, however, the ANC gained 62.6% of the vote and 252 seats in a 400 National Assembly, contrasted to 20.4% and 82 seats for the NP, 10.4% and 43 seats for the IFP, and the remaining 6.5% and 23 seats for four other parties. Regionally, the ANC gained effective majorities in seven out of the nine provinces - yet one-party rule was enshrined in none and the NP joined the IFP in securing effective control over a territorial/provincial base.

Both the negotiation process and the electoral process were flawed but, importantly, the principles of proportionality and of the accountability of the presidency to parliament were crucial to reconciling racial and other minorities to the transition.

Towards An Appropriate Electoral Model for Anglophone Africa

Following Beetham (1994) and Reynolds (1995), this present survey has argued strongly that the combination of a PR electoral system with a parliamentary, rather than a presidential, form of government is most likely to enhance the prospects for democracy in Africa. This refers most immediately to the classic advantages of PR over the plurality systems for divided societies. PR allows for greater representativeness in legislatures than the plurality system, and thereby facilitates wider inclusivity and identification with the political system, and is more likely to require the mutual accommodation of different political parties in either formal coalition or informal collaboration. However, such virtues will be compromised unless they are connected to a sound basis for parliamentarianism: in other words, for the maximum effect of PR, parliaments must be able to exert a real measure of control over executives, and to be able to subject governments to a genuine accountability.

The theory may be fine, but the reality is that of those Anglophone African countries which present themselves as multi-party democracies, only South Africa approximates the optimum model. Elsewhere, the plurality system operates in all countries other than Namibia, whilst only in Lesotho (where presidentialism is blocked by the monarchy) is prime-ministerial government retained. Nor, for all the approbation extended to South Africa's present arrangements, is there substantive evidence that change towards the model is afoot anywhere - save perhaps in Lesotho, where at least the vanquished opposition parties are now citing the advantages of PR.

This is scarcely surprising for in any country major constitutional changes are only normally broached in response to crisis. In any case, South African democracy may be highly admired, but it has not yet been severely tested, and would-be emulators might well be advised to await its greater maturity. Consequently, it will serve little purpose to speculate whether and what aspects of the PR/parliamentarism package might come to be implemented in which countries. Rather, it may be more useful to offer some brief general comments as to what this review suggests about the relationship between electoral systems and the quality of any born-again multi-party democracy in Africa.

A first point is repetition of the obvious one that electoral systems are only one aspect of a constitutional and political package which, in a multi-party system, must seek to achieve balance between representative government and an effective executive. What must be stressed is that in Africa the return to multi-partyism has been made by countries coming from a variety of starting points: from military rule in some, from semi-competitive one-partyism in others, and from non-competitive one-partyism in yet others. Furthermore, each and everyone of them is coming with their own historical baggage, whether it be a background of division and civil war, heavy-handed dictatorial rule, and/or failed experiments in socialism. No single electoral and constitutional package can therefore be expected to fit the requirements, or the practicalities, of such diverse experiences.

Nonetheless, as elaborated by Reynolds (1995: 97-8), it can be proposed that when electoral systems do come up for debate, they should aim at maximising legitimacy by ensuring parliaments are representative of the entire electorate and not just a plurality or majority; achieving accessibility, so that no political persuasions or groups feel excluded; rendering politicians and governments accountable to the voters; providing incentives for parties to accept differences, rather than exacerbating fundamental conflict; and finally, encouraging cross-cutting parties that appeal to issues and values rather than to ethnic and/or regional identities. Comparative review of our case study countries suggests quite clearly that the PR elections in South Africa and Namibia produced parliaments that were more representative, accessible and reconciliatory than those in the countries which retained the plurality system. To be sure, the national list system in South Africa has rendered MPs very distant from the voters - but the post-electoral allocation by the ANC in particular of geographic responsibilities to its individual MPs suggests that under the final constitution there may eventually be a mix of PR with a limited re-introduction of the constituency system.[4] The firm link between the MP and constituency, which is one of the most important benefits of the plurality system, need by no means be lost under an appropriately structured system of PR. Meanwhile, although there is little evidence as yet of the emergence of parties which cut across ethnicity and region in any of the countries under review (save in Nigeria, where the umbrella two-party system was artificially-engineered), PR would seem to offer much greater long- term promise in this regard.

For all that UNITA initially rejected the outcome of the 1992 election in Angola, and for all that Renamo remained in the 1994 election in Mozambique under massive international pressure (Harrison 1995), only PR could have provided any base for inclusive and prospectively sustainable settlements in either country. Together with the examples of successful transitions in Namibia and South Africa, this should send out messages to constitution-makers in West Africa, where Nigeria, Sierra Leone and The Gambia all await a return to civilian rule, and where the plurality based election of 1992 in Ghana was, with some substance, dismissed by the opposition as rigged (Oquaye 1995; Boahen 1995). When contemplating their transitions, however, these latter countries might equally usefully consider the wisdom of avoiding electoral presidentialism.

The shift to executive presidencies, and to the separation of presidential and parliamentary elections, was widely linked (although not in Nigeria and The Gambia) to the move to one-party rule. However, in ex-British Africa, although not all presidential elections were competitive (voters in one-party Tanzania and Zambia had the right only to reject a single-party nominee and in Sierra Leone in 1985 an incumbent president did not face a challenge), it was only in Nigeria, where the elections of 1979 and 1983 were conducted under US-style arrangements, that there was a fundamental break with the Westminster legacy. Consequently, a reversion to parliamentarianism, whereby the leader of the majority party in parliament becomes head of state and titular president, could relatively easily be effected in Zambia, Tanzania, Kenya, Malawi and Ghana. This could also easily be linked to the appointment of a prime minister, charged with conducting day-to-day business, where some political distance between parliament and president were deemed necessary for the dignity of head of state.

However, the major point is that, for all that PR can provide for a representative and multi-party parliament, only one person can become president. If the major prize of an election is control of the executive presidency, even French-style run-offs or requirements that successful candidates secure a minimum level of support from diverse regions around the country cannot undo the winner-takes-all logic of the election - unless, as in transitional South Africa, the constitution dictates a government of national unity. Furthermore, if the office of president is separately legitimated and empowered, the ability of parliament to render the executive accountable is unavoidably compromised.

It is not, perhaps, coincidental that Botswana, the one Anglophone country which has maintained multi-party democracy continuously from independence, has avoided going the route of electoral presidentialism. Nonetheless, as indicated by Good (1995), even in this case the accretion of powers to the executive at the expense of the legislature has led to emergence of what he terms a 'liberal authoritarianism' which calls into question the depth and quality of that democracy. We return, therefore to the basic point: the choice of the most appropriate electoral systems may be crucial for shaping and entrenching multi-partyism in Africa, yet unless elected institutions have the constitutional and political capacity to control governments, democracy will at best be hollow, and at worst a sham.

Notes

1. Mackenzie (1958) remains one of the most comprehensive and accessible overviews of electoral systems available.
2. These electoral statistics were provided by Professor Roddy Fox of the Department of Geography, Rhodes University. His calculations are based upon constituencies as defined by the Kenya Parliamentary Constituency Review Order 1987, Legal Notice No. 309 of 11 November 1987.
3. Cammack, personal communication to Roger Southall, 20 September 1995.
4. As provided by the final constitution, the election of 1999 will be conducted under the same rules for the National Assembly as in 1994. However, there is provision for the possibility of electoral change.

3 Electoral Corruption and Manipulation in Africa: the case for international monitoring

JOHN DANIEL AND ROGER SOUTHALL

In the old world of the cold war, international monitoring of Africa's elections was the exception rather than the norm. The Zimbabwean and Namibian 'liberation' or 'founding' elections of 1980 and 1989 respectively, and the post-Amin Ugandan election of 1980, were probably the most notable of those exceptions. However, in the radically changed international climate of the 1990s, external monitoring, often in conjunction with a domestic operation, is a standard feature of the African electoral landscape. As Gisela Geisler (1993:630) has put it, 'international interest in the fate of democracy in Africa is a phenomenon of the post-cold-war era'.

This 'phenomenon' has spawned the latest in a line of expatriate invaders. Once, in a more optimistic era, they generally tended to be 'developmentalists'; some were also idealists. But in more recent - and harsher - times, they have made way for the tough bureaucrats of multilateral financial institutions like the IMF and World Bank and of bilateral creditors. Today, these new expatriates are more likely to be 'democratizers'; many, to be sure, still with high ideals and the best intentions but now also the collective representation of donor-driven economic and political 'conditionalities' - the 'good governance' enforcers of constitutional and structural reform.

It is precisely because it is often seen as part of some wider agenda, as well as the fact that its actual effectiveness is challenged, that the international monitoring of African elections has become a contentious issue. However, before we examine this controversy, it may be profitable to sketch the background against which the case for monitoring must be put.

37

Electoral Corruption and Manipulation in Africa

The liberation elections which heralded Africa's decolonization ushered into power political parties which, for the most part, could lay reasonable claim to enjoying mass popular support. However, most of these new nationalist regimes turned out to be much more fragile than had been anticipated. On the one hand, the states they inherited often lacked mass (or regional) legitimacy, administrative coherence and political capacity, resulting in diverse tribal, class-based or popular challenges to their rule. On the other, they dominated their polities in that they were central to the allocation of resources in what were overwhelmingly undiversified economies. This rendered them subject to the discontent of those excluded from patronage or disappointed by the material fruits of independence.

These first-generation ruling nationalists claimed to embody the national interest. Yet, they often were challenged by opposition parties which claimed to be no less nationalist themselves. Hence it was that following the transfer of power, ruling parties espoused the virtues of national unity, stability and development and sought to consolidate themselves in office (and, if possible, so avoid removal by the military). Yet most - albeit reluctantly in some cases - came to recognize the importance of conducting post-independence elections in order to retain a semblance of a claim to popular legitimacy and support.

However, the critical fact is that they did not, for the most part, regard these elections as genuine contests for popular support. Instead, they saw them as an essential means for the consolidation of their hold on office. Elections were, therefore, all too often manipulated and perverted for the purpose of laying claim to a spurious legitimacy.

Variations on the theme of electoral manipulation in Africa are almost endless but, in broad terms, we can identify eight main forms of malpractice. These are: (i) the imposition of restrictions on the activities or even existence of an opposition; (ii) abuse of voter registration procedures; (iii) manipulation of the size of constituencies; (iv) restrictions upon the selection or registration of candidates; (v) the unfair use of state resources; (vi) the amendment of constitutions in favour of the ruling party; (vii) the abuse of voting and counting procedures; and (viii) the overturning of unfavourable results. Each of these will be examined below.

Restrictions upon opposition activity Much has been written about the shift from competitive to one-party systems during the early era of post-independence politics in Africa. Suffice it to say here that those countries in which this development did not take place have been the exception rather than the rule. Even in Botswana, where the multi-party structure of democracy has never been formally challenged, the hegemony of the ruling Botswana Democratic Party (BDP) has been such that the party has never been under any national electoral threat (Parsons, 1984:47-54; 1986). The similar dominance of the *Parti Socialiste* in Senegal secured it handsome victories in the competitive elections of 1983 and 1988 (ACR, 1982-83:B555; 1987-88:B129-31).

Historically, the form that restrictions upon opposition have taken have varied considerably. Broadly, however, it can be argued that the move to one-party states tended to be rather more coercive (via use of overt intimidation, arrest, detention of opponents, postponement of elections etc.) where opposition parties constituted a substantive challenge to the ruling party. Hence, whereas the move to one-partyism in the then Tanganyika (where Nyerere's Tanganyika African National Union (TANU) collected 83 out of 84 seats in the pre-independence election in 1960) was relatively consensual, in Ghana under Nkrumah the 1964 plebiscite on whether the constitution should be amended to declare the country a one-party state was preceded by official persecution of a vigorous opposition (Austin, 1970:414-21). Similarly, violence against its candidates and supporters led to the withdrawal of the Sierra Leone People's Party (SLPP) in the election of 1973, and presaged the declaration of a one-party state by the ruling All People's Congress (APC) in 1978 (Hayward and Kandeh, 1987:32-5). In short, in many states, if opponents of a government were not physically eliminated, they were harassed or detained (Zolberg, 1966:82-92).

The outcome, in electoral terms, was either contests in which opposition parties registered no more than a token presence (Zambia in 1968) (Ollawa, 1979:248), or one-party elections which were either semi-competitive, as in Tanzania from 1965, Kenya from 1969, Sierra Leone from 1978 and Zambia from 1973 (Cliffe, 1967; Hyden and Leys, 1972; Hayward and Kandeh, 1987; Chikulo, 1981); or non-competitive, as in Ghana in 1966 when, after the earlier promulgation of a one-party state, British practice was followed in declaring all unopposed candidates automatically elected (Zolberg, 1966:82). Similarly non-competitive have been each of the post-independence elections in Zimbabwe, and none more so than the latest 1995 poll.

Abuse of voter registration procedures   There can be no elections without voters. As summarized by Mackenzie and Robinson (1960:467):

> Even under complete universal suffrage there are limits on the eligibility of persons to vote, such as age, nationality... in addition, it is essential for

orderly contests that each elector should be assigned to one constituency and only one, so that he can vote only in his proper place. These matters cannot be decided by adjudication within the polling station, and must be settled well in advance. Furthermore, under any system there must be a check to ensure that no voter votes twice.

On this basis, Moyo (1992:150) argues that up-to-date and reliable voters' rolls are fundamental to the running of free and fair elections. Today, there are few African countries in which universal adult suffrage does not officially obtain, even if newly democratic South Africa is unusual in following western practice by having reduced the voting age from 21 to 18 years of age. However, the practice of denying the vote to those deemed likely to support officially unfavoured candidates has been borrowed by a number of governments from colonial example. The French, for instance, in the Cote d'Ivoire, sought to eliminate voters from the electoral register who were thought to favour the *Parti Democratique de Cote d'Ivoire* (PDCI) during the early, radical years of its existence (Zolberg, 1966:137). And the British in Kenya, under the African franchise law of 1956, denied the right of otherwise qualified members of the Kikuyu, Embu and Meru tribes to register unless they could prove that they had actually aided the administration during Mau Mau (Mackenzie, 1958:24).

In post-colonial Africa, the failure to update voters' rolls has often been as much an act of omission as of commission (Moyo, 1992:148-51). Indeed, in some countries, the enumeration of the population and the accurate registration of voters have clearly been beyond the capacity of the state. It may be more argued, therefore, that for an election to be judged unfair on the basis of inaccurate registration, it has to be proven that such inaccuracy has systematically favoured one party over another. Otherwise, a registration process may be judged as flawed but as not necessarily having in itself impinged upon the criterion of fairness. A case in point might be the South African election of 1994, where the absence of a national voters' roll (although voters were registered) contributed to considerable administrative chaos but is not thought to have affected the overall result significantly.

Yet such examples aside, there have been widespread complaints in a number of formally competitive and semi-competitive elections that registration procedures have worked specifically to deny the vote to suspected opposition voters, as in Lesotho in 1970 (Leeman, 1985:18-19). Alternatively, as in the Ghanaian election of 1992, the registration of as many as 1.4 million voters more than was statistically possible almost certainly advantaged Jerry Rawlings' National Democratic Congress (Oquaye, 1995 : 267). Yet nowhere in Africa has the compilation of voters' lists been more manipulated than in Nigeria 'where - put most crudely - population equals power' (Beckett, 1985:93), and where, for instance, in 1983 the ruling National Party of Nigeria is thought to have worked through the Federal Electoral Commission to boost the number of northern voters in its favour (ACR, 1983-84:B512-3).

Manipulation of the size of constituencies Elections to most assemblies in Africa, as elsewhere, have taken place on the basis of territorial constituencies, under both plurality and proportional representation (PR) voting systems. The delimitation of constituencies is thus always of major importance, as the manner in which voters are distributed between constituencies affects the fortunes of individual candidates and of political parties.

The extreme case of abuse of delimitation normally involves gerrymandering single-member constituencies so as to give greater value to the votes of one party than another. Yet 'no system of PR has been (or can be) devised in which the political fate of individuals is not to some extent affected by the way in which boundary lines are drawn on the electoral map' (Mackenzie, 1958:107). In Africa, manipulation of constituency size has taken place under both PR and plurality systems, although what is perhaps surprising is how little (rather than how much) it has taken place under the latter.

Following passage of the *Loi-Cadre* in 1956 and the resultant creation of assemblies in all the territories of France *Outre-Mer*, universal suffrage elections were held upon the basis of multi-member constituencies under list-system PR. However, it was not long before Guinea under Sekou Toure had opted to transform the entire country into a single constituency, under which a party obtaining a simple majority of the vote would secure every seat in the assembly. It was, however, actually the ruling PDCI in Ivory Coast which became the first to put this system into operation, 'moving from 60 assembly seats and 19 constituencies in 1957, to 100 seats and 4 constituencies in 1959, and finally to 70 seats and a single constituency in 1960' (Zolberg, 1966:80). The system was subsequently adopted also by Mali in 1964 and Senegal in 1963 (Zolberg, 1966:79-81). From there, it was but a short step to the formal elimination of opposition and the move to a one-party state.

Given the potential for political interference, it is customary for delimitation exercises to be undertaken by officially neutral electoral commissions. Yet commissions only advise; ultimate decisions to implement boundary recommendations are taken by governments. Concerted bias in favour of the ruling party, or officially favoured candidates in one-party semi-competitive elections, may therefore be considered to be deliberate.

Few studies of plurality elections in Africa have paid detailed attention to this issue of constituency size. An exception is Parson's study of the 1984 election in Botswana, in which he concluded that there was little evidence of systematic gerrymandering (Parson, 1986:2-8). Similarly, although Bavu (1989:93) has pointed to a remarkable disproportion in constituency sizes under Tanzania's one-party electoral system, he can only instance a couple of constituencies (Arusha and Ngara) which were apparently created in response to ethnic demands and the 'interests of individual politicians'. However, in contrast, Fox (1996) demonstrates conclusively that unequal constituency size systematically favoured KANU in the Kenya election of 1992, just as the over-representation of rural voters in white South Africa was systematically increased during the 1950s and 1960s to the National Party's advantage (Lemon, 1987). Constituency boundaries were also manipulated to advantage the Uganda People's Congress (UPC) in the fraudulent elections of 1980 (A Local Observer, 1988; Kasfir, 1991:257).

Restrictions upon the selection or registration of candidates Whether under the PR or plurality systems, one of the easiest ways of eliminating either intra-party or extra-party opposition to incumbent elites has been denial of the opportunity to challengers to stand for elections.

As noted in chapter two, one of the strongest criticisms of list-system proportional representation is the control it can give to party managers over the selection of candidates. A graphic example of such abuse was provided by the system adopted by the PDCI for the election of 1960 - a system rapidly adopted by Guinea and Mali as well. According to Zolberg (1966:80)

> ...the party developed a clever technique for dissuading potential candidates from filing [for party nominations] independently. Its own nominees [were] not made public until a few minutes before the deadline; hence, hardly anyone with even the slightest chance of obtaining a place on the dominant party's ticket would jeopardize this chance by betraying his uncertainty and impatience; and when the PDCI ticket [was] finally made known and some [found] they were not on it, there [was] no time to consult with other individuals willing to take an equal chance.

Elsewhere, under the plurality system, the dominance of ruling parties has been not uncommonly reinforced by official disinclination to accept the registration of opposition candidates. In the first nationwide local government elections in Kenya, for instance, 'technical faults' were found in the nomination papers of all but six of the opposition Kenya People's Union candidates, so that KANU candidates were virtually all returned unopposed (Leys, 1975:226). Rather different, but with much the same result, was the case of the 1985 'election' in Lesotho, which saw all 60 ruling Basotho National Party (BNP) candidates returned unopposed following a change in electoral requirements which massively increased the election deposit and demanded that each candidate's nomination be backed by 500 supporters - in a country which was then becoming increasingly subject to official violence (Southall, 1995a:19).

Even more blatant were the measures, ranging from outright trickery to murder, used to bar opponents of the UPC standing in the election of 1980 in Uganda (A Local Observer, 1988; Mutibwa, 1992:140-1). Such tactics found their echo in the Zimbabwe election of 1990, in which a number of Zimbabwe Unity Movement (ZUM) candidates withdrew their nominations, allegedly because of intimidation and death threats (Moyo, 1992:69).

An equally cynical device has been the manipulation of citizenship to deprive opponents of the right to stand for election. In 1973, one of three opposition politicians elected to Swaziland's parliament, Thomas Ngwenya, found himself suddenly stripped of his citizenship and deported on the grounds that he was born 100 yards inside South Africa on land claimed then, and to this day, by the Swazi government (Daniel and Vilane, 1985:54-67). More recently, the government of Frederick Chiluba disposed of the challenge of former President Kenneth Kaunda (whose parents were born in present-day Malawi) by securing a constitutional amendment which limited presidential candidates to those born in Zambia to Zambian-born parents. Meanwhile, in Kenya, the response of the Moi government to the formation of an opposition party headed by Richard Leakey, the prominent white Kenyan vocal in his criticism of official corruption and brutality, has been to brand him as a colonialist, a racist and a foreigner (*Mail & Guardian*, 28 July - 3 August 1995).

Use of state resources to favour the ruling party   In almost all elections in post-colonial Africa, access to state resources in terms of influence over the media, control over the security forces, and availability of government transport and funding, as well as the often crucial right to determine the timing of elections, has systematically favoured ruling parties. So standard is such practice that it becomes invidious even to cite examples, save to note that such advantages have by no means always been determinate, as the Malawi Congress Party, which continued to dominate the airwaves, found to its cost in both the referendum on restoring a multiparty system in 1993 and the subsequent election of 1994 (Cammack, in this volume). Interestingly, it seems that it is only in the case of certain semi-competitive one-party elections (notably in Tanzania) that effective financial limitations seem to have been imposed upon candidate spending (Harris, 1967:35).

Amendment of the constitution in favour of the ruling party Apart from the legalisation of one-party systems, incumbent parties have self-interestedly re-arranged the electoral terrain in two main ways: first, in most ex-British territories, by strengthening the executive through the creation of elective presidencies; and second, by provision for the appointment of nominated members to legislatures. In contrast to Francophone countries which adopted presidentialism at independence, British territories inherited Westminster-style constitutions which centred government around the leader of the largest or majority party in the legislature (or in the elected lower house in the case of bicameral parliaments). Botswana (where the President is the leader of the largest party in parliament) and Lesotho (where presidentialism was blocked by the monarchy) were to prove the only countries to (formally) retain this inheritance, whilst in Swaziland a monarchical despotism abolished any pretence to democracy whatsoever. Elsewhere, a move to executive presidencies, which involved a separation of presidential and parliamentary powers, and which was widely linked to the introduction of a one-party state, was inaugurated in Ghana in 1960 and usually also provided for a separation of presidential and parliamentary elections.

The subordination of parliament to presidential power was buttressed by the latter being able to lay claim to direct popular legitimacy. However, whereas in one-party Tanzania and Zambia the electorate was offered the choice of rejecting the single party's nominee for president, one-party presidential elections elsewhere (for instance, in Sierra Leone in 1985) were rendered farcical by lack of alternative candidates (although less absurd than in Malawi, where in 1970 Banda was declared President for life). In contrast, although the first presidential election in Zimbabwe in 1990 was competitive, the electoral authorities were reluctant to do or say anything which could be construed as working against Mugabe's interests (Moyo, 1992:72).

Provision for the appointment of members of parliament, directly or indirectly by the executive, was an accompaniment of the drift to presidentialism and the erosion of parliamentary authority. In the newly united Tanzania, for instance, only 107 members of parliament were elected in the one-party election of 1965, 15 were indirectly elected by approved institutions, and fully 67 were nominated (although this figure included 41 MPs from Zanzibar). More saliently, the foundation for multi-partyism in Zimbabwe was significantly eroded in 1990 by the introduction of a unicameral legislature, 30 of whose 150 members were to be appointed by the president. With 13 out of 120 elective seats uncontested, this gave the ruling Zimbabwe African National Union-Patriotic Front (ZANU-PF) an effective 43 seat lead before the election was even started (Moyo, 1992:30 and 165-81).

Abuse of voting and counting procedures A time-honoured way of fixing an election is, of course, by rigging the vote. This may be done at the point of voting, or at the point of counting.

Allegations that lack of neutrality by electoral officials has facilitated such abuses as the stuffing of ballot boxes with fraudulent votes, and/or that the counting of votes has been rigged have been common fare in African elections: the Ghanaian plebiscite of 1960, the Lesotho election in 1970 and the recent South African election of 1994, particularly in Kwazulu-Natal, and the Rawlings election of 1992, are all cases in point (Austin, 1970:393; Leeman, 1985:18-19; Szeftel, 1994:468; Oquahe, 1995:259-75). Such corruption has often been judged either to have been unnecessary or ineffective. The CPP would have won the plebiscite anyway, whilst in Lesotho the BNP still failed to secure a fair win in 1970. In Kwazulu-Natal, however, the extent of chaos and fraud was on such a scale that determining a true result became impossible, and the decision to award the Inkatha Freedom Party a controlling majority was a negotiated one, 'one additional concession by the ANC' (Szeftel, 1994:469). In contrast, the Ugandan contest of 1980, where the count was taken over in mid-process by the pro-UPC Military Commission to negate a win by the Democratic Party, provides one of the most clear-cut cases of an election having been stolen by a manipulation of the result (Mutibwa, 1992:142-3).

More ambiguous was the abolition of the secret ballot for the KANU candidate selection processes prior to the one-party Kenyan election of 1988 in favour of open queuing by party members behind their favoured candidates. Under this system, provision was made for candidates who obtained 70 per cent support of those queuing to be returned unopposed. (In the remaining cases, where candidates had not been so returned, all voters could then choose between several candidates in each constituency at the general election.) These arrangements sent 65 politicians to parliament unopposed, with 123 of 188 electoral seats contested by secret ballot. Whilst this controversial system aroused considerable protest on the grounds that open voting encouraged coercion, corruption and bribery, it boosted both party membership and voter turnout on election day. Against this, it was seen as a ruse to weaken the central party machinery in favour of increased personal control by the President (Shields, 1988). When Mackenzie (1958:127) wrote nearly four decades ago that 'open voting is now virtually obsolete in elections to legislative assemblies, even in societies where the level of literacy is low', he reckoned without KANU's one-party procedures.

The overturning of unfavourable election results This might be called the corruption of last resort. If all else has failed, some losing ruling contenders have been prepared to call the whole show off. The key examples, prior to the Nigerian military's behaviour in 1993, are the conspiracy of the losing SLPP with the army to reverse the victory of the APC in Sierra Leone's election of 1967 (Hayward and Kandeh, 1987:51) and the negation of the win of the opposition Basutoland Congress Party (BCP) by the ruling BNP in Lesotho in 1970 (Macartney, 1973).

The resilience of the electoral process None of the abuses catalogued above were invented in post-colonial Africa. However, their combination and interaction in the majority of elections which took place during this same period might suggest that the continent's electoral experience was a wholly negative one. Yet this has not been so, for in contrast, the literature on African elections indicates much that is positive.

First and foremost, despite its turmoil, 'the political process in independent Africa presents a striking illustration of the resilience of the electoral process'. This may lie partly in what Hayward (1987: 18) terms the many meanings of elections, yet

> much of it rests in the commitment of Africans to some level of participation and choice in the governmental process. It is clear that elections in Africa are not just the stuff of politicians, that the masses in many African states, sometimes much more than the elites, have a preference for electoral forms and processes.

Second, precisely because the idea of elections has taken such deep popular root, few elites and governments are able to claim legitimacy without eventually subjecting themselves or their preferred successors to some form of electoral test.

Third, as a number of experiences would aspire to show, African politics is not simply the downward spiral of doom and despair that is so often portrayed. Much recent evidence indicates that countries can return from civil war and civil and military authoritarianism. Indeed, this is what the recent continental drive for democratization has been all about. The importance of elections is that they are central to that process. However, in a continent where the popular right to electoral choice has been so sorely abused, there is a *prima facie* case for ensuring that when they do take place, governments should come under as much pressure as is possible to muster to ensure that elections are genuinely free. That is what electoral monitoring is all about.

Election Observing and Monitoring

In much of the literature on elections, the terms 'observing' and 'monitoring' are often used loosely and interchangeably, synonyms for the same function, referring to some form of eyewitness and fact finding. From this perspective, observing is merely poll-watching, 'a particular form of fact finding' (Rwelamira and Ailola, 1993:210). In most cases it forms only a part of election monitoring, a more extensive and multifaceted exercise which can take several forms, not all of which will or need be present in any one electoral environment. It can range across the following activities:

- direct management and administration of the total electoral process. This is rare but was the case in the United Nations-managed election in Cambodia in 1992;
- supervision and control over, but not the administration of, the election. This was the case in Namibia in 1989 where the UN had authority over the South African government-administered election;
- administrative management of the election under the supervisory control of either the host government (as in Lesotho in 1993) or an independent commission appointed by the host government;
- electoral assistance to a host government ranging from technical help in the form of equipment (maps, ballot boxes, voting booths, generators etc.) to experts in the drafting of electoral laws, codes of conduct etc.;
- electoral monitoring with an additional security or policing component as in the Haitian elections of 1990 and the 1992 elections in Angola.

Other activities and variations can be found but the point is that observer missions, limited to little more than poll-watching, are 'the mildest form of international monitoring and....offer the international community limited means of influencing the actual process' (Rwelamira and Ailola, 1993:228).

However, monitoring cannot be reduced to observing or simple poll-watching. Garber (1990), Rwelamira and Ailola (1993), and Anglin (1992), among others, have identified a host of monitoring objectives. Of these, the four most important would seem to be:

- fact finding for the purposes of attesting to the fairness and freeness - or otherwise - of the election. Key to this task is ensuring that the election is conducted according to internationally-accepted criteria. It also involves detecting election-day fraud or irregularities in the balloting and counting processes as well as bolstering the ability of election-day officials to adhere to the rules of the game, even in the face of pressure;

- securing domestic and/or international legitimacy for the process and its result. This can be a complicated and contentious question. But what is certain is that the mantle of legitimacy will not be achieved without the positive sanction of the monitoring mission;
- promoting a sense of security and confidence in the electorate so that the voters will feel free to participate in the process;
- ensuring that the process runs its full course and that if free and fair, the will of the electorate is realised. In other words, this means creating the conditions whereby the winners are allowed to win and the losers accept that they did in fact lose.

All these objectives clearly have enormous implications for African governments - and electorates. Consequently, especially where non-nationals are involved, the nature of electoral monitoring has become highly controversial. In essence, the debate around whether electoral monitoring is a necessary accompaniment of democratization in Africa revolves around two major questions. These are, first, whether or not it constitutes an affront to African dignity and sovereignty; and second, whether or not electoral monitoring achieves its objectives. We will now examine both these issues in turn.

The sovereignty critique   International monitoring is attacked in some quarters on the grounds that it amounts to an abridgement of national sovereignty. All governments, it is argued by this critique, are guardians of their nations' integrity and have the right to resist external interference in their internal affairs. For instance, this was the response of the apartheid regime when the possibility of external monitoring of the South African transition process leading to elections was raised by the South African Council of Churches in May 1992. At the time, the negotiation process was stalled by a wave of violence, which many opponents of the government suspected was being orchestrated by elements connected to the security forces. But (then) President De Klerk dismissed the proposal as a gross infringement of South African sovereignty and as a grave challenge to the legitimacy of his government (Anglin 1994:6). In the event whilst there was no official monitoring process, the election was subject to the scrutiny of a host of monitors variously backed by the European Union, foreign governments, NGOs and churches.

The fact is, however, that many incumbent African governments resent the expression of distrust in their integrity or competence implied by calls for elections to be monitored. Furthermore, an element of anti-colonial feeling argues that if the elections in such countries as the United States and those of the European Union do not need monitors, such obligations should not be imposed upon African governments. Indeed, the sense that international monitoring is part of a neo-colonial design is shared by certain critics of African governments, such as Oquaye (1995:272). In a sharp attack on the Commonwealth Observer Group during the 1992 election in Ghana, Oquaye identifies international monitoring as 'part of the new international order' imposing economic and political conditionalities on Africa.

There is no question that a degree of international involvement or oversight of elections raises delicate questions. When a domestic election is taken over and run by non-national forces (as in Cambodia in 1992 and, to all intents and purposes, in Lesotho in 1993 and Mozambique and Malawi in 1994) or when the outcome is dependent on the pronouncement of outsiders, then an erosion of sovereignty has taken place. However, even if we accept that any notion of the absolute sovereignty of states has always been a myth, the trend towards the greater interdependence of states necessarily implies that all governments are increasingly hedged around by external constraints which range from international laws to exposure to the global media. In particular, human rights concerns are becoming increasingly internationally regulated. It is as part of this package that, as Bjornlund, Bratton and Gibson (1992:406) observe, 'the practice of observing and monitoring elections is gaining increased acceptance around the world'. Indeed, as they further note:

> The Conference on Security and Cooperation in Europe ... adopted a declaration in June 1990 requiring all member states to accept the presence of international observers for national elections. And the United Nations General Assembly and Secretary General have endorsed the practice of election observing, including by non-governmental organizations.

Such developments indicate that those governments (such as Zimbabwe) which reject an observer presence on grounds of sovereignty are increasingly likely to endanger their international standing. This would seem to have been recognized by both the governments of Zambia, which actually invited a high-level election-observer presence for its 1991 elections, and of Namibia which, whilst deeming it inappropriate that foreign personnel should be involved in the administration of its first post-independence election of 1994, indicated that foreign observers would be welcome (Simon, 1995:111).

In any case, any 'sovereign right' of governments to conduct elections on their own must increasingly be related to their capacity to do so. Apart from providing for 'freedom and fairness', external involvement in or actual management of elections has become essential where the state has either, in effect, ceased to exist (as in Uganda in 1980 and Cambodia in the early 1990s); or where its administrative reach has become limited to only parts of the country (as in Mozambique in the aftermath of the civil war with RENAMO). Indeed, in such cases, the international legitimation which may flow from external endorsement of elections may well serve to buttress, rather than undermine, the sovereignty of electoral victors which, as in the case of the Angolan elections of 1992, may otherwise be disputed by disgruntled losers.

Yet issues of capacity apart, the major case against the sovereign right of African governments to reject international monitoring is quite simply that so many of them have exhausted their popular legitimacy and trust. Until most recent times, it is only in a handful of African countries (notably Botswana, pre-coup Gambia and Mauritania) that electorates have been able to trust their rulers to provide the space and conditions for genuine electoral competition. Consequently, for all that the connection between monitoring and the 'good governance' agenda of western governments may be post-cold war, disingenuous and suspect, the moral obligation now lies squarely with African rulers to demonstrate their commitment to free and fair elections. If electoral monitoring does, indeed, represent something of an assault upon national sovereignty, then more importantly, it should ideally constitute a guarantee of popular sovereignty.

Does monitoring achieve its objectives? Writing about the Ghanaian election of 1992, as well as upon the controversial Kenyan election of 1993 where she herself was an observer, Geisler (1993: 621) challenges not just the efficacy of international monitoring but also its moral legitimacy. Analysing the two cases, she charges the Commonwealth Observer Group (COG) in Ghana with 'superficiality and lack of professionalism' and an 'often eclectic application of democratic standards'. Furthermore, she alleges that the COG deliberately ignored the negative comments and observations of the US-based NGO observer groups from the Carter Centre and International Foundation for Electoral Systems (IFES). In other words, suggesting that the COG was prepared to overlook manifest electoral abuses in the interests of expediency, she also implies that they may have shared the concern (*The Economist*, 14 November 1992) that 'Ghana's good conduct with regard to economic restructuring might well have declined with good democratic conduct'.

She is no less critical of the COG effort in Kenya, suggesting that:

> political considerations seemed to hold sway over their judgement of the elections. Their unanimous acceptance of these seriously flawed elections contrasted sharply with the verdict of national observer groups and so many disgruntled voters. Hailed as the most important test-case of donor-imposed political conditionality, the Kenyan elections contributed to tarnishing the reputation of both the donors and the international observers (1993:624).

Citing *Le Monde's* (10 January 1993) view 'that the unacceptable "grabbing of power" by African politicians had been merely replaced by "snatching victory out of the ballot box" and that observers inadvertently help to legitimize this process', Geisler concludes by arguing that:

> There is much to suggest that such cynicism may have become a sad reality. Accurate and reliable assessments of elections do not feature high on the agenda of donors, international observation exercises remain so superficial that conclusions are either too vague or empirically untenable, and the political attention span of most donors do not reach far beyond polling day (1993:634).

There have been other cases where the COG has acted in a similarly dubious way, most notably the fraudulent 1980 Ugandan election. In these three cases, the COG did not allow the facts on the ground to sway it from a political judgement which had likely been pre-determined by forces in Britain and/or the Commonwealth Secretariat: most certainly in the Ugandan case, London was convinced that Obote was the only leader with the capacity to restore political order in post-Amin Uganda (Kintu-Nyago, 1996). Such instances are not unlike the suppression of a report by European Union monitors which was highly critical of many aspects of the South African election of 1994, and which appears to have confirmed that the result in Kwazulu-Natal was fixed among the parties in order to ensure that the IFP secured a place in the government of national unity. The point, as one official put it, was that the election 'produced the result everyone wanted' (*The Independent*, 20 March 1995).

Nonetheless, the overall picture of electoral monitoring in Africa is better than these three cases suggest. On the one hand, that there have been cases where the monitoring effort has been flawed, insufficient or subjected to immense external pressure to endorse a result desired by powerful international actors. In the Ugandan election of 1980 and arguably the Kenyan election of 1992, the final verdicts of international monitors would seem to have legitimated outrageously rigged or unfairly structured outcomes. On the other hand, there have been cases where the international monitoring presence has played an important role in assisting or underwriting a difficult transition from authoritarianism to democracy: the 1991 elections in Zambia (even though many Zambians complained that overseas monitors manipulated local monitoring groups and actually promoted splits between them) (Bjornlund et al, 1992), in Lesotho in 1993 (Daniel, 1994), in Malawi in 1993 (Cammack in this volume), and, most significantly in South Africa in 1994 (despite the irregularities, as described above, which were conveniently overlooked)(Anglin, 1994). Indeed, as Geisler (1994) notes in a paper which tempers her previously wholly critical evaluation of monitoring, only active intervention (with offers of practical assistance to officials and presiding officers) saved the 1994 election in large areas of South Africa (particularly black urban and peri-urban areas as well as in the Bantustans) from ignominious collapse.

Having established that the African electoral record is such that there is a definite need for some form of external validation, and that electoral monitoring can be a support to the democratization process, the question is under what conditions is it most likely to achieve its objectives, and what forms should it take?

Rendering Monitoring Effective

International monitoring cannot in itself provide free and fair elections. It can only attempt to ensure freedom and fairness once the political commitment to the holding of formally competitive elections has been made. Thereafter, however, experience suggests that five major elements need to be in place for monitoring to be rendered effective.

External forces must commit themselves to democratic outcomes. As indicated above, the growing extent of monitoring in Africa is an accompaniment of post-cold-war pressures for the democratization of authoritarian regimes. Consequently, in the present era of structural adjustment and political conditionality, the will and resolution of the external financial forces involved in any particular case, be they the major western investors or the international financial institutions, may often be critical in establishing the framework for competitive elections. In Ghana in 1992, for example, their intervention, together with internal pressures for democratic reform, was crucial in promoting the end of authoritarian rule:

The external factor - which is the main reason why the elections were held at all - was linked with the principle adopted by the World Bank and the West that aid would be given in future by the application of the 'good governance' principle (Oquaye, 1995:261).

The record shows that whilst these outside financial and diplomatic forces compel democratic contests to happen in the first place, as in the cases of Lesotho and Malawi, or facilitate local movement towards elections, as in Zambia, alternatively it also demonstrates that they can live with less-than-democratic outcomes (as in the cases of Kenya and Nigeria) provided their essential interests are not affected adversely.

Of course, in cases where election losers block transitions to democracy or where incumbent governments dubiously structure their electoral return, the record also shows that western governments will likely plead powerlessness to intervene to produce a democratic outcome. They may justify their inactivity by arguing that such intervention would constitute neo-colonialism and be an infringement of African sovereignty. It would be better, they will almost certainly continue, for them to exert renewed pressure for democratization behind the scenes.

The problem about such 'quiet diplomacy' is that it is non-transparent and we can never be sure about its extent, force, tactics or even existence. Consequently, for western governments and international financial institutions to be kept up to the mark, it seems necessary to ensure that when international monitoring takes place, it should involve a variety of external organizations and interests, be they drawn from such international bodies as the UN, Commonwealth and European Union or from the plethora of interested NGOs (ranging from the International Republican Institute to Oxfam). Increased international African involvement should also be particularly welcomed, although this should most definitely extend beyond any official delegations of the Organization of African Unity to include representatives of continental civil society, increasing numbers of whom have now gained experience in observing or supervising their own domestic elections.

What is clearly at issue here is that whereas international monitoring will be at its most effective where there is unambiguous external pressure for a democratic outcome, a diversity of international monitoring groups is necessary to contest occasions when powerful external forces are embarrassed or reluctant to pose awkward questions. International monitoring, to be effective, cannot be allowed to become the sole property of interested governments or financial institutions, even though these latter will often have a major role to play.

The legitimacy of electoral monitoring must be accepted by the key domestic players. The point of electoral monitoring is to provide for neutral supervision or observation of elections whose administration and results are likely to be disputed. Its purpose is to provide for a basis of trust in the electoral process. This presumes that political contestants have come to accept, reluctantly or otherwise, the basic rules of electoral competition and the right of international monitors to interpret them and to adjudge their electoral behaviour. President Kaunda initially refused to countenance the presence of monitors, and only issued the invitation to them after the Movement for Multiparty Democracy made that a condition of their participation in the election. This further implies that governmental institutions, especially the electoral authorities, play a neutral role supportive of monitors.

Electoral monitors must themselves exhibit a commitment to neutrality and to the integrity of the electoral process. Unless electoral monitors are accepted by political contestants as more committed to a free and fair process than they are to any particular outcome, any verdict they deliver, and the point of their being present to referee, will be subject to challenge which may derail the election process.

Difficulties may arise if particular monitoring groups are viewed as pursuing agendas which are deemed to be hostile to political contestants. Such a situation would most normally occur where domestic human-rights-oriented NGOs become involved in the monitoring process, as often they will have been involved in struggles for democratization. In Zambia, in 1991, NGOs could broadly be seen as aligned with the MMD; in Lesotho, in 1993, as opposed to a return to power by the BNP; and in South Africa in 1994, international as well as domestic observers were informally recognized as overwhelmingly favouring a triumph for the ANC. What this implies is that, whilst it would be contentious to block any group which chooses to observe the election, 'international and indigenous private organizations [should] collaborate in building a comprehensive election monitoring capacity'. Such cooperation should lay down rules which all observer groups, whatever their background, are required to follow which would seek to require their practical neutrality. Furthermore, it may further allow for the individual representatives of different organizations to be despatched in mixed groups around the country, thereby encouraging the development of consensus views upon the electoral process.

Beyond providing logistical advantages and ensuring that what is usually limited observer capacity is used economically and sensitively, a collaborative network with an agreed representative and organizational structure which is recognized by the national electoral authorities will also provide the quasi-official status which monitors may require if they are called upon to intervene in disputes on the ground and, if necessary, to assert the integrity of the electoral process. Furthermore, existence of a recognized network of monitoring groups may provide the framework for the delivery of unanimous verdicts as to the freedom and fairness, or otherwise, of an election. This, for instance, proved important in Lesotho, where the 65 seat to nil victory by the BCP was initially rejected as rigged by the BNP and, further, served to undermine the lawsuits that were filed by various of the latter's disgruntled candidates (Sekatle 1995). On the other hand, such a collaborative framework does not exclude, and should not exclude, the delivery of dissenting verdicts by particular observer organizations.

Effective electoral monitoring requires an appropriate level of intervention. Electoral monitoring is about securing trust. The more likely the electoral process is to be contested, the greater the need for involvement by electoral monitoring, and vice versa. A high level of involvement by electoral monitoring organizations is less required in Botswana, with a series of free and fair elections already to its credit, than in countries staging transition or post-transition elections (as in Zambia in 1996) where a tradition of electoral competition remains to be consolidated. Similarly, the degree of external involvement in the administration and staging of the election will vary with the capacity and coherence of the state concerned. How the level of involvement will be decided will depend upon the circumstances - yet what can be argued is that electoral monitoring, to be credible and effective, should be prepared, if necessary, to go beyond mere observing by questioning the rules of the game as instituted by ruling authorities. As illustrated above, there is a large variety of ways in which elections can be skewed and, at the very least, electoral monitors must be prepared to comment openly upon uneven constitutional as well as electoral terrain.

Electoral monitoring requires adequate funding. A final requirement of any monitoring exercise is the continued political and financial commitment of external forces. If the western powers, which ultimately fund monitoring conducted under the auspices of organizations such as the UN or the Commonwealth, lose interest in the democratization process, it is unlikely that NGOs - whether international or domestic - will be able to substitute adequately for them, not least because they themselves are so often directly or indirectly dependent upon funding by governments. This may, in turn, tempt financially dependent NGOs and international organizations to tailor their verdicts to what they may think is required, especially if individuals are keen to retain membership of a monitors' 'flying circus' ('Goodbye everyone, see you in Zambia, or Kenya, or Mozambique next year!'). Similarly, external donors may prove reluctant to back NGOs with a reputation for delivering politically awkward critiques of electoral processes.

Nonetheless, despite such dilemmas, and despite the dangers that poorly implemented monitoring can undermine rather than promote democratic government, the idea of electoral monitoring as an accompaniment to African elections is here to stay (at least so long as debt management and governance remain on the agenda) and the reputation of governments which choose to prevent it will suffer accordingly. Yet its effectiveness will continue to depend not only on external funding and support, but also on African governments being prepared to accept it as an integral and necessary element of any legitimating, and legitimate, general election.

4 The 1989 Elections and the Decolonization of Namibia

LIONEL CLIFFE AND DONNA PANKHURST

The November 1989 elections in Namibia marked that country's shift from war to peace and from colony to independent state. An extended transition had begun early in that year with the establishment of a direct United Nations presence inside the country, and then, in April, a cease-fire in the long war between fighters of the South West African People's Organisation (SWAPO) and the occupying security forces of South Africa. The following six months were intended to permit the development of a new political climate in which SWAPO operated alongside others as an open political party and the administration and media were even-handed (despite being in South African hands). The United Nations Transitional Assistance Group (UNTAG) monitored the cease-fire, the administration of the transition, and the election of a Constituent Assembly (CA), whose role was to be to define the institutional forms of the independent state and society. On the assumption that the CA would use its powers to transform itself into a legislature, the election was also, indirectly, for a parliament and government. At issue was thus far more than simply who won the contest and why.

Six years on from the start of the transition, in which time there has been a second, post-independence election, it is also possible to offer some preliminary assessment of the political system that has emerged, and to query the prospects for democratization over the longer term.

Colonialism, Liberation Struggle and Negotiated Transition

Two legacies of geography and colonialism can be picked out as giving Namibia its distinctive character. First, it is a large country, four times the size of Britain, whose tiny population of less than a million and a half is bizarrely scattered. In a territory some 700 kilometres long, almost half the population are located within 50 kilometres of the northern border, where they inhabit the former 'reserves' of Ovamboland, Kavango and Caprivi, virtually the only areas of this mainly semi-arid country available to African residence under apartheid where smallholder farming was possible. A further 15% of the population are found in the capital, Windhoek. The other 'reserves' are even more arid, suited more to livestock than farming, and are sparsely populated by Herero, Nama, Damara and other peoples who were subject to brutal genocide and relocation under German colonial rule early in the century. Under apartheid, over 80% of the countryside was legally reserved to whites (German and South African settlers), who still farm or ranch huge tracts with small groups of semi-servile resident or 'contract' workers.

The colonial situation imposed different social and economic roles on these differing and widely separated ethnic groups. The northern peoples were corralled into reserves cut off from the 'police zone' which was demarcated over the rest of the country and into which only adult male Africans were allowed to move as migrant workers for the mines, fishing industry, farms and even the South African labour market. In other respects the reserves were not subject to direct interference, but neither were they the scene of any development, except to some extent by Lutheran and other missions. For the first half of the century it was the peoples to the south, who had been hounded out of their original home areas and dumped in semi-arid pockets between white farms and ranches, that were cast as farm labour. It was they who experienced the severity of the day-to-day administration of the police zone.

The colonial political economy, where exports and revenues derived overwhelmingly from mines owned by a mix of South African and foreign corporations and where white settlers monopolized the land and such internal markets as existed, generated extreme polarisation. It also led to the proportion of national product exported rather than retained in the country reaching a record scale. Thus, one set of fundamental issues at stake in the transition was how far these enormous inequities, and the repatriation of the country's surpluses, would be reversed.

The second distinctive element in Namibia's legacy was the system of administration of the colony and the effect of this on later politics. The savage rule of Germany ended with the First World War and thereafter South West Africa (SWA), as it was then called, was consigned by the League of Nations to South Africa as a Mandated Territory. South Africa then succeeded to a United Nations Trusteeship over SWA in 1945. Then, during the 1950s, as protests against the overrule by Pretoria came to be voiced internationally, the UN gradually attempted to withdraw South African control. However, various UN Resolutions and even the verdict of the International Court of Justice were ignored by South Africa, which imposed the same apartheid laws and institutions as at home. Separate administrations were established for the different ethnic groups (including the whites), and political leaders were groomed and enabled to set up local patronage networks. Whites were represented directly in the South African Parliament, and many joined the ruling National Party (NP).

Yet international pressures steadily became too strong to be ignored and South Africa changed tack in the early 1970s, proclaiming its commitment to a separate and eventually independent SWA. To this end, it set about orchestrating its own internal political solution by gradually involving ethnic politicians in a partially responsible government. These were then brought loosely together in a confederal group of parties, the Democratic Turnhalle Alliance (DTA), organized around a white core which had broken from the NP.

Meanwhile the liberation struggle had begun in earnest. Two nationalist groups emerged at the end of the 1950s. One grew up at the initiative of the Herero chiefs, but soon went beyond them to form the SWA National Union (SWANU). The more substantial, which partially overlapped, built upon Ovambo migrant workers, initially in South Africa, and eventually took shape as SWAPO. They were greeted with intense repression, and as a result, first steps to prepare for armed struggle were taken by SWAPO activists in exile from the early 1960s. These led to some ambushes and other incidents in the far north east of the Caprivi Strip, which was opened to access from Zambia once that country became independent in 1964.

Faced with an unpropitious geo-political situation and the might of South Africa, armed struggle at that stage tended to be seen as a complement to international pressures and diplomacy, and some leaders always viewed it in those terms. However, the prospects for infiltration into the more heavily populated Ovambo areas further west were dramatically improved with the independence of Angola from Portugal in 1975, although these were also to remain complicated by the fighting within Angola between the MPLA government (supported by Cuban troops) and the rebel UNITA movement supported by South Africa and backed by actual SA invasions. Nevertheless, SWAPO was able to mount widespread incursions throughout Ovamboland and even further east and south by 1976-77.

The South African response was to escalate counter-insurgency, to indigenise it by recruitment of a SWA Territorial Force (SWATF), and to continue its military operations in Angola. It also entered into negotiations with a 'Contact Group' (CG) of western governments that set itself up as mediators to get Pretoria to accept a UN Plan for the independence of Namibia, set out in Security Council Resolution 435 of 1978. This UN Plan provided for the full independence of Namibia as a unitary state through a transition which would involve a UN Transitional Assistance Group (UNTAG) to monitor a cease-fire, a political process leading to elections for a CA, and the handing over of power by South Africa to a representative government. The subsequent UN role was unique in that the UN was not merely invited in by warring parties but could claim a central presence under international law. In the event, it used its powers and legitimacy only to a limited extent.

South African reluctance to implement the Plan, either to buy time, extract concessions or as part of its 'total strategy' for the region (Davies and O'Meara, 1985; Wood, 1992; Cliffe et al, 1994) were given a boost internationally with the elections of the Thatcher and Reagan governments. In the ensuing ten years before Pretoria agreed to implement a transition along the lines of the UN Plan rather than its own internal solution side-lining SWAPO, further concessions were made. One of the several that were accepted by the CG and foisted upon SWAPO directly affected the proposed elections: the CA would be required to pass the constitution by a two-thirds majority. Thus the target for all parties in any election would be not just to seek a majority, but 66.6%, or to deny that critical figure to opponents. South African government strategy was thus to ensure that its allies obtained at least a blocking third of the CA if they could not keep SWAPO out of power.

A further suggestion, favoured by the US, was to have a conference of all parties before the transition to agree a draft constitution. That was not accepted but instead in 1982 a set of constitutional principles were set out. These curtailed the CA's freedom of operation and also made basic constitutional issues subject to decision by the power-brokers of international diplomacy and South African intransigence. They specifically set out individual rights that entrenched existing property and thus inhibited any redistributive policies in the future. They also contained strong implications about pluralist political forms designed to curb any SWAPO ambitions for the typical nationalist model of a single-party system. This issue was to take on more salience even for radical opinion in the light of revelations about the anti-democratic practices of SWAPO that came out in connection with its own detainees (see below) and in subsequent analyses (Leys and Saul, 1995).

These extended and partially hidden negotiations also resulted in one area of imprecision that was to sow seeds for major confusion when the transition process began. UNSCR 435 originally allowed for the demobilization of combatants from both sides: the confinement of the South African Defence Force (SADF) and SWATF to barracks and the withdrawal of the former from the country in stages; and the gathering of guerillas of SWAPO's People's Liberation Army of Namibia (PLAN) who were in the country into assembly points, presumably similar to those in Zimbabwe's transition in 1979-80. But no such detailed provision for SWAPO fighters inside Namibia was included in later arrangements between the CG and South Africa, the latter claiming later that SWAPO had no such presence.

While negotiations over such issues went on through the 1980s, South Africa continued with massive incursions into Angola. Indeed, until 1988 it remained in doubt whether South Africa would accept any version of UNSCR 435. What helped to tip the balance were battles in southern Angola in 1986-7 which were fought to a stalemate, indicating for the first time that the SADF did not have battle superiority nor command of the air. A multi-dimensional settlement involving South African and Cuban withdrawals from Angola and the implementation of the UN Plan for Namibia were the alternative to further costly escalation.

Inevitably such complex agreements involved not only the warring elements in Angola, including South Africa and Cuba, but also the CG (principally the US), and the USSR, the African Front-line States as well as SWAPO. Not surprisingly, therefore, the formula for the transition in Namibia was a considerable compromise.

The Political Climate of the Transition

The lack of precision and gaps in the UN Plan for Namibia increased the potential for former mortal enemies to strive to translate whatever edge they inherited from the period of struggle into electoral advantage. Their ability to do this both affected and was influenced by the overall political climate.

SWAPO saw its crucial trump card as its overwhelming popular support. It believed any minimally open political process would allow it to translate that support into votes and into power. However, this did not stop it trying to steal a march at the start of the transition by infiltrating guerillas into northern Namibia ahead of the cease-fire in April.

South Africa and its appointed Administrator-General (AG) took over absolute power from the Transitional Government at the beginning of the transition, and remained in unambiguous control of running the election. This meant that the coalition of opposition to SWAPO had access to the resources of state structures, including their coercive power. Of course, the AG's staff were formally committed to cooperating with UNTAG, and they, and the DTA itself, claimed that no official support was given to any parties. However, their supposed neutrality was always open to question, and revelations in mid-1991 revealed details of an orchestrated campaign by the South African state to use intimidation, massive financing of parties and manipulation of events and their reporting in the media to shape the election and the whole transition process (*The Guardian*, 11 June 1991).

The Aborted Cease-fire and Subsequent Demilitarization

The transition began badly with a destabilising ambiguity over the demobilization arrangements for any SWAPO fighters inside Namibia. In the early hours of 1 April, the SADF reported an 'invasion' by PLAN. Immediately, the supposedly disbanded Koevoet squad of the South African Police, notorious for its brutality, initiated hostilities. There followed in the next few days some of the bloodiest fighting seen in Namibia in the whole long war, with more guerillas, civilians and SADF killed than in any other engagements inside Namibia, perhaps 250 or more deaths. The two sides only reached a 'stand-off' by mid-April (Brigadier Opande, Kenyan deputy military commander of UNTAG, *Interviews*, 8 and 9 September 1989). During those days the UNTAG and FLS representatives were trying to arrange a cease-fire, but it was not until mid-May that the plan's implementation was officially resumed and SADF and SWATF were once more confined to base.

These events profoundly threatened the peace process and the transition itself, and prompted the AG to announce that the arrangements for the elections were indefinitely postponed. So, how were they allowed to happen and what effect did they have on the political climate?

Acrimonious debates over the resourcing of the UN operation had meant that the UN military did not begin to arrive until late March. By then fewer than 1,000 of the intended 4,650 military component were on the ground, with few vehicles and little equipment. The UN Secretary General's Special Representative (UNSGSR), Marthi Ahtisaari, did not himself arrive until 31 March (Jaster, 1990). Late on 1st April the UN Secretary General 'reluctantly' gave approval for some SWATF units to be released from bases to back-up the police. He claimed that he was faced with 'the alternative of accepting a decision by South Africa to decide that it could no longer be bound by UNSCR 435, and the settlement proposal' (Cedric Thornberry, UNTAG spokesperson, 5 April 1989) and for SADF then to deal with the threat in their own way and without any restraint. The next day the UNSGSR approved the reactivation and rearming of six SWATF battalions to 'assist the SWA Police'.

Confusion about provisions for the disarming and monitoring of PLAN fighters within Namibia provided opportunities for the parties to try to push forward their own political strategies, part of which rested on the extent of SWAPO's presence in the country. The South Africans wanted the propaganda advantage of claiming that the PLAN fighters had invaded from beyond Namibia's borders. On the other hand, it was of great symbolic significance to SWAPO to have its people actually in Namibia. Geneva Protocols (between South Africa, Angola and Cuba) specified that PLAN fighters should withdraw some 150km north of the border with Angola, a proposal which itself discounted SWAPO's claims that there were PLAN fighters already in Namibia. SWAPO claimed that as they had never been a direct party to the Protocols, they were not bound by them, and claimed the right to restrict its forces to bases inside Namibia. However, no concrete provision was made for any PLAN fighters that were in Namibia, as the Geneva Protocols did not cover what was to go on inside Namibia. Yet evidence from the PLAN fighters who did come into the country overwhelmingly contradicts the view put out by the South Africans that this was a belligerent invasion. Eye-witness accounts, even of South African soldiers themselves, suggests that the PLAN fighters were indeed intending to surrender to UNTAG (Cliffe et al, 1994:88-9). Nonetheless, the decision by someone in the PLAN high command to send fighters back home was at best extremely ill-conceived, even if it could be claimed not to contravene the cease-fire agreement.

South Africa subsequently won the right to ensure that no PLAN fighters were to be allowed to be demobilized within Namibia, and most made their way back to Angola without the assistance of safe-passage arrangements secured by negotiations between Angola, Cuba and South Africa. By 15 May this was officially complete, although several more fighters were to die in the process.

Demobilization of the South African-controlled forces was to be a much murkier and drawn-out affair, with considerable delays in the dismantling of command structures, and deception of the UN as regards the retention of weaponry (Cliffe et al, 1994:92). Koevoet, like the other South African-controlled forces, continued to be paid, and remained effective beyond the time set out in the plan, even after many of them they had officially been demobilized and/or absorbed into the police force.

The incursions thus provided the justification for the dreaded forces of Koevoet to be once again let off the leash, under the guise of the police force and with only very limited monitoring by the UN until the very eve of the elections. Their renewed ability to operate with legitimacy constituted the single most serious intimidating factor which called into question the very freeness of the election. Moreover, the remobilization of SADF and SWATF, authorized by the UNSGSR, gave credence to the South African version of April's events. This legitimized the massacre, made it more difficult to monitor the activities of Koevoet thereafter; and generally placed UNTAG in a position of responding to South African initiatives. It also delayed all UNTAG's other preparatory tasks until mid-May. Together these moves enhanced South Africa's control over the transition process.

The social and political climate continued to be tense and full of hostilities during almost the entire period between April 1989 and independence in March 1990. Shootings, kidnappings, throwing of hand grenades, beatings and even assassinations took place. However, persistent violence and the most systematic intimidation of voters and parties was considerably limited by the presence of UNTAG staff, hundreds of foreign observers and the reports of monitoring groups, such as the Church Information Monitoring Service.

Structural intimidation was also widespread. Many people who had jobs or pensions from particular ethnic administrations, or were caught up in patron-client relationships, or indebted to officials, chiefs and headmen, chose not to vote in any way that would jeopardize their situation. Employees and farm-workers, trapped in feudal relationships with their employers, were often either subject to pressure to vote for the party suggested by their boss (usually DTA), or were refused permission to vote at all. Structural intimidation was also integral to the electoral process itself. Registration and voting took place in magistrates' courts, at white farms, and in old army bases, all places associated with colonial oppression; registration and electoral officials were from the AG's staff; and in some places police were prominently placed at registration points/polling stations, often with guns.

Instances of SWAPO violence and intimidation did occur, and may explain why SWAPO ex-detainees were not more prominent in campaigning. On the whole, however, considerable restraint was displayed by SWAPO, which was determined not to offer any excuse for delaying or halting independence. By contrast, DTA recruited ex-members of the security forces, mostly from Koevoet, and particularly in Ovamboland and Kavango, to work in military-style units usually under white leaders who maintained close links with other ex-Koevoet members in the police force. UNTAG was never able to fully control their tactics of outright intimidation and violence, particularly in Ovamboland where the most widespread, overt and bloody intimidation occurred right up to the beginning of polling (Cliffe et al, 1994:101-2). Neighbouring Kavango and Caprivi, formerly heavily militarized districts, were similarly afflicted. Elsewhere, in less militarized regions, open conflict between the supporters of different parties was more the norm. In Windhoek there were several confrontations, but the most serious incident was the assassination of the senior SWAPO figure, Anton Lubowski. Meanwhile, UNTAG itself was not free from attack, and direct harassment of black voters continued to the point of voting in Swakopmund.

Nonetheless, the election was declared to be free and fair by the UNSGSR, and most observers concluded that the violence and intimidation had not affected the result to any significant degree. The massive SWAPO victory in Ovamboland was reassuring on this score, but unanswered questions remained as to how much stronger SWAPO's support would have been elsewhere in the north had the climate been different.

Finally, although the UN certainly set some store by a transformation of Namibia's racially-biased media before the election, the state-controlled South West African Broadcasting Corporation did not reform its pro-South Africa bias until the UNSGSR intervened in mid-September, after which equal access was granted to all parties, and some impartial information about the election process itself was provided by UNTAG.

The Administration of the Transition and the Elections

The regulations governing the conduct and type of election were always assumed by the South Africans and SWAPO to have a bearing on the result, and so were themselves matters for contestation. That the election was to be for a CA, through some system of proportional representation (PR), was agreed in 1986, but the details of the election itself had to be negotiated once the UN plan was underway. South Africa regarded PR as being closer to its interests than a plurality system, as this would increase the chances of small parties being represented, and promoted the idea of voters having two votes and/or there being two lists to ensure some direct representation of 'ethnic groups'. The system eventually agreed upon was that of a single national constituency, whereby each party put forward a single list of candidates from whom a number proportional to the votes received over the whole country would be elected.

This much was agreed long in advance, but other crucial matters concerning the eligibility and registration of voters, the registration of parties, and mechanisms for polling and vote counting, were left to be resolved by the AG, subject to the approval of the UNSGSR. This meant that the South Africans were able to retain the initiative in drawing up regulations in all these matters, with Ahtisaari only intervening with the right of veto, although he consulted other parties widely. As merely monitor and supervisor of the elections, UNTAG was in many ways put in an almost impossible situation, but the limits to their action were certainly interpreted in a conservative manner by the UNSGSR. International responses to the initial AG proclamation which set out a draft of the regulations were condemned as 'outrageous', 'completely unacceptable' and 'even worse than we could have expected' (*The Guardian*, 23 July 1989), and had in fact been part of a similar framework for elections held in 1978 which had been declared null and void by the UN (UNIN, 1989). However, whilst Ahtisaari initially condoned the draft regulations, intervention from the international community and directly from the office of the UN Secretary General in New York ensured that some revision did occur.

There were three main areas of contention about what was an complex voting and counting procedure. First, the proposed verification procedure would have required all voters to place their votes in envelopes with their registration numbers on the outside, thus violating the secrecy of the ballot. This condition was removed. Second, voters were to be allowed to vote anywhere in the country, which gave considerable room for manipulation. This was subsequently limited, in that voters were now expected to vote where they had registered, but could apply to vote elsewhere, in which case their ballots would be sent separately to Windhoek as a 'tendered ballot' to be counted along with identification documents, and with measures to ensure secrecy. Third, only disabled or illiterate voters were to obtain explanations or help in writing their vote, and such assistance would only be offered by South African officials. The final regulations stipulated that an UNTAG supervisor would always be present when help was being given.

Voter education thus had to be rushed in the short period left after the regulations were settled and, in Ovamboland, the location of some polling booths was not decided until four days before the election began on 7 November. Moreover, the registration of parties and voters had to take place before these details were agreed, and the registration of voters was itself a highly contentious matter because of the difficulty in defining and proving Namibian citizenship. A wide definition was accepted which included people whose parents had been born in Namibia or who had been resident for at least four years prior to 1989. This made many South Africans and Angolans eligible, including some engaged in counter-insurgency operations, refugees, and other immigrants - people who were hardly expected to vote for SWAPO. On the other hand, regulations requiring documentary proof of birthplace, rather than the commonly accepted evidence of sworn statements from parents, presented problems for many people, and possibly disenfranchised three thousand SWAPO supporters. By some estimates 'missing' voters could have represented as many as four seats for SWAPO (Cliffe et al, 1994:120-6).

UNTAG, the AG and many other observers denied that there had been any significant exclusions. The close match with predicted figures based on population estimates was cited as evidence, but these were based on calculations from the 1981 census, which itself is thought to have undercounted, and furthermore no adjustments for returnees, or people from Angola or South Africa, were made in the predictions of eligible numbers. The *pattern* of registration following this yardstick also varied, with regions of under-registration tending to be those which results showed as having a high degree of support for SWAPO.

People turned out in large numbers from the first day, eager to cast their vote. In many parts of the country, DTA made its presence felt around polling booths, distributing free food and drink, with roads and supporters decked in party colours. However, there was not much overt evidence of intimidation outside the polling stations to get committed voters to stay away or to change their allegiance.

Technical problems occurred in Ovamboland because such large numbers of people voted at each station. On the second day, many had run out of ballot papers, printing ink, ballot boxes and envelopes for tendered ballots. A number of factors were of concern to observers: illiterate voters were often not given help, and even literate ones struggled as no African languages were used on the papers; only Afrikaans and English. Furthermore, UNTAG officials often played a quite secondary role and party agents often remained quite passive at the stations.

However, the remarkably high turn out, with 83% of votes being cast on the first three days, seemed to confound observer reservations about the fairness and freedom of the elections, and the UNSGSR officially proclaimed them to be so on 14 November. Although many observers concluded that parts of the process were certainly not very free, it was a common conclusion that the overall result was roughly fair.

The Parties and the Issues

Ten parties contested the elections,[1] but the main battle was always between SWAPO and DTA which, between them, eventually shared 85% of votes cast. The other contestants were reduced from a much larger number which existed when the UN plan first begun to be implemented (some were only established in 1989, with others having a longer history). Many of these small parties came together to form five of the six fronts which contested the election (the DTA making the sixth). Each of these five fronts obtained one seat in the CA.

Many observers divided the contestants between two camps - *non-collaborationist* and *collaborationist*, dominated by SWAPO and DTA respectively, along with the two contestants which represented the interests of the previous regime, the Action Christian National (ACN), an alliance between the National Party of South West Africa and the Deutsche Aktion/Deutsch Sudwest Komitee, and the Federal Convention of Namibia (FCN), an alliance of six minor parties.

In 1989 SWAPO consisted of two separated structures seeking integration: one returning from exile; one emerging from internal repression. The external wing had developed organizational forms appropriate to international diplomatic representation and promoting armed struggle. Its leaders had lived in exile for 25 years or more, and had not submitted their position or programme to a Congress or any other form of accountability during that period. However, they had been involved, with international advisers, in policy formulations through the UN Institute for Namibia in Lusaka, which had produced weighty studies of Namibian realities and position papers. Its other personnel consisted of fighters, party functionaries, intellectuals and students. They only began to return to the country in the five months before the election, party president Sam Nujoma only in October. SWAPO in exile had built up a significant resource base with support from the UN, the OAU and non-aligned and socialist states, but little was made public about funding during the election period.

SWAPO had always maintained an internal wing, with a legal existence, but it had been so harassed by the South African administration that it had never been able to develop a fully visible, national structure or even much of a presence in parts of the southern and central regions. Yet many leading figures in the churches, professions, schools and among mineworkers and students had chosen to identify with it and their number grew rapidly in the late 1980s.

Other members in this non-collaborationist camp included the United Democratic Front (UDF), an alliance of eight parties, and the Namibia National Front (NNF), an alliance of five parties.

By contrast, DTA had the experience of contesting and prevailing in elections for ten years and also had very considerable resources of funds, vehicles and supplies. The source of DTA's considerable finances was never revealed during the transition period, and indeed the alliance denied it received any funds from the Namibia Foundation, the one source that was publicly known to bankroll many small parties, having appeared in 1989 to support multi-party democracy and group rights. However, revelations in July 1991 from South Africa's 'Inkathagate' scandals revealed that the South

Africa government funded several anti-SWAPO parties. The implication that the South African government was also dictating DTA's overall strategy can be read into some of the other revelations, and indeed DTA did eventually admit to having benefited from South African funding (*The Guardian*, 26 and 27 July 1991).

Other members in this camp included the Nambia Patriotic Front (NPF), Christian Democratic Action (CDA), the Namibian National Democratic Party (NNDP), and SWAPO-Democrats (SWAPO-D). The parties' manifestos showed a surprising degree of consensus on a range of issues about Namibia's future. All were committed to a multiparty representative system of cabinet government, and all promised services in health, education and so on, and all promised hard work. The position of parties was revealed more closely from observing the campaigns: the parties' stance towards each other overshadowed any debate or distinct positions on other issues. The stance taken by contestants towards each other represented a political position as regards Namibia's history and potential future.

SWAPO articulated a less radical position on transforming inherited economic and social structures than might have been expected and, most significantly, did not campaign on the land issue except in the north, and then only in vague terms. Instead, SWAPO sought to assert its position as the single authentic voice of the Namibian people struggling for national liberation against South African rule. At its rallies, SWAPO stressed the need for reconciliation but also the importance of rejecting all the collaborationist parties.

In contrast to the white-interest ACN and the Rehoboth separatist FCN, DTA did not campaign for any specially entrenched 'group rights'. Rather than projecting any positive image of their own, the DTA parties instead indulged in negative electioneering, intimating that SWAPO had some covert agenda involving political repression, one-partyism and a radical social and economic programme.

The main issue with which the other parties tried to taint SWAPO's image, and against which SWAPO became most defensive, was that of its detainees, Namibians imprisoned and often tortured by SWAPO in camps in Angola and Zambia. This also became a vehicle for the articulation of ethnic politics: it was argued that the majority of those detained, and those who had still not been repatriated, were non-Ovambo, drawn especially from Coloured, Damara, Nama and other communities in the south, and it was in these areas that the issue had most impact. SWAPO stood accused of having imprisoned as many as two thousand people between 1980 and 1990, usually on charges of spying or of being South African agents, and that between five hundred and one thousand were still being detained or had died in detention. It was still claimed at the end of 1989 that five hundred had not been released, in spite of denials by SWAPO and a special UN mission which more or less exonerated SWAPO.

Table 4.1 Namibian Constituent Assembly results 1989 - total votes and seats for each party

Party	*Valid votes	% votes	CA Seats
ACN	23,728	3.5	3
CDA	2,495	0.4	0
DTA	191,532	28.6	21
FCN	10,452	1.6	1
NNDP	984	0.1	0
NNF	5,344	0.8	1
NPF	10,693	1.6	1
SWAPO-D	3,161	0.5	0
SWAPO	384,567	57.3	41
UDF	37,874	5.6	4
Total	670,830	100.0	72

* Excludes rejected votes.

The detainees issue undermined SWAPO's international image, and led to local arguments about funding and other support, particularly by churches. It also mobilised detainees' relatives and their communities against SWAPO and made viable a political movement opposed to SWAPO but untainted by the collaborationist label - the UDF, drawing particular support from its heartland in Damaraland, being the most vociferous. Attempts were made by some SWAPO leaders to handle the issue by explaining the context in which so many people had been arrested as spies, and apologizing for the most extreme forms of treatment. However, the prospect of a commission of enquiry was refused, and a number of SWAPO's senior leaders were conspicuously silent in their lack of public remorse. Such a stance was gleefully picked up by SWAPO's electoral opponents, many of whom did not have clean hands themselves.

The final results gave SWAPO a comfortable majority (57.3%) of the valid votes cast entitling it to 41 out of the CA's total of 72 seats. This was, however, short of the two-thirds' majority that would have given them control of the CA. The overall results are presented in Table 4.1. DTA was the only other sizeable party with 28.6% of the popular vote, entitling it to 21 seats, 3 short of the one-third of the total required for a blocking veto within the CA. The UDF with 5.6% of the vote and its strong local support around Damaraland, and the ACN with 3.5%, were the only other parties to win more than one seat. Three other parties with around 1% each obtained a single CA seat.

SWAPO was the winning party in only eight of the 23 electoral districts (EDs), but that meant little as they were not constituencies and varied a hundred-fold in terms of voters. However, it does indicate the regional nature of its support. SWAPO's majorities were in the bigger districts which included 68% of registered voters. The different social and regional voting patterns are seen more starkly in Table 4.2. Ovamboland is a case apart, deserving separate consideration because of its size alone, and also because the result was so radically different from elsewhere. It showed such a majority (92%) for SWAPO that it can be considered a virtual one-party region. The overwhelming nature of this support needs to be explained.

At the opposite end of the spectrum there were a range of many, mostly small EDs (our last category of areas in table 4.2), where DTA received the largest vote, and in all but two of which SWAPO's vote was 30% or less. One exception was the remote Caprivi strip where SWAPO polled almost 40% but still had to concede a majority to DTA (52.4%). The other was Okahandja, a white farming area near Damaraland. These EDs included almost all the areas of white farming and the 'reserves' of most of the ethnic groups other than Kavango and Ovambo. Overall, DTA obtained only a bare majority, 50.3%, in this category of EDs. It is nevertheless the case that in the 22 EDs outside Ovamboland, which area alone delivered 70% of SWAPO's total vote, the DTA received more votes than SWAPO: 180,787 to 158,946.

In a middle category of EDs, SWAPO received 30-70% of the vote and a bigger share than any other party. These included three mining and fishing areas and the northern 'reserve' of Kavongo where SWAPO had a majority, and Windhoek, where it had 46%, plus a handful of white farming districts where SWAPO headed the list with about one-third of votes, where DTA shared the rest with significant minorities either to UDF or ACN.

Table 4.2 Namibian elections 1989 - patterns of differing SWAPO voting strength

Type of regional result	Electoral Districts	% of votes cast	SWAPO %	DTA %
SWAPO overwhelming (Ovamboland)	1	36.5	92.3	4.4
SWAPO plurality (1)	7	31.9	49.4	34.2
SWAPO minority (2)	15	31.7	24.0	48.4

Notes:
(1) Karibib, Kavango, Luderitz, Maltahohe, Swakopmund, Tsumeb, Windhoek.
(2) Bethanie, Caprivi, Damara, Gobabis, Grootfontein, Herero, Kaoko, Karasburg, Keetmanshoop, Mariental, Okahandja, Omaruru, Otjiwarongo, Rehoboth, Outjo.

Seeking Explanations

Both in predicting and in explaining the Namibian election results there has been much recourse to a simple explanation in terms of 'ethnicity'. It most certainly was the basis for most pre-election predictions, and for the parties' own calculations and strategies. But, as our three-way categorization in Table 4.2 makes clear, Ovamboland apart, the returns indicate mixed party support in most regions. Although parties' support varied regionally, there is no monopoly of party support on the part of any ethnic group. In fact, the ethnic make-up of most districts is mixed, especially where there are towns and in areas of commercial farming. As few districts are ethnically homogeneous, a simple 'ethnic-bloc' analysis is not possible for an ED as a whole.

Nor does the evidence exist to see whether party support in EDs with localities occupied by distinct ethnic groups (for instance, the three 'tribes' in different parts of Caprivi, or the small Herero 'reserves' included in

Damaraland or Gobabis, or the Nama area that became part of Keetmanshoop) correlates with these distinct areas. Counting was in fact done separately for each polling station but those figures, which would have made possible such calculation, were never released. The authors did, however, manage to obtain some of these results, from 29 polling stations out of an estimated 70, in Kavango.

Although that electoral district is one of the most ethnically homogeneous (over 80% Kavango), it might have been expected to reveal another kind of 'ethnicity', that of a 'clan' or 'chiefdom', or at least the influence of patronage. The district is made up of four chiefdoms, and it was widely expected that the westernmost of these, Kwangali, whose chief was thought to be pro-SWAPO, would vote SWAPO and the other areas would be DTA strongholds. The available figures for the polling stations, while showing some geographical distinction in voting (roughly 60% SWAPO west of Rundu town, just over 50% around the town, and about 40% immediately to the east), indicate that differences were only marginal. Both parties commanded significant support across all the polling stations, with only one exception - the smallest, with an overwhelming vote for one party.

There is an even more fundamental objection to applying the simplistic 'ethnic' label to the voting pattern. To the extent that there is any correlation between an area and party support, as in Ovamboland, the label is not in itself an *explanation*. Rather, it is that correlation which itself needs to be explained. If the majority of Herero in fact voted for the DTA, or the Ovambo overwhelmingly for SWAPO, why was that so?

In part, ethnic voting patterns could have been expected as a legacy of political practices and structures established by the South African administration, which had created tribal structures, set up second-tier authorities, and supported the tribal DTA alliance. As a consequence, such 'open' politics as existed in Namibia over the previous twenty years had centred around patron-client relationships channelling often misappropriated funds from the second-tier authorities. Elections held during the colonial period were accompanied by intimidation and patronage channelled through the same ethnic structures of authority. Many observers supposed that the use of similar techniques in the independence elections would promote results reflecting the party political allegiances of 'ethnic' leaders. Thus prediction and, to some extent, analysis after the event took the form of reading off regional results from the political hues of socially-dominant individuals and groups, whether chiefs, well-known political leaders or employers. However, these historical factors only partially explain Ovamboland, the only virtually one-party area and arguably the most resistant to patronage politics.

A further complication in trying to estimate any 'ethnic' factor is that it figured differentially in the public stances of the main contenders. DTA's constituent elements and other small parties did make explicit calls to a local ethnic identity and certainly built more systematically on patronage networks than SWAPO, whereas the latter had always articulated a conscious, pan-Namibian nationalism. Both main contenders had a broad leadership covering all ethnic groups: but DTA had built up theirs by an alliance of tribal 'barons', whereas SWAPO's leaders came from all areas and tried, at least in their public stance, to transcend an ethnic identity. The matter of the role of 'ethnicity' in Namibian nationalism was thus one of those items of difference about alternative futures at issue between the two sides (Dollie, 1989). A further implication of this particular area of contestation is that the extent to which party support followed any discernible ethnic pattern would be a measure of the success of the DTA/RSA conception of nationalism as opposed to SWAPO's 'nation-statism'. It is ironic then that the only clear-cut instance of such a pattern was the overwhelming Ovambo support for SWAPO.

Where intimidation and patronage were thought to have been minimal in their occurrence and effect, some other sets of explanation have to be found for the preponderance of ethnic groups voting en bloc. It may simply be that ethnicity roughly coincides with some other category, such as class: for example, those Ovambo people resident in the southern and central parts of Namibia constitute a large proportion of the industrial working class, and it may be that the explanation for their voting for SWAPO in those areas is because of their shared interests as workers, rather than as Ovambos *per se*.

Another standard approach to analysing election results is to look for correlations between political consciousness and actual voting behaviour on the one hand, and the social and economic profile of the electorate. But in circumstances where opinion polls were impractical in the atmosphere of intimidation and fear, one can only do this indirectly by indicating some factors which could have determined outcomes for particular regions. Here we can only examine the vote for each party to consider possible explanatory hypotheses.

The Bases of Party Support: Minor Parties

We can separate the results for each party into four groups. Here we consider (i) those that failed to win a CA seat - 3 parties; (ii) those that won only *one* seat - 3 fronts; and (iii) those that won a handful, namely the UDF with 4 and ACN with 3. After that, we will examine support for the DTA and SWAPO.

The failures   Three parties - SWAPO-D, CDA and NNDP - between them obtained less than 1% of the national vote and can be dealt with summarily. None of the three could command even any small pockets of local support. Only in one ED did any of these parties manage to acquire slightly over 1% of the vote (CDA had 1.4% in tiny Bethanie).   Clearly their positions, their leaders and organization had no basis for appeal to voters, nor even the prospect of patronage.   Moreover, each of them could be seen as little more than a vehicle for a personality with long political credentials.

The single seat parties   Three fronts - FCN, NPF, and NNF - managed to secure one CA seat each, the NNF only by benefit of the 'remainder' formula. Between them they polled only 26,579 votes, 4% of the total.   FCN and NPF both received a significant minority of votes in one area, whereas NNF picked up a few votes across most of the country with no area significant.

The specific patterns of their support can be summarized thus.   FCN had espoused some degree of devolution of central powers and 'group rights', but it secured almost half of its 10,542 votes from Rehoboth, where it polled almost 30% of all votes. Its significance was thus confined principally to the Rehoboth Baster, but even then simply as the main opposition party. NFP secured significant shares of the total vote in only two EDs, both Herero-speaking: Hereroland (12.6%), where it had third place, and Kaokoland (19.9%) where it beat SWAPO into third place.   These two districts contributed 41.3% of the Front's national vote. However, in no sense was the NPF 'a Herero party': it only gained minority support in those areas, and did manage to win a few hundred votes in each of a number of EDs mainly in the centre and east of the country and in Windhoek.

NNF was also expected to obtain support in Hereroland. Although its share there (4.6%) was higher than in other EDs, it received just 1-2% of the vote throughout much of the country and was never even in third place in any ED. If anything it had slightly higher shares of the vote in the towns, including Windhoek. This would be consistent with the inclusion in this alliance of some sophisticated, left-wing political groups of teachers and professionals.

Minor parties gaining more than one seat   The UDF's most obvious success was in Damaraland, where it gained an absolute majority of all votes, the only case where a minor party secured over 50% in any ED. This vote confirmed the local strength of its main constituent party, the Damara Council, and on its own that area guaranteed one seat in the CA.   However, the ED included Arandis, the dormitory township for the Rossing uranium mine; but UDF made very few inroads there into what was SWAPO's overwhelming support among the estimated 4,500 registered mineworkers and their families. Some of the rest of their support was regional: in five EDs close to Damaraland (Karibib, Okahandja, Omaruru, Otjiwarongo, Outjo) UDF's share of the vote was between 10% and 24%.

The ACN alliance stood on a platform of preserving the rights of the white communities and of 'maintaining standards'. The presumption must be that its 23,728 votes came overwhelmingly from whites. Its highest share of the vote by far was in Karasburg, the border ED where so many South Africans voted.

The Bases of Party Support: The Main Contenders

SWAPO's strength was overwhelmingly in Ovamboland, which alone contributed 57.8% of its vote, and where its appeal successfully reached all areas, social strata and classes. Kavango, where it won over 50%, was another area of large support, but SWAPO's more mixed success there reflected a rather more complex political history during the colonial period and the war. SWAPO also won minority support in centres of organized labour, the mines and the major towns. Counting these latter workers and migrants, a very large proportion of Ovambos obviously did vote for SWAPO, but over the whole country significant proportions of people of other ethnic groups did so too. SWAPO's appeal was, however, much less nationwide than it had anticipated.

What first has to be explained is the extent of this SWAPO vote in Ovamboland and among Ovambo; why did no significant section of the population vote against the party? Clearly its origins among Ovambo and among migrant workers has not been seriously challenged. The area's proximity to the fighting throughout the 1970s and 1980s, its supply of recruits both from among peasants, workers and school students reinforced these linkages with the movement. Support for the party, even before 1989, seems to have been strong among educated youth, teachers and the churches. The possible identification of these and other 'professionals' with either the Department of Bantu Administration or the Transitional Government may have been reduced because the provision of instruction in English in the region's schools, unlike other areas, may have excluded them from preferment in local and national administrations which used Afrikaans. It is also evident that the several large entrepreneurs and many hundreds of small traders and shop and bar keepers also backed the party, even though they had prospered from a local economy fuelled by the presence of SADF, SWATF and counter-insurgents. Moreover, it is clear that the party must even have obtained the votes of some of those who were directly benefiting from the existing structures - members of ethnic battalions and Koevoet, local administration employees, and their dependants.

An 'ethnic' explanation has been put forward to explain not only the Ovambo result but SWAPO getting over 50% in the main towns, Luderitz, Swakopmund (including people from Walvis Bay) and Tsumeb, and almost half in Windhoek. No survey data allow us to say whether Ovambo migrants and workers voted SWAPO in the same large proportion. But comparing proportions of votes with the census population in these EDs suggests that workers in the mines and in fishing from other ethnic backgrounds also gave strong support to SWAPO. Subjective evidence suggests how the mechanisms of this tendency for class identification with SWAPO may have worked themselves out. In Arandis, the miners' township for Rossing Uranium, part of Damaraland ED, a leader of the Mineworkers Union (*Interview*, 1 January 1989) explained how the local branch had debated which party to back. Some consideration was given to smaller parties - NPF, NNF and WRP - with a progressive, pro-workers' platform, but their records were not considered to be strong enough to provide a solid alternative to SWAPO, which was seen as likely to deliver most for workers in future. As a reaction, some 75 members, mostly Damara, resigned from the union. Some indicative evidence, then, of a workers' block vote for SWAPO marginally qualified by 'ethnic' loyalties.

Kavango was the other large area where SWAPO won over 50%. Its involvement in the war, after the 1970s, was not as direct as in Ovamboland but its support among youth, teachers and in the church seemed to have been a partially effective counter to the patronage politics and widespread intimidation by Koevoet. In Caprivi, another border reserve, SWAPO also won a significant share even though it was the DTA president's home base. Elsewhere, SWAPO was not a majority party but everywhere obtained significant proportions of the overall vote. In the central, commercial farming areas dominated by whites it won roughly one-third of the vote, and in some of them was indeed the largest single party. But it obtained less than a quarter in the south and in the Herero-speaking areas.

These proportions in the south and centre certainly undercut SWAPO's claim to represent the 'nation', and represented a poorer result than they expected. Thus, for instance, a party organizer in Keetmanshoop reckoned that SWAPO would get two-thirds of the vote - 'despite the detainee issue' (*Interview*, 28 October 1989).

There are two kinds of explanation for the performance in these areas. Apologists would stress the lack of any pre-existing party infrastructure and the difficulty in challenging built-in patron-client patterns. An alternative perspective (e.g. Susan Brown, personal communication, June 1990) suggests that SWAPO actually lost popular support in the months leading up to the elections. Statistical evidence of any such trend is not available, but there are some straws in the wind which do indicate a swing against SWAPO in 1989. Some commentators point to a below-par attendance in 1989 at the annual memorial of the struggle against the Germans by some Nama led by the ancestor of SWAPO's internal leader, Henrik Witbooi. He himself (*Interview*, 28 October 1989) thought that, while justifying detention as necessary in war, the issue would cost SWAPO a two-thirds majority nationally.

Another contributory factor that might explain why SWAPO managed to win only a significant minority in many central and southern areas was hinted at by one of the party's regional election directors, who admitted (*Interview* 23.10.89) that SWAPO had 'little to offer the poorest' of the rural population in Hereroland. This statement not only implied that SWAPO's support was among the town population, those who were schooled and professionals, but pointed to a policy failure of being unable to articulate a land or resource distribution or other income-generating formula that would benefit farm labourers and peasants.

The DTA scored highest in the south of the country and in other farming areas, plus Hereroland and Kaokoland, but nowhere reached as much as 66% of the vote. Yet it is equally true that in only three EDs, two of them being Luderitz and Damaraland, it obtained less than a quarter of the vote. One set of explanations is that its support built upon the patronage of local affiliated parties that had access to the resources of second-tier administrations, plus the backing of a majority of white, farmworkers, and residents from Angola and South Africa. But its support extended beyond these elements with a direct interest in the status quo. It is hard to calculate numbers but the manipulation of the detainee issue probably did lead many to calculate that the DTA was the only viable alternative to dominance by a single party with a questionable record of repression. It may also have benefited from its image as a party of resources that could deliver.

DTA's great failure was in Ovamboland where they gained only 4%. An estimate of those employed in the administration there (although many were teachers) plus ethnic battalion and Koevoet personnel, let alone their adult dependants, was far more (some 15,000) than the vote of only just over 10,000 they received. Moreover, these figures suggest that the widespread campaign there of intimidation failed to deliver votes, even if it prevented registration, and may have been counter-productive, although the same conclusion cannot be assumed for Kavango and other areas where intimidation was common.

The Transition to Independence

The elections to the CA and its subsequent deliberations settled the institutional structures that would provide the legal basis of the new state: they constituted the new parliament; and installed SWAPO as the new government. The constitutional principles brokered by the CG in 1982 restricted the sovereignty of the CA and the Namibian people, but SWAPO chose not to challenge their legitimacy. SWAPO thus accepted not only a commitment to multi-party democracy but also the recognition of property rights and limits on its ability to tackle structural inequalities in Namibia's economy and society. Having less than two-thirds of the seats still allowed it to more or less control the detailed drafting of the new constitution as only a simple majority was required for each article and clause, with the two- thirds being necessary only for the final vote on the constitution as a whole. The drafting of the constitution was done secretly in committee, and no major disputes between the parties were publicly aired (but see Cliffe et al, 1994:201-12 for details of the committee discussions).

The detainee issue at first threatened to disrupt the proceedings of the CA with a demonstration outside the *Titenpalast* on the first morning, and it underlay both the public and committee discussions about fundamental human rights, which resulted in removing the provision in the draft document which had allowed preventive detention. Land and property rights were heatedly discussed in private, but a united front was presented in public. During the discussion of presidential power, which resulted in considerably greater limitations being placed on it than in the original draft, the thorny question of bicameralism began to appear, and it was this question that divided the committee most severely. SWAPO was forced to agree to a second legislative chamber, to be called the National Council and comprising two representatives from each of the new regional councils. The CA was to become a National Assembly, in future electable by a national PR system.

After the election, but before formal independence in 1990, the various political alliances of the opposition fronts began to crumble, and there were splits in the parties. A number of key figures joined SWAPO or DTA. SWAPO had decisions to make about its own transformation, considering the role of the party in relation to the state; the basis for party membership; and the role of interest groups. These issues had quite contrasting regional dimensions. In Ovamboland the issues were whether and how to win over the dissenting one-tenth of the population, consolidate one partyism, and recast the role of the party within the district. In other places where SWAPO was simply the most popular amongst several parties, the issue was more about trying to make inroads into other parties' support. In the many districts where SWAPO had only minority support it faced a real dilemma about how to proceed. Some SWAPO leaders used their ethnic links with communities to try to increase the party's support, such as amongst Herero people, and another common tactic was to persuade influential individuals to join the government, if not the party. By contrast, little was done to appeal to trade unions or the poor, whether rural or urban.

Thirteen new regions were eventually delineated in 1992 through a redrawing of the political map, abolishing the old bantustans, combining communal and commercial farming areas, and dividing Ovamboland into four regions (Sidaway and Simon, 1993). Each of these regions contained single-member constituencies from which representatives would sit in the National Council. The first regional elections took place in December 1992, and had about 70% of the 1989 turnout voting in the ninety-five constituencies.

SWAPO won all but four of the regions, and so the result was not seen as one which revealed massive popular discontent, but rather one which suggested a polarization as the small parties lost representation. DTA won more constituencies in three regions and one was split between DTA and UDF, but no parties other than these three were represented in the twenty-six member National Council, which was inaugurated in January 1993. SWAPO also had majorities in thirty-nine of the forty-eight local authorities carved out of the regions, with DTA controlling seven and UDF having two (Cliffe et al, 1994:227). This is not to say that discontent was not building up by this time, particularly amongst the rural and urban poor, for many of whom life remained very difficult, but it did not translate into electoral opposition.

In 1994 full-scale elections took place for the National Assembly and for the President, and again there was some anxiety that SWAPO's lack of prioritization of the welfare of the poor, might, even in its northern heartland (Pankhurst, 1995), translate into diminished electoral strength. Instead, SWAPO increased its majority from the 1989 position to well over two-thirds. The registered electorate was increased by 120,000 from that of the independence elections (Simon, 1995:108), mostly from the increase in young voters, and as many of the South African residents who voted in 1989 were no longer eligible in this election, the number of 'new' voters was even greater than the figures suggest.

Eight parties contested this election: SWAPO, DTA, UDF, The Democratic Coalition of Namibia (a new group of disaffected DTA and ACN), SWANU, the Monitor Action Group (successor to the ACN), the FCN, and the tiny Workers' Revolutionary Party. Campaigning was low-key, and the event very peaceful, with high profile voter education, largely funded from United

States' sources, producing a turnout of 76.05% of the electorate for both polls (Simon, 1995: 108-10). The opposition lodged complaints with the Attorney General about electoral irregularities in four polling stations of the north where the number of votes cast exceeded the number of voters registered, although the Electoral Commission found that there was an 'acceptable explanation' (Simon, 1995:112), and the issue did not develop into a serious political crisis.

Sam Nujoma was re-elected President with 74.46% of the vote, whilst his only opposer, the DTA candidate, Mishake Muyongo, achieved 23.08% (Simon, 1995:112). SWAPO achieved 72.72% of the vote for parties, whilst DTA remained the only credible opposition with 20.45% overall. The squeeze on the smaller parties resulted in only the DCN, MAG, and UDF having any representation in the National Assembly besides the two major parties. There was no significant change in the regional support base of the parties from 1989 (but see Simon, 1995:113 for detailed regional analyses), and, as in the 1989 elections, few white or 'coloured' people appeared to have voted for SWAPO. The loss of South African voters from the roll seemed to have translated into a decrease in support for DTA, and the increase in young voters to have overwhelmingly gone to SWAPO.

The increase in SWAPO's strength reawakened concerns about possible moves towards a one-party state, but the reality seems closer to the phenomenon of the one-and-a-bit-party politics found in Botswana, in which the trappings of multipartyism and periodic electoral competition are ensured but do not present any real threat to the dominance of the ruling party. SWAPO signalled that it intended to retain the mechanisms of democratic accountability, insisting that in the event of making any constitutional amendments it would hold a referendum. The main amendment discussed in this context was extending the right of the President to hold office for more than two terms.

Conclusion

SWAPO achieved an electoral victory in 1989 within a structure whose design and manipulation still lay, to a large degree, in the hands of South Africa. To win against these constraints demonstrated the very real support for SWAPO which existed in the country at independence. That it did not meet the challenge set earlier by the South Africans and the CG, that of obtaining the two-thirds' majority needed to write the constitution, did not seem to matter very much. The result was celebrated as an outright victory by SWAPO, and its failure to win two-thirds of the vote went some way towards allaying opposition fears that an over-dominant party would be hell-bent on introducing a one-party state at the earliest opportunity. In the subsequent negotiations about the constitutional amendments, SWAPO conceded the need for a bicameral legislature, a limited presidential term and the protection of property rights - and relinquished claims for government to have the right of 'preventive detention'. These were all concessions which SWAPO might have been expected to resist more fiercely than it did, considering its stance in previous years before the election, but it seems that the need to take up the reigns of power was more pressing than prolonging negotiations.

To some extent it would appear that SWAPO's willingness to accept a constitutional compromise represented a shift in political outlook which pre-dated the election. It could be argued that SWAPO was willing to relinquish these powers because it did not require them to follow its political programme, which was based on minimal direct state intervention in the economy. Such a stance certainly seems evident in its record since independence: its stalling on the issue of land reform and poor record on employment-creation contrasts markedly with the good relations the government has maintained with international business and Namibian owners of capital (Pankhurst, 1995; Simon, 1995). That the party was able to follow this programme whilst still retaining electoral support meant that there was no need for it to alter the constitution radically, except in the matter of the presidential term. The degree of its commitment to democratic accountability will only be fully revealed, however, in the event of growing popular disaffection being translated into support for an opposition party or presidential candidate.

Note

1. In addition to SWAPO, the other nine parties were: ACN - Action Christian National; CDA - Christian Democratic Alliance; DTA - Democratic Turnhalle Alliance; FCN - Federal Convention for Namibia; NNDP - Namibia National Democratic Party; NNF - Namibia National Front; NPF - Namibia Patriotic Front; SWAPO-D - SWAPO Democrats; and the UDF - United Democratic Front.

5 Democratization and the 1991 Elections in Zambia

CAROLYN BAYLIES AND MORRIS SZEFTEL

Zambia's 1991 multi-party elections stand as a model of peaceful regime transition. The United National Independence Party (UNIP), which had ruled Zambia since independence in 1964 and as the sole legal party since 1973, was removed by a landslide victory for the Movement for Multi-Party Democracy (MMD) which had coalesced out of disparate demands for multi-party democracy only 15 months before. The speed with which the one-party state was dismantled and its government evicted was dramatic, but the revolution was a partial one. Zambia effectively experienced the replacement of one dominant party by another, with UNIP's strength reduced almost entirely to a regional rump in the country's Eastern Province. Moreover, many aspects of political culture, organization and practice remained intact and were ultimately to undermine many of the gains of 1991. Nevertheless, the elections were a genuine expression of citizen participation and proved an effective means of changing the country's leadership.

It is too simplistic to describe a uniform authoritarianism across sub-Saharan Africa, much less its being challenged by uniform pluralistic initiatives. Not only has there been a wide variation of post-colonial experience, and different forms of authoritarian, patrimonial, democratic or quasi-democratic rule, but the particular balance between participation and repression characterizing any given state has had a significant bearing on both the nature and 'success' of political change. Zambia's Second Republic (1972-91) was characterized by a one-party system under a constitutionally supreme party (UNIP) and a high level of concentration of power in the presidency, with limited local government and a parliament which, while permitting debate, served essentially to rubber-stamp party policy. A state of emergency inherited at independence remained in force throughout, enabling the exercise of arbitrary power. Attempts were made to co-opt or neutralize any competing bases of power, including the trade unions. Those who were too vocal in their dissent within the party were invariably excluded or removed from office; those excluded found their efforts frustrated and, in some cases, their liberties curtailed by the state security apparatus (cases of torture were highlighted by the Human Rights Commission established by the new government after 1991).

Yet certain constitutional guarantees remained in the one-party state, however weakly observed, and enough room for manoeuvre existed for an independent press to emerge, for church leaders to criticize the regime, for the trade union movement to retain a degree of independence and for a movement for multi-partyism to emerge. If the regime was authoritarian, the rhetoric of participation favoured by its president was not completely devoid of meaning, and his constructed ideology of Humanism at least provided a basis for questioning how far the society remained a humane and just one.[1] Perhaps the limits of the regime's authoritarianism were illustrated when the elections produced a peaceful transfer of power. President Kenneth Kaunda appeared on television the next morning to concede defeat and his successor, Frederick Chiluba, the former leader of the Zambia Congress of Trade Unions (ZCTU), was sworn in hours later. Uniquely in post-colonial Africa, government had changed hands without violence, and without force (or its threat) being required to underwrite the results of the election.

Contradictions of the Zambian Political Process

Underlying the Zambian post-colonial political process was a legacy of colonial exploitation - uneven development, integration into the global economy through the production of a single export commodity (copper), the domination of multinational mining corporations, and the relative exclusion of Zambians from social and economic resources. It left a society without control of capital or skills, without a bourgeoisie or the institutions of bourgeois society. This gave centrality to the role of the state: access to its offices and its resources was the key feature of politics; competition for that access became bitter and all-consuming. It ensured that the multi-party structures inherited at independence in 1964, and the governing petty bourgeoisie which operated them, would be insecure, weak and ineffective.

The 1964 independence constitution gave Zambia a pluralist political system dominated by an executive presidency. At independence, this pluralism resolved itself into two competing parties - UNIP and the older ANC (African National Congress). In the 1964 elections, ANC could win only 10 of the 75 seats contested and had become confined to the Southern Province and a few neighbouring areas of Central Province. UNIP's domination made it unlikely that the ANC could ever seriously challenge UNIP for power.

The weakness of the multi-party system was thus entrenched from the beginning. Post-colonial politics were shaped by conflict and competition *within* UNIP rather than between parties. In part, such divisions arose precisely because of the weakness of the opposition, which meant that there was little need for internal unity after independence had been won. Above all, however, it arose from the nature of political mobilization and organization in the context of economic underdevelopment. UNIP membership offered instrumental rewards: access to the state apparatus in a society where there were few other avenues of social mobility. UNIP's recruitment of support gave strategic significance to political leaders who were, in essence, regional and sectional political brokers, all inevitably competing with each other for influence and power at the centre. Clientelist politics thus dominated UNIP's activities. Party and government positions had constantly to be distributed among different groupings so as to minimize dissatisfaction. Politicians constantly weighed and measured this distribution, their own influence dependent on their ability to reward their followers. Essentially, the system made the executive an arbiter of access so that policy became hostage to the distribution of spoils.

The process plunged the party into crisis almost from the start; the UNIP national executive elections in 1967 were fought between two large coalitions of interests - with one sweeping the board. Since cabinet position was then tied to party office, 1967 produced a major reshuffle of posts and an end to factional (tribal) balancing. In consequence, a new opposition, the United Party, was formed by one of the defeated factions and won every seat from UNIP in Western Province in the 1968 elections. When the 1967 party elections were set aside in an effort to restore the practice of balancing the distribution of portfolios among various interests, the faction which had won in 1967 became embittered and, after numerous disputes, eventually formed another opposition party (UPP) in 1971 which threatened UNIP's hold over its Copperbelt and Northern Province heartland. It was this that led to the imposition of a one-party state in 1972 (Gertzel et al., 1984).

The response of the state was to increase its control over political activity; progressively, 'government' replaced 'politics'. The 1964 constitution and colonial emergency regulations had placed considerable power in the hands of an executive presidency: now it was used to manage political competition. Party office became dependent on executive patronage, a strategy exemplified in the slogan 'It Pays to Belong to UNIP'. Ultimately it led to the creation of a 'One- Party Participatory Democracy'. Kaunda was quite explicit about the motives for this:

The One-Party Democracy will help us to weed out political opportunists ... It has been fashionable in the past for any Party member ... to threaten to quit, or indeed quit, the Party to join the opposition; for any civil servant ... to threaten to quit ...; for any businessman denied a licence or a loan on perfectly legal grounds to run to the opposition, in the hope that if they formed the Government, he would be favoured. This era in which the politics of patronage has been a feature of life is gone (ibid: 17).

The One-Party State, Presidential Power and the Management of Patronage

The one-party state did not end patronage politics so much as give the centre control over it. Parliament, cabinet and party became increasingly subordinate to presidential dictat. As Gertzel has observed, 'the dominant institution in the one-party state was not the party but the presidency, in which resided enormous power' (1984:102). This power was used to marginalize political activity. The security apparatus was developed to oversee and defend the process. Bureaucrats and military officers were promoted into government positions ahead of elected politicians. In 1980, local government reform effectively disenfranchised the bulk of the electorate in local elections. Where shortages or inefficiency brought the government into public disfavour, Kaunda took to blaming individual politicians publicly; the list of notables thus sacked grew. In time, however, the process helped to undermine the one-party state: UNIP atrophied, losing any real political function and credibility; and Kaunda came to be regarded as a despot and blamed for poor government performance.

The single-party system can be seen as an attempt to contain structural political conflict within the context of chronic underdevelopment. However, in an economy such as Zambia's it was unlikely that factional demands could ever be satisfied. The attempt to do so badly distorted an already unevenly developed mono-economy. The creation of a huge state sector fell victim to the effort to control resource distribution as jobs and rewards were shared out by the centre; the public sector, particularly its corporations, became engulfed by political patronage. A system of price subsidies on basic commodities constantly squeezed producers in the hope of placating consumers. Throughout, the bureaucracy took its cut.

The one-party system obstructed the development of an autonomous civil society. Initially, the one-party state had opened up political office and government patronage to many middle-class strata. However, the extent to which those in high positions were personally beholden to the President provoked resentment. When a declining economy imposed increasing costs on them, including the growing inadequacy of state patronage and the lack of opportunities for initiatives outside the framework of the party, this resentment became all the sharper. The plethora of organizations and publications which emerged once restrictions had been lifted in 1990 testify to the desire of an elite strata for an end to presidential power. Ultimately, this spectrum of interests and opinion coalesced around the MMD.

Economic Crisis and Political Disaffection

From 1973, there was neither economic growth nor high copper prices, international debts mounted and the contradictions of clientelist politics became intolerable. Declining government revenue continued to subsidise the large public sector as well as the price of basic foodstuffs for the urban population. But whether government policy was motivated primarily by an attempt to retain its urban, working-class base (Bates and Collier, 1993; Hawkins, 1991) or to protect rent seeking on the part of the state elite (Callaghy, 1990) or to cater to the interests of multinational capital within the copper industry (Shafer, 1990), it became increasingly difficult to sustain the combination of welfare and patronage measures which had characterized UNIP's rule. Between 1975 and 1986 Zambia was forced by the IMF to attempt (unsuccessfully) seven different stabilization and adjustment programmes. Almost without exception, these produced contraction, inflation and unemployment. In December 1986 a round of price increases provoked food riots in which people were killed by security forces. Kaunda subsequently renounced the IMF stabilization programme, stating in an interview that he hoped that the IMF could devise an adjustment programme which would not require him to shoot Zambian citizens.

Economic malaise, debt and stabilization crises imposed huge political costs on the government. It was blamed by the West and the IMF for not implementing the stabilization measures properly (Callaghy, 1990; Bates and Collier, 1993) and by the populace for introducing them at all. A variety of articulate dissidents, drawn from business, the trade unions and students, began to criticize it openly. Although the business community owed much to the sponsorship of UNIP, it had also been critical of government policies such as proposals for industrial democracy and called for privatization of state enterprises. Union leaders, particularly when ZCTU was led by Chiluba, were fiercely critical of party and government. By the beginning of the decade,

Chiluba laid the blame for the crisis on UNIP and Kaunda personally (*Africa Economic Digest*, 11 March 1991). What united business and unionists was a growing tendency for them to favour market capitalism in preference to state direction. In this they spoke to a popular mood at home and abroad.

It is interesting that these groups, the chief beneficiaries of the regime, ultimately turned against it because the economic reforms it was forced to adopt by its creditors compromised their relative privilege, undermined their security and reduced their standard of living. There is some irony in the fact that these interests were so central to the creation of MMD, which ultimately embraced the very structural adjustment policies which had turned them against Kaunda and UNIP. ZCTU, for example, castigated structural adjustment in the 1980s because it imposed so much hardship on union members (Hamalengwa, 1992). Parastatal employees similarly chafed at retrenchment and the freezing of salary levels. Bates and Collier (1993) suggest that business and commercial farmers too were alienated by adjustment policies. Thus, different class forces coalesced around the view that the source of the trouble was the government and its authoritarianism.

The demise of the Second Republic was rooted in contradiction. A regime which had proclaimed its Humanism so enthusiastically, opposing exploitation and warning against inequality, generated great inequalities and created a group of privileged individuals opposed to liberalization measures - and able to justify this in terms of concern for 'the common man'. At the same time, economic decline also led the 'common man', in the shape of organized labour, to protest against the policies too. Yet this opposition ultimately produced a government which enthusiastically implemented these same reforms.

If Zambia's situation hardly parallels that of Eastern Europe, the overthrow of single-party systems there encouraged demands for the same in Zambia. Even more important was the new emphasis of international creditors, multilateral institutions and western governments alike, on 'good government'. Many of the meetings and conferences convened to press for reform during 1990 and 1991 owed something to the support and resources made available by the 'donor community'. Attempts by Kaunda to strengthen his election campaign (for instance, by 1991 salary increases for defence and security forces) were effectively scuppered by the country's creditors. Structural adjustment conditionalities in 1991 required a freeze on many capital projects and an increase in consumer prices on staple maize meals of up to 275%. Kaunda appealed to donors to permit a six-month freeze on these increases until after the elections. The response was that any delay would result in pledged loans being withheld. The donors insisted that the government 'should divorce the economic programme from politics' (*Weekly Post*, 1: 1991). Like the MMD, the donors appeared to blame Zambia's economic misfortunes on the UNIP government's mismanagement (see, for example, the Carter Report).

The Popular Dimension of Democratic Politics

Popular protests emerged with some suddenness in Zambia. If discontent was prevalent in the early eighties, there was also a certain resignation. The 1988 elections, for example, produced a 55% poll and Kaunda, the only candidate for the presidency under the single-party system, received a 'Yes' vote of some 90% (Chiluba, 1995). But by the end of the decade there was growing impatience with the situation, fuelled by many of the forces and events we have noted. At the end of 1989, the leader of ZCTU called openly for a return to multi-party democracy in Zambia (Chiluba, 1995: 64-5).

The basis of the alliance which swept the MMD to power was forged some years earlier. President Chiluba's account stresses a gradual meeting of minds of the leaders of Zincom (for business) and ZCTU (for labour) from the early eighties, fostered ironically at annual UNIP conventions where both found they were calling for similar policy changes (1995: 69). Opposition voices also emerged within a number of civic or professional bodies created by the educated urban elite. Many were long established but now became more openly critical and, in some cases, stood in for a political opposition prohibited under the single-party constitution. The role of the churches was particularly significant in opening up and pursuing lines of debate. The country's first independent newspaper was *The Mirror*, published by the churches, who also sponsored a small paper for workers which began to appear on the Copperbelt in 1982. Later a host of other independent papers, most notably *The Weekly Post* (now *The Post*), would join them. A mixture of political commentary and rigorous criticism of economic developments characterized meetings of the Economic Association of Zambia, a body active in the early seventies which now emerged as an important forum for opposition views.

The period was one of considerable ferment. In 1990 a protest march by university students was confronted by security forces. The students were joined by market vendors in a public show of anger. Later, a riot over increased prices of maize meal left 25 dead. Military coup attempts occurred in 1988 and June 1990, the last producing widespread public celebrations before it was realized that it had failed. There was, for the first time, open criticism of the President within UNIP in 1990 and 1991. In mid-1991 strikes occurred throughout the urban areas, and there was a proliferation of opposition groups and conferences calling for a multi-party system.

In this climate, the government's determination to resist demands for democratic change was progressively eroded. By late 1989, UNIP was resolved to concede change but to do so in such a way as to retain power. An internal inquiry about the implications of developments in Eastern Europe was launched in 1989. In March 1990, UNIP's Fifth National Convention met to discuss ways of democratizing the party and heard calls for a broader process of democratization, including the abolition of the one-party state (ZIMT, 1992: 3). A subsequent UNIP National Council agreed to hold a referendum in October about such a change. After the 1990 coup attempt and the display of public support for it, however, plans for a referendum on the future of the one-party system were replaced by a decision to move straight to multi-party elections. The constitution was amended to permit other political parties and pave the way for elections. If the MMD was critical of this process, which it saw as an attempt by UNIP to hold elections before the opposition had time to organize properly, it nevertheless now had the political space in which to organize and compete.

A group of professionals, business leaders and trade unionists formally established the MMD in mid-July 1990 at the Garden House Hotel outside Lusaka. An interim executive was appointed pending a national conference and elections. This executive was headed by Arthur Wina, Zambia's first finance minister and a prominent businessman, and other key figures of the Zambian bourgeoisie. It also included some younger intellectuals who had been responsible for organizing the meeting, among them Akashambatwa Mbikusita-Lewanika from Western Province and Derrick Chitala, from Northern Province, who were to be ministers in the first MMD government. Representatives of the labour movement included two former ZCTU leaders noted for their opposition to UNIP, Frederick Chiluba and Newstead Zimba. Chiluba accepted the interim position of organizing secretary to the MMD and drew on his continuing trade union links in organizing the party across the country.

Not surprisingly, this organization supported him when the MMD elected its first executive. After being formally registered as a political party in early 1991, a national conference of the party elected both a National Executive Committee (NEC) and a shadow cabinet. Chiluba defeated Arthur Wina for the presidency with Levi Mwanawasa, a lawyer and former Solicitor General dismissed by Kaunda, as vice president. The NEC reflected wide regional support for the movement, its leadership being drawn from all provinces although Luapula, Northern and Western were particularly strongly represented and Eastern very poorly. There was perhaps greater representation from business and the legal profession than academics. But there were no women in either the NEC or shadow cabinet - and the poor were conspicuously absent as well.

President Chiluba concedes that the various elements which came together in the MMD made a 'somewhat unlikely grouping' (1995: 73). He emphasizes the role of the ZCTU under his leadership, arguing that the labour movement had been active throughout the eighties in campaigning for support for change and had closely followed the dramatic changes taking place internationally in the latter part of the decade. He considers his statement in December 1989, calling for a return to pluralist politics, as initiating the local campaign for a return to multi-partyism. But he also concedes that the alliance of elements pushing for change had developed strength over virtually a decade.

The comments and writings of others indicate that initiatives, meetings and planning was long underway on many fronts among many interests. Among business people, unionists, lawyers, students, intellectuals, disgruntled UNIP leaders and several former military officers, there was a determination to restore multi-party democracy in order to remove Kaunda and UNIP from power. Although other parties were formed (by mid-1995 over 30 had been registered), many represented little more than their leaders. It was the MMD's ability to link together so many disparate groups, representing a diversity of aspirations and a wide range of grievances (both political and personal) against UNIP and Kaunda, that quickly made it the one significant force.

The Conduct of the Elections

Zambia's elections in 1991 were subject to intensive monitoring, both by local groups and by various external observers, including the Carter Foundation and Commonwealth representatives. Local monitoring initiatives reflected an enthusiasm for democratic process and expressed a growing civic consciousness. Their participants represented a range of NGOs concerned to guard human rights, gender equality, the rule of law, and freedom of association and speech.

The government was initially reluctant to permit external monitoring or to accept that the climate of suspicion required outside observers, but eventually relented. In July 1991, a local monitoring body, ZIMT, was registered under the Societies Act to support the achievement of a 'democratic and fair' multi-party election in Zambia (ZIMT: 12), its initial membership including some prominent churchmen. Suspicions about its links to government led to pressure on the churches to distance themselves from it and form a separate monitoring body. After a meeting during which the Carter team encouraged interested groups to agree a common approach to monitoring, a number of NGOs and church representatives stayed behind to discuss the possibility of closer coordination of their work. ZIMT representatives preferred to retain their own organizational independence but others - including PAZA (the Press Association of Zambia) and the Women's Lobby - joined the churches to form ZEMCC.

A number of worries were expressed by the various monitoring groups. They included concerns about the government not implementing a full voter registration after it agreed to multi-party elections, the inadequacy of procedures for dealing with lost voter registration cards, the government's insistence (in the face of international representations) that ballots be counted at district centres rather than at polling stations, media bias, issues of campaign finance and the continuing state of emergency.

The failure to produce a new voters' roll was particularly significant. The list of registered voters was effectively based on the voters registration exercise carried out prior to the last general election in 1988. When preparations were in hand in 1990 to hold a referendum, there was some updating of the roll but it was only a partial exercise. Hence many were unable to vote in 1991 because they had reached voting age (18) after the last registration, had moved to another constituency or had lost their card.

Zambia traditionally operated a system of requiring voters to produce both a voter's card and a national registration card. Operating two separate systems of registration entailed considerable expense, but a further difficulty arose from the fact that the voter's card was easily mislaid, being used only on the occasion of an election. To offset this problem, the elections' office was authorized to issue temporary voters' certificates to up to 10% of the registered voters in a constituency during the four days prior to an election, so long as national registration cards were produced by those whose names were already on the voters' roll. It provided a partial corrective, but was also subject to abuse. Its very need highlighted the restrictions on democratic participation which operated in 1991 and which have been exacerbated in subsequent years.

Table 5.1   1991 Zambian presidential election results - by province[2]

Province	Chiluba /MMD vote / %	Kaunda /UNIP vote / %	Gross % poll
Central	74,355 74.41	25,575 25.59	38.01
Copperbelt	296,502 91.35	28,085 8.65	55.1
Eastern	44,483 25.35	126,961 74.05	49.35
Luapula	83,039 88.98	10,189 10.92	47.14
Lusaka	128,709 76.53	39,446 23.46	43.62
Northern	119,685 85.05	21,038 14.95	44.97
NWP	46,950 70.19	19,941 29.81	42.69
Southern	128,589 85.22	22,299 14.79	43.59
Western	75,150 81.37	17,207 18.63	41.33
Total	997,462 76.25	310,741 23.75	46.35

Source: Republic of Zambia, 1991 Presidential and Parliamentary Election, Provisional Official Election Results, Government Printer, Lusaka, n.d.

Table 5.2   1991 Zambian parliamentary election results - by province[2]

Province	MMD vote / %	UNIP vote / %	Others vote / %	Gross % poll
Central	70,547 72.60	26,385 27.15	234 0.24	37.15
Copperbelt	265,040 89.12	30,991 10.42	1,375 0.46	50.62
Eastern	41,263 25.05	120,604 73.23	2,833 1.72	48.06
Luapula	69,364 85.78	11,497 14.22	-	41.03
Lusaka	130,830 75.75	39,073 22.62	2,817 1.63	45.00
Northern	116,648 84.42	20,775 15.04	750 0.54	44.21
NWP	43,529 66.95	19,506 30.01	1,987 3.06	41.86
Southern	125,372 84.23	22,146 14.88	1,324 0.89	42.86
Western	89,935 82.86	17,766 16.37	842 0.78	48.33
Total	952,528 74.80	308,743 24.24	12,162 0.96	45.28

Source: Republic of Zambia, 1991 Presidential and Parliamentary Election, Provisional Official Election Results, Government Printer, Lusaka, n.d.

The Elections and their Outcome

The campaign generated considerable enthusiasm, encouraging some predictions of a 90% voter turnout. Both sides expressed confidence of victory though, in the absence of opinion polls, such judgements were entirely subjective. In the event, there was a much lower poll than anticipated but the MMD won decisively with 76.25% of the presidential vote (on a poll of 46.35% of registered voters) and 74.8% of the parliamentary poll (on 45.28%) taking 125 of the 150 assembly seats. UNIP's parliamentary vote was just 24.24% while less than 1% voted for all other parties combined (Table 5.2). Frederick Chiluba accordingly became the second President of Zambia.

Table 5.3   **Winning percentages in Zambian parliamentary[3] contests (highest and lowest by province)**

Province	highest winning %	winning party	lowest winning %	winning party
Central	86.44	MMD	50.80	MMD
Copperbelt	96.78	MMD	69.75	MMD
Eastern	93.4	UNIP	58.94	UNIP
Luapula	93.6	MMD	79.70	MMD
Lusaka	82.28	MMD	51.26	UNIP
Northern	96.31	MMD	61.30	MMD
Nthwestern	86.86	MMD	50.63	MMD
Southern	92.23	MMD	77.72	MMD
Western	91.16	MMD	51.08	MMD

While reflecting overwhelming support for the MMD, there were some regional differences. UNIP won all 19 seats in the Eastern Province, as well as Rufunsa and Feira in Lusaka Province, Kabompo West, Chavuma and Zambezi West in Northwestern Province and Isoka East in Northern Province. In most cases - whether the victor was UNIP or the MMD - the win was decisive, with many winning percentages as high as 80 or 90% but there was some variation and a number of constituencies with narrow margins of victory. As shown by Table 5.3, the MMD's support in parliamentary elections was uniformly high in Copperbelt, Luapula and Southern Provinces and (except for Isoka East) Northern Province, with no MMD candidates receiving less than 60% of the valid votes. In Luapula the MMD won all seats with at least 79% of the vote. UNIP's victories in Eastern Province were also broadly secure. In a few constituencies, mostly in Western Province, contests were tightly fought, but these were exceptional.

Table 5.4   1991 Zambian parliamentary elections - gross percentage polls: constituencies with highest and lowest polls in each province

Province	highest % poll	winning party	lowest % poll	winning party
Central	48.84	MMD	26.65	MMD
Copperbelt	63.37	MMD	24.85	MMD
Eastern	66.63	UNIP	39.24	UNIP
Luapula	67.09	MMD	35.80	MMD
Lusaka	51.34	MMD	29.94	UNIP
Northern	70.51	MMD	32.04	MMD
Nthwestern	52.97	UNIP	27.16	MMD
Southern	59.11	MMD	26.70	MMD
Western	47.65	MMD	26.90	MMD

There was some variation both within and across provinces in the gross percentage poll. In the parliamentary elections (Table 5.2), Copperbelt registered the highest average turnout (50.62%) and Central Province the lowest (37.15 per cent). But variations between constituencies were more significant. As Table 5.3 shows, the lowest was on the Copperbelt

(Kafulafuta) with just 24.85 per cent while the highest was in Northern Province (Kanchibiya) with 70.51%.

The Significance of the Elections

These elections, then, resulted in the government changing hands and a new political party dominating the political landscape. But what can be said about those who were elected? Did the election reflect a change in who has power and who governs in Zambia? Did it mark a change in the configuration of social forces underlying and influencing the state? What sort of policy changes did it set in motion? Events and tendencies since the elections indicate that the structure of Zambian politics remained largely unchanged despite democratic elections and constitutional change. What 1991 did was to add multi-party competition to a system of presidential power. It did not change presidentialism and it did not change the imperatives which drove clientelism and competition for access to the state.

Narrowness of the political elite

While the 1991 elections excited considerable enthusiasm and the entry of some who were new to active politics, on the whole the contestants from both parties were relatively homogeneous in terms of age, gender and level of income or class position. Very few women were nominated or elected. Although some of those standing were younger, the elections did not mark the handing over of power to a new generation. Rather, most faces were familiar and identifiable as veteran politicians: the 'old guard' (press criticism of MMD was later to employ the jibe of 'recycled politicians'). And although the presidential candidate had once been head of the ZCTU and a number of other contestants had a trade union background, rather more were professionals or businessmen. Indeed, at least a third of MMD candidates had businesses or farms and several of the most prominent indigenous owners were counted among their ranks.

The pool of MMD candidates included a number of former politicians who had suffered dismissal from office, exclusion from election, arrest or detention without trial. There were also those who considered their economic interests thwarted under the Second Republic or who objected to the arbitrariness which increasingly characterized the UNIP government. Though unified by their opposition to President Kaunda, they straddled a number of internal divides and in some cases made uncomfortable bedfellows. There were several who aspired to high Cabinet office (an unusual number to the presidency itself) and whose disappointment with the positions actually obtained after the elections promoted rapid disaffection from the MMD leadership. Yet there was also considerable talent and a depth of expertise among those elected to office. Eight MMD candidates, for example, had been ministers in previous governments and another had held junior ministerial rank. Two more had served as Solicitor General. At least five had been District Governors. If drawn from a relatively narrow social base, therefore, the candidates were neither lacking in ability, nor in experience. Yet candidature for elections is only one, rather specialized, component of political participation. A broader view of such participation must include the dynamism and scope of activity within civil society. In this regard, though there have been attempts in recent years to encourage grassroots community action or, alternatively, to build on local initiatives through which community members define and act on their concerns, the bulk of local NGO membership is relatively highly educated and urban, and the bulk of civic organizations' activities are confined to urban areas. Thus, while participation in politics in the broad sense flourished after 1990, the band of actors involved was relatively narrow. Yet it is still useful to take note of the lines along which this narrow band was defined - that is, its urban, male and professional or business character.

Tribe, nation and citizenship

The 1991 elections confirmed the validity of the MMD's claim to be a national party. Even in Eastern Province, it frequently received 20 to 30% of the vote. Nevertheless, discordant accusations of regional or 'tribal' favouritism or manipulation were articulated regularly after the elections: over the composition of the first cabinet; in the resignation speeches of some disaffected MPs; in claims that ministers and deputies were disproportionately drawn from particular provinces; in criticism of proposals to rename the international airport and Lusaka University after political figures from Northern and Southern provinces; in appointments to certain cabinet posts; and in attempts to woo the leaders of certain opposition parties to (or back to) the MMD.

References to tribalism and regionalism were particularly prominent during 1993 and 1994 when disaffected MMD leaders set up the National Party and (given the prominence within it of leaders from Western, Northern, Northwestern and Southern provinces) seemed capable for a time of building a viable opposition. Though it gained only five seats in by-elections, its performance still alarmed the MMD, which resorted to the language of tribalism in order to discredit it. There were other occasions as well when government leaders felt obliged to deny tribal bias, as when it expelled two of its founding leaders, Chitala and Mung'omba (*Zambia Daily Mail*, 18 September 1995). The comment of Newstead Zimba at the time, that none could complain about tribalism given that the cabinet was 'balanced' (ibid.), reflects a considerable sensitivity to such complaints.

For all that, there was a certain displacement of concern over tribalism toward the issue of citizenship. This 'game' started during the 1991 election campaign when UNIP claimed that Chiluba was not a Luapulan by origin but a Zairois. If this smear was the basis for subsequent government actions, it has proved a costly one for UNIP. Two UNIP officials (confidants of Kaunda) were deported to Malawi in 1994 because they were alleged to be Malawians. Subsequently, MMD leaders and newspapers have depicted former President Kaunda as a Malawian and even claimed that the country had been under foreign control for 27 years. After depositions by a few witnesses, the Constitutional Review Commission submitted a draft constitution in 1995 which included a clause barring any Zambian whose parents were not born in Zambia from standing for the presidency. The clause, widely referred to as 'the Kaunda clause', was seen as a blatant attempt to prevent the latter from challenging Chiluba in 1996. Interestingly, the government White Paper on the draft constitution systematically rejected virtually every recommendation by the Commission aimed at shifting powers from the presidency to parliament; but it adopted the Kaunda clause. In turn, opposition figures and some of the press, notably *The Post*, alleged that Chiluba's family came from Zaire.

Further, a movement resurfaced in Western Province after the elections, demanding the restoration of special status for the kingdom of Barotseland, a status abrogated by the UNIP government. It continued to press these demands into 1998. Tribe, citizenship and nationality have thus attained a new prominence in political discourse.

Policy directions - in whose favour?

The MMD manifesto and its government's initial budgets embraced economic liberalization and structural adjustment, as had the UNIP government in its final months. But the speed and enthusiasm with which it implemented the initial economic reform policies distinguished the MMD from UNIP. Its first budget affirmed its commitment to privatization and support for private enterprise. If health, education, defence and infrastructural investment were targeted for support, the reduction of the public sector was paramount.

This gave little comfort to parastatal and government employees. In spite of the fact that the president was a former trade unionist, and some policy gestures were directed towards giving adjustment a 'human face', economic reforms invariably placed a strain on formal sector employees and urban consumers in general. Shortly after the elections, the price of maize meal - the staple diet - was doubled. It was argued that setting the economy on course would ultimately benefit all, but short-run policy accorded most closely with the interests of international capital and local business. Indeed there was little reference in the first budget speech under the MMD government to any group other then entrepreneurs. The MMD victory thus ushered in policy changes which firmly committed the government to reforms which, under UNIP, had been adopted only piecemeal, grudgingly and often only temporarily. The pace of reforms subsequently slowed, but the direction has not varied.

Political participation and voter turnout

A relatively low poll was one of the notable features of the 1991 elections, contrasting with the anticipation of much higher turnouts. While higher than the gross percentage poll of the 1973 elections (the first under the single-party constitution) which was just 39.4%, it was lower than the 66.7% in 1978 or 55% in 1988. This downward trend continued. Elections were a constant feature of Zambian political life after 1991, with local government elections being held in 1992 and 45 by-elections taking place between the general elections and mid-October 1995, with vacancies having occurred in more than a quarter of all parliamentary seats. In the local government elections the gross percentage poll was only 13.9%. The average poll in the by-elections through April 1996 was only some 18%, a dramatic decline even on 1991. But again there was considerable variation among constituencies, ranging from highs of 38.5% in Chadiza (August 1992) and 38% in Chasefu (November 1993) to lows of 5.79% in Lufwanyama (October 1995) and 6.7% in Lukashya (April 1994).

In general, by-election turnout was higher in Eastern Province than elsewhere, averaging 26.5% there against a low of 11.3% in Northern Province. Polls tended to be highest in constituencies where by-elections were won by UNIP (23.1%) and lowest in those won by MMD (16.4%). It might be tempting to interpret this as a sign that voters were more likely to turn out where there was a genuine contest. Yet such differences were of marginal significance compared with the sharp decline in voting overall. The average decline in the gross poll was of the same general order, regardless of which party won.[4]

But what do variations in percentage polls signify and more particularly to what extent did low polls, especially in by-elections, represent voter fatigue or apathy? President Kaunda complained after the election of 1991 that 'mothers' had not voted and though this particular claim has been disputed (Longwe and Clarke, 1991), there may well have been some categories of under-represented voters. Some commentators suggested that poverty entails such a preoccupation with the struggle to meet basic needs that many, especially in rural areas, had little time to devote to voting. Reference has also been made to problems of transportation, remoteness of polling stations, last minute changes in the location of polling stations, or simply frustration with the government (Fodep, 1993). While a range of factors help to account for low voter turnout, it is important to appreciate that calculations are based on numbers of registered voters, which have remained constant for years, while the number of potential voters has steadily increased.

Thus, declining polls were at least partly a function of declining proportions of citizens on the voters' roll who were still resident in their constituency of registration, with those constituencies experiencing the greatest out-migration suffering greatest distortions. One estimate put the degree of 'wastage' due to such factors as deaths and moving away as high as 25% over four years (Baylies and Szeftel, 1984:56). But while polls may have under-represented the proportion of registered voters still resident in constituencies who exercised their ballot, there is another equally important respect in which they were a poor measure of electoral participation. The absence of a comprehensive voter registration exercise in recent years effectively disenfranchised not just those who had moved but also those who had come of voting age in the interim. The great majority of Zambians are under the age of 25, and yet a sizeable chunk of this younger generation (perhaps as much as 22% of the potential electorate in 1995) remained disenfranchised, despite reaching voting age.

It is not possible to calculate exactly how many citizens were effectively disenfranchised; but even if it was not as high as the 50% suggested by Derrick Chitala (*Times of Zambia*, 14 October 1995), it undoubtedly was a key factor in determining the remarkably low levels of electoral participation in the nineties. Should a full registration be achieved, the 'youth' vote is likely to be of particular importance to any party seeking power. What is clear is that, quite apart from any inadequacies of leadership or representative accountability, democracy and elections are something that have happened to someone else as far as a large proportion of the population are concerned.

Continuing Legitimacy and Popularity of the MMD

Registration problems apart, it is likely that the sharp decline in participation was rooted in disappointment about the achievements of the MMD government. A critical feature of Zambia's political landscape since the 1991 elections was the tendency of the governing party to fragment, with MPs and party officials either resigning or being expelled amid charges of corruption, tribalism and lack of democratic accountability. Stanford Hiazo, MMD MP for Mumbwa, for example, claimed when he resigned that many members of the new government had abused their offices and enriched themselves: 'men who had nothing on October 31, 1991 have become overnight billionaires'. The list of abuses, he said, was 'endless' (*Weekly Post*, 12 November 1993). Inonge Mbikusita-Lewanika claimed that the MMD had 'lost the revolution it had initiated, as people began to look after their own narrow interests' (*Weekly Post*, 22 March 1994). In other cases, individuals were openly self-seeking. Thus Daniel Munkombwe, deserting UNIP to MMD in the wake of former President Kaunda's return to the UNIP leadership, stated that since the MMD had a preponderance of seats at both parliamentary and local government levels, political logic demanded that he make such a move (*Sunday Times of Zambia*, 15 October 1995).[5]

Since 1965 Zambia, like Kenya, has had a rule which ties parliamentary seats to the party under whose banner they were won. Thus, defection requires MPs to offer themselves for re-election. In 1993 and 1994 the courts in Zambia were asked to adjudicate on those cases where MPs had not resigned but had been expelled by the MMD and had tried to continue to sit as independents. The courts held that the same rule applied, thus opening the way for the MMD government to purge MPs who did not toe the executive's line. In contrast with UNIP, which suppressed autonomous political activity outside the party, the MMD has been extremely zealous in purging leaders and local officials suspected of opposition to Chiluba. Of the 47 by-elections called between 1991 and April 1996, 25 were the result of resignations or expulsions, often followed by transfer of party allegiance. Most were defections from MMD, but several of the most recent involved departures from UNIP or the National Party. In some cases incumbents were able to regain their seats but, in general, it proved difficult for most of them to do so.

In many ways, the political situation after 1991 mirrored that which occurred after 1964. In 1964, UNIP's overwhelming victory over the ANC meant that the discipline of inter-party competition was absent and intra-party conflict over the spoils of office and access to the state became the dominant feature of politics. The overwhelming MMD success in the 1991 elections left it in a similar position in relation to UNIP and opened the way to internal division. If anything the situation was worse after 1991. UNIP's unity had been forged in the independence struggle; competing leaders retained a measure of respect and comradeship to temper their competition. Such links were largely absent in a recently formed coalition of disparate forces concerned essentially to restore a multi-party system and unified mostly by opposition to the former regime and its president. Moreover, the differences of outlook between business, labour and intelligentsia (all in turn divided by regional and sectional allegiances) were always likely to make unity difficult - and so it proved. Immediately after the elections problems emerged in forming a government and some notable leaders refused to serve.

It is not surprising, therefore, that internal wrangling, jockeying for position and discontent when anticipated preferment was not attained, characterized the years since 1991. Further, to the extent that the political elite was largely urban-based while still requiring rural support to maintain its position, it is equally unsurprising that mobilization along regional or ethnic lines continued. This, in turn, created a tendency to breed accusations of favouritism and to encourage intrigue. Essentially, multi-party electoral politics did not replace the sectional clientelist politics which so characterized UNIP. Rather they were grafted onto it and perhaps made the more virulent by the weak cohesion of the MMD and by the new market opportunities created by economic liberalization, which have fostered unprecedented levels of elite corruption. In this context, it is perhaps more surprising that the MMD government maintained its integrity and its level of support for as long as it did.

The MMD was divided along lines of region and ethnicity but also along ideological and generational lines. Indeed, ethnic divisions were a by-product of leadership divisions rather than their cause. It is interesting to consider the groups which left or were driven out of the party or government in the years since the 1991 elections. They included the old UNIP free-market liberals, perhaps the most prominent of whom were the late Arthur Wina and Emmanuel Kasonde, the MMD's first finance minister and architect of its liberalization and adjustment strategy. They also included some of the old UNIP party stalwarts, the most prominent of whom, Humphrey Mulemba, left to lead the National Party. Individuals drawn from the non-indigenous racial minorities, most prominently Guy Scott and Rolf Shenton, also figured among those who departed, as did lawyers and human rights activists who provided much of the early impetus for democratic reform, particularly Mwanawasa, the MMD's first vice-president, and Rodger Chongwe, its first legal affairs minister, who initiated the Constitutional Review Commission. The departure of the latter element has clearly weakened the early enthusiasm of the MMD for constitutional reform and for reducing the presidential character of political power.

The exodus also included many of the intellectual cadre so important in articulating the demands for democratic reform around 1990, particularly Chitala, Mung'omba and the late Baldwin Nkumbula, although the latter rejoined the MMD shortly before his death. The *Weekly Post* (16 November 1993) claimed to have received numerous letters protesting at the 'recycling' of political leadership, asking 'where are the young?' By late 1994, this group had self-consciously styled itself as the 'Young Turks' in a pointed reference to generational differences. It expressed increasing impatience on questions of reform, accountability, corruption and the pace of democratization. The group was fluid in make-up and divided from the older generation as much by outlook as age. In 1995, Akashambatwa, one of its most important voices, suggested that its hopes for a 'social market economy' had been pushed aside by a dash to a free-for-all market and personal acquisitiveness. He, like Chitala and others, soon found themselves in opposition.

UNIP for its part persisted as an opposition party, presenting a less corporatist, less statist face than of old. Its support base was disproportionately in Eastern Province, although its Central Committee was carefully recruited from all provinces and its president, Kebby Musokotwane, was from Southern Province. Although there were few signs that it could break out of its stronghold areas to a significant extent, it remained the best organized and resourced party and thus a threat to a divided government promoting unpopular reforms. In 1993 the government accused a faction of UNIP of plotting extra-constitutional subversion (citing a document popularly termed the 'Zero-Option' plan) and briefly restored the state of emergency. After this, there was relative peace between the parties until the end of 1994, when it was announced that former President Kaunda was re-entering politics. There was some talk of his forming a new party, but the prize of UNIP's wealth and organization were a powerful attraction and there followed intense internal wrangling before Kaunda was restored as head of the Party in June 1995. This in turn led to defections from some of those who felt they had been pushed aside, including the entire executive in Southern Province.

By-elections in Eastern Province were largely a consequence of the death of sitting MPs, but two were the result of defections from UNIP to MMD - including Dingiswayo Banda, a minister in the first independence cabinet and leader of the opposition in the National Assembly. Of 12 by-elections for seats formerly held by UNIP through October 1995, the party retained 9, including all those in Eastern Province. It also gained three Northern Province seats where incumbents defected from MMD (but did not themselves contest the by-elections) in Mbala, Mpulungu and Mkushi North. MMD in turn lost a number of seats to the National Party following a series of defections in the summer of 1993. By-elections the following November were a crucial test of how far the new opposition party could make inroads into MMD support. In the event the ruling party held seats in Pemba in Southern and Malole in Northern provinces, but lost three in Western Province and one each in Northwestern and Southern (although the latter was subsequently regained at a later by-election as the NP itself began to suffer internal divisions).

The degree of effort which the MMD put into its by-election campaigns perhaps belied the impression that it tried to convey of being secure about its majority. The elections were characterized by complaints of bullying and allegations that government frequently distributed food relief to constituencies in the days before polling. The government countered that the maize distribution was carried out by NGOs, but the repeated coincidence of the activity fuelled suspicions of electoral malpractice (*Times of Zambia*, 28 August 1995).

Allegations also concerned misuse of government vehicles (*National Mirror*, 15-21 October 1995) and the selective and privileged use of temporary voters' certificates by the MMD. During the Feira by-election in August 1995, for example, UNIP representatives alleged that the improper use of voters' certificates constituted rigging of the elections. They claimed, moreover, that in an earlier campaign in Mwandi 500 voters' certificates were issued to the MMD compared with 150 received by UNIP (*Zambia Daily Mail*, 27 August 1995). Quite apart from the question of inequitable treatment, allocation of such certificates through parties had dubious legality, since it was the responsibility of the electoral commission and its representatives to issue such certificates to voters who had lost their voter's card. UNIP's allegations in Feira were in fact refuted by ZIMT (*Times of Zambia*, 30 August 1995), but the persistence of problems in this area is indicated by the Elections Office declaring that, in view of complaints about forgery, no certificates would be issued for the Msanzala by-election in October 1995 (*Times of Zambia*, 14 October 1995).

Campaigns were also frequently characterized by minor skirmishes and acts of violence, as in Lundazi where a group of MMD supporters attacked two individuals carrying a ballot box, demanding to see its contents (to allay their suspicions that it contained already completed ballots) and in Lufwanyama where four people were allegedly stabbed (*Times of Zambia*, 11 November 1995). At Feira, in August 1995, youths had been brought in from Lusaka and camps of UNIP and MMD cadres were reportedly stationed on either side of the main road (ibid.). The defeated candidate in the Lundazi by-election in October 1995, Dingiswayo Banda, placed particular blame on his former colleague, Dr Kaunda, who he said had arrived with four truck loads of youths who had intimidated villagers (*Zambia Daily Mail*, 16 October 1995).

In spite of such incidents, the final verdict of election monitoring organizations was generally that by-elections have been reasonably free and fair. Fodep's report of the local government elections in 1992 noted only petty irregularities (Fodep, 1993: 10-16). However, it is also true that when critical reports were issued, such as Fodep's worries about maize distribution at the time of the Chikankata by-election in October 1994, they drew a sharp rebuke from the government.

Overall, the MMD's record in retaining seats in by-elections was respectable, particularly when account is taken of the prolonged drought and great economic hardship brought on by structural adjustment policies over which the government presided. Virtually all by-elections recorded reduced majorities for the winners, with a average decline of about 18%, albeit noticeably steeper in seats won by the MMD (at 20.7%) than UNIP (at 12.3%). Indeed, there were three cases where the victor received less than 50% - Mwansabombwe where the MMD won with just 44.8% of the vote, Mwandi with 44.5% and Chilanda in September 1995 with 43.91%.

In general the record of by-elections showed a decline in the MMD's popularity, but the distribution of parliamentary seats by party indicated that this decline was not sufficient to undermine its dominance of national politics. Even so, the bitterness of political rhetoric suggested a persistent sense of insecurity on the part of the government. One MMD official went so far as to suggest that UNIP should be banned as the only means of preventing political violence and civil strife, particularly as the 1996 general elections approached (*Times of Zambia*, 12 October 1995).

Certainly, throughout 1995 (and particularly when Kaunda became UNIP president again) the government sought to harass the opposition at every turn. In 1996, much of the UNIP central executive was detained and charged with treason, only being released shortly before the elections. The 'Kaunda clause' brought into question basic democratic rights of political competition and drew angry criticism from donor representatives.

The 1996 Presidential and Parliamentary Elections

The 1996 parliamentary and presidential elections served as a stern test of the popularity of the MMD as well as of how far the consolidation of the democratization process embarked upon in 1991 had gone. Controversy over the new Constitution and over the perceived inadequacies in the registration of voters characterized the buildup to the elections and ensured that they were held in a charged atmosphere. When it became clear that Kaunda would indeed be barred from standing, UNIP declared that it would boycott the elections, a position also taken by the Liberal Progressive Front. Other opposition parties, however, decided to participate, the leader of the Zambia Democratic Congress arguing that they wished to test the legitimacy of the electoral process and demonstrate a commitment to the pursuit of all peaceful avenues of action. In the event the MMD won overwhelmingly, taking 131 of 150 Parliamentary seats - 6 more than in 1991 - albeit with a lower percentage of the vote in the parliamentary contests - down to 60% from 75%. President Chiluba was accorded an even more resounding personal victory in the presidential contest. Against 4 opponents in 1996, he won 73% of the votes, only slightly below his 76% in 1991. The Government hailed the result as an enthusiastic endorsement of its policies and practice by the Zambian people, in elections that had been free and fair, that had seen a free registration of voters, free access to the media for opposition parties and no violence on polling day (*The Post*, 21 November 1996).

Others, however, were less convinced. Various elements within the donor community expressed regret that the elections had not accommodated all political competitors. Most local election monitoring groups, including Fodep, ZIMT and a new organization set up in the months before the elections, the Committee for a Clean Campaign (CCC), declared the elections to have been seriously flawed, in part because of irregularities in the campaign and voting procedures, but most importantly because of deficiencies in the voter registration exercise and a conviction that provisions of the new constitution restricted rather than ensured equal opportunities for political participation across the population. The election results were also disputed by some opposition politicians. Former President Kaunda declared the initiation of a campaign of civil disobedience and petitions were lodged in the courts criticizing the electoral process and the conduct of the Electoral Commission. The 1996 elections thus proved locally and internationally divisive, opening rather than resolving questions about the democratic character of Zambian political development and about the validity of the elections themselves.

Conclusion: Democratic Progress

An assessment of the significance of the 1991 elections in Zambia and of subsequent government performance must consider how far did each contribute to or represent progressive democratization. Did the elections mark a substantive shift in political practice and the nature of the political system?

The constitutional change which enabled multi-party elections to occur was certainly of central importance to a process of democratization. A lifting of the state of emergency was significant for reducing the ease with which arbitrary authority could be exercised, although there was a setback some months after the election on this score when a state of emergency was temporarily reintroduced. However, the reintroduction of political pluralism did not of itself alter the relationship between Parliament and President, alter patterns of clientelism or remove the potential for a politics oiled by, if not steeped in, corruption.

Even so, a rhetoric of good government characterized by transparency, competence and openness was adopted. Various bodies were established or strengthened, including the Anti-Corruption Commission, the Drug Enforcement Agency and the Human Rights Commission. If the independent press has often been an irritation to government, eliciting a vitriolic and occasionally bullying response, it has not been shut down. And if somewhat halfhearted, an attempt has been made to institute a code of conduct for parliamentarians. Yet the pace of change on some fronts has slowed, if not reversed. While bilateral donors would claim that they are doing no more than taking the government to task on promises contained in the MMD Manifesto, their excursions into monitoring the pace of political reform have certainly put pressure on the government to which it, in turn, has often reacted angrily.

At the same time, there has been considerable cause for concern about democratic progress. Attention has focused in particular on the use of the Public Order Act to prohibit meetings of some opposition parties, on what some regard as harassment of the independent press, on failure to advance the cause of gender equality, on a more general unwillingness to enshrine a bill of rights in the constitution, on a reluctance to countenance the Constitutional Review Commission's recommendation that a new constitution be enacted or ratified via a constituent assembly and referendum. There is increasing criticism of the state's use of arbitrary force against opposition elements and abuse of its power to prevent pluralist politics from flourishing.

The process is an ongoing one. In some respects the very fact that organizations of civil society are raising their voices to express concern or that opposition parties continue to organize are themselves indicators of a healthy democracy. Measures of democratization are in any case often elusive, with little consensus being demonstrated either among external donors or members of the government. Zambia's elections in 1991 surely constitute a significant milestone in the search for democracy, but it is still unclear on what road the country is travelling.

Notes

1. Humanism was generally regarded as a vague set of homilies designed to justify almost anything the regime did. But it imposed on the country a discourse which constantly invoked sentiments of equality, considerate treatment of others, fair treatment and so on. Its role in fostering such sentiments only becomes clear in contrast to the acquisitiveness unleashed by liberalization after 1991.

2. There were 41,441 rejected ballots - 3.07% of votes cast in the presidential vote and 45,093 rejected in the parliamentary voting. Votes for each party are given as percentage of valid votes cast. DP, NADA, NPD and independent candidates have been lumped together as 'others'. DP got 120 votes in the Copperbelt; NADA obtained 489 in the Copperbelt and 1206 in Lusaka - a total of 1,695; NPD received a total of 803 votes - 234 in Central, 158 in the Copperbelt, 352 in Lusaka and 59 in Southern provinces. Independents obtained 9,544 votes made up of 608 in Copperbelt, 2,833 in Eastern, 1,259 in Lusaka, 750 in Northern, 1,987 in North-Western, 1,265 in Southern and 842 in Western.

3. The percentage poll in the parliamentary contests did not always coincide with that in the presidential election. In Kanchibiya the gross poll in the latter was just 46.62% with 94.07% going to the MMD candidate.

4. The average decline in constituencies won by the MMD: 27.6%; UNIP: 26.6% and NP: 25.6%. Three constituencies have had two by-elections. In all cases the decline is calculated from the figure for the poll in 1991, not from the poll of the previous election.

5. Munkombwe was one of the country's most prominent farmers and the chairman of UNIP in Southern Province. After the 1991 electoral defeat, Kaunda was succeeded as UNIP leader by Kebby Musokotwane, his former deputy and a prominent Southern Province figure. Musokotwane did not enjoy the confidence of many of the Eastern Province leadership of UNIP which, by default, had become the core of the party. When the government arrested a number of them, including two of Kaunda's sons, over allegations that they were plotting to overthrow the state, there were open accusations that Musokotwane rather than the MMD had engineered the crisis. Some of the detainees were tortured and one later died. The bitterness about this incident resulted in Musokotwane finding it difficult to obtain enough nominations to allow him to contest the UNIP presidency against Kaunda in 1995.

6 Kenya: The Survival of the Old Order

ROK AJULU

Kenya's sixth general election took place in December 1992. Its significance lay in three main areas. First, apart from the so-called 'Little General Election' of 1966, these were the first multi-party general elections since independence in 1963. Second, contrary to much pre-election expectation, the ruling Kenya African National Union (KANU), which had come under internal and external pressure to allow a return to multi-partyism, was returned to power, albeit with a minority of the vote. Finally, the elections brought to an end the one-party state created when all opposition was outlawed in 1969 and inaugurated a formally democratic dispensation.

Eight political parties contested the elections. Four were small, with marginal constituencies. The most significant of them were the Kenya Social Congress (KSC) led by a former MP, George Anyona, and the Kenya National Democratic Alliance (KENDA), led by a former University lecturer, Mukaru Nganga. Otherwise, the main contestants, apart from KANU, were: Oginga Odinga's Forum for Restoration of Democracy - FORD Kenya or FORD (K); Kenneth Matiba's breakaway FORD Asili or FORD (A); and Mwai Kibaki's Democratic Party - DP.

Previously, presidential elections, which accompanied contests for parliament, had been based on the plurality electoral system. However, a constitutional amendment prior to the 1992 election stipulated that the winner in the presidential race now had to obtain, besides a simple majority, at least 25% of the votes cast in at least five of Kenya's eight provinces. It further specified that if none of the presidential candidates managed to attain this goal, a run-off would be held between the two leading candidates. The provision also mandated the President-elect to form a government from his or her own political party whether or not such a party had won a parliamentary majority.

The results for the 171 contested parliamentary seats (17 KANU candidates had been returned unopposed when registration ended) were as follows: KANU with 26.6% of the total vote took 83 seats, giving it 100

110

overall; FORD (K) secured 18.4% and 31 seats, FORD (A) 22% and 29, DP 20% and 23; and Anyona's KSC, the Party for Independent Candidates (PICK), and Kenya National Congress (KNC) took one seat each. However, KANU's presidential candidate, the incumbent Daniel Arap Moi, was the only one to win 25% of the vote in five provinces, and thereby retained the presidency, although he secured only 36% of the vote against the 63% obtained by the opposition candidates together. The multi-party general elections thus narrowly returned President Moi and KANU to power.

Table 6.1 1992 Kenya general elections - breakdown of registered voters and constituencies, by provinces

Province	Registered voters	% of reg. voters	Number of seats	% total seats
Nairobi	673,814	8.53	8	4.26
Coast	661,427	8.37	20	10.64
N. Eastern	141,088	1.79	10	5.32
Central	1,224,981	15.51	25	13.30
Eastern	1,221,196	15.46	32	17.02
Rift Valley	1,919,672	24.30	44	23.40
Western	851,191	10.87	20	10.64
Nyanza	1,205,132	15.26	29	15.42
Totals	7,898,501	100.00	188	100.00

Source: Ajulu and Fox, 1994.

KANU's victory was principally due to the distribution of parliamentary constituencies being skewed in favour of its strongholds in the North Eastern, Rift Valley, and (to some degree) Coast Provinces. In each of these provinces, constituency boundaries were drawn so as to grossly over-represent individual voters. In contrast, in opposition strongholds in the more populated Nyanza, Western, Nairobi and Central Provinces, it required, in some cases, four times the number of voters to win a single seat. Table 6.1 demonstrates this relationship clearly. In Nairobi Province, 673,814 voters or 8.53% of total registered voters had only 8 seats whereas North Eastern Province's 141,088 voters, representing 1.79% of voters, had 10 seats. Again, Central Province with 15.51% of voters had 25 seats while Coast Province's 8.37% of the electorate returned 20 MPs.

Table 6.2   1992 Kenya general elections - registered voters and constituencies in three Rift Valley districts

Kerio District		Baringo District		Nakuru District	
Const.	Reg. voters	Const.	Reg. voters	Const.	Reg. voters
Kerio East	21,444	Baringo East	11,003	Nakuru East	90,469
Kerio West	29,813	Baringo North	26,925	Nakuru Town	100,322
Kerio Central	19,328	Baringo Central	39,522	Molo	120,705
Kerio South	29,616	Baringo South	43,055	Rongai	43,235
				Nakuru North	41,883
No. of consts.	Reg. voters	No. of consts.	Reg. voters	No. of consts.	Reg. voters
4	94,201	4	120,505	5	396,614

Source: Ajulu and Fox, 1994.

The argument is further illustrated by Table 6.2, which compares registered voters and distribution of constituencies in three selected districts in Rift Valley Province. Together, these accounted for 31.8% of voters in the province: Kerio's 94,000 voters represented 4.9%, Baringo's 120,505 constituted 6.3%, and Nakuru's 396,614 accounted for 21%. However, whereas Kerio and Baringo each had four seats, Nakuru was allocated only five, the average number of voters per seat in the three districts being 25,053, 30,126 and 79,323 respectively.

Table 6.3   1992 Kenya general elections - distribution of seats by province

Province	DP	FORD-A	FORD-K	KANU
Nairobi	0	6	1	1
Coast	1	0	2	17
N. Eastern	0	0	1	8
Eastern	9	0	1	19
Central	10	14	1	0
Rift Valley	2	2	2	32
Western	0	7	3	9
Nyanza	1	0	20	7
Total	23	29	31	93

Source: Ajulu and Fox, 1994.

To grasp the implications of this skewed distribution of seats, a word about Rift Valley ethnic distribution is appropriate. The northern parts of the province are mainly occupied by the Turkana and Samburu. To the south are the small groups which together form the broader Kalenjin ethnic group, and towards the Tanzanian border are the Masai, spread over the two districts of Narok and Kajiado. These were the core of the ruling KANU minority alliance, giving it 17 unopposed seats. Between the two is the Agikuyu group, descendants of squatter labourers who migrated from Kiambu and Nyeri districts following dispossession by white settlers and their fellow Agikuyu chiefs at the turn of the century. Distributed proportionately, the Kikuyu vote could probably have accounted for twice the 5 seats it had in the Province.

Table 6.4   1992 Kenya general elections - presidential vote by province

Province	Kibaki (DP) No./%	Matiba FORD (A) No./%	Moi KANU No./%	Odinga FORD (K) No./%	Others - /%
Nairobi	69,715	165,553	62,410	75,888	
	18	44	16	20	2
Coast	32,201	33,399	188,296	42,796	
	10	11	62	14	3
North Eastern	3,259	7,188	46,420	5,084	
	5	11	72	8	4
Eastern	392,481	79,436	290,372	13,673	
	50	10	37	2	1
Central	373,147	630,194	21,918	10,668	
	35	60	2	1	2
Rift Valley	98,302	214,727	981,488	75,465	
	7	16	71	5	1
Western	14,404	214,060	219,187	98,822	
	2	38	39	17	4
Nyanza	51,988	10,299	117,554	581,490	
	6	1	15	75	3
Totals	1,035,497	1,354,856	1,927,645	903,886	

All this lends credence to opposition claims that over the years, KANU had gerrymandered the constituencies in its favour. Be that as it may, the elections demonstrated that nearly 30 years after independence, ethnicity still remained the central focus of political mobilization. This is reflected in the patterns of regional representation demonstrated by Tables 6.3 and 6.4, which show the distribution of parliamentary seats and presidential votes by province.

To place these tables in perspective, a further word is necessary. Kenya has more than 40 ethnic groups ranging in numbers from a few hundred to several million. The four largest occupy four distinct provinces: the Kikuyu (21% of the population) live overwhelmingly in Central Province; the Luhyia (14%), a fragmented collection of some 16 sub-groups who have never voted as an ethnic bloc, in Western Province; the Luo (13.5%) in Nyanza; and the Kamba (11%) in North Eastern Province, which they share with the Meru (5%). Meanwhile, as noted, the Kalenjin (11%) occupy the Rift Valley along with the Masai, Turkana, the Samburu and a large population of Kikuyu 'immigrants'. The rest of the Rift Valley and the North Eastern province is very sparsely populated and accounts for no more than 7% of the total; Coast Province is occupied by a number of small ethnic groups constituting 5%, and Nairobi Province is metropolitan but is predominantly composed of ethnic groups with the highest degrees of proletarianization, namely Kikuyu/Meru, Luo, Luhyia and to some degree, Kamba.

In these circumstances, ethnic support for particular parties and leaders is relatively easy to identify. The KANU victory came mainly from the Rift Province among the Masai, Kalenjin, Pokot and Samburu and from sections of the Western and Coast Provinces, and represented an alliance of minority ethnic groups. In contrast, support for the three main opposition parties came mainly from the majority ethnic groups and sub-divided mainly along ethnic lines. Odinga's FORD (K) drew mainly from Nyanza among the Luo and to a lesser extent from the neighbouring Luhyia; Matiba's FORD (A) obtained the backing of the two Kikuyu districts of Kiambu and Muranga and, with Martin Shikuku, a Luhyia, as its deputy leader, split the Luhyia vote with KANU; and Kibaki's DP secured its support from his home district, Nyeri, and shared the neighbouring Kamba vote with KANU. The Luhyia and the Kamba were the only major ethnic groups to split their vote between KANU and the opposition parties.

In the independence elections of 1963, it had been KANU (then led by Jomo Kenyatta) which had represented the alliance of the majority ethnic groups, when the Kikuyu, Luo, Kamba and sections of the Luhyia had voted more or less as a single bloc, while the opposition Kenya African Democratic Union (KADU), in which Moi was a key figure, had represented an alliance of the minority ethnic groups - Kalenjin, Masai, sections of Luhyia and some coastal ethnic groupings. In 1992, Moi now led a KANU that drew on much of the old KADU constituency, while the opposition now competed for the votes of much of KANU's original heartland.

This chapter offers an explanation as to why the transition to multi-partyism in Kenya took the particular form it did, and thereby ensured the survival of the old order. It takes the elections of December 1992 as a basis for this assessment and argues that, given the balance of forces during the period

1990-92, a far-reaching transition was not possible: instead, the transition process was always likely to lead to a legitimation of the old order. That political contestation emphasizes an ethnic dimension does not necessarily mean that the explanation for this cannot be sought from within a paradigm of class analysis. Rather, it may be argued that in socio-economic formations of this type, ethnicity becomes the medium through which class politics is mediated. For this, it is important to return to the debate about the specificity of the post-colonial state and to focus on the centrality of the state in post-colonial Africa, particularly its role as the only significant focus of accumulation and patronage in economies of this type. To paraphrase Moore (1987), the state is strong in the sense that the state sector comprises a large section of the economy, and its bureaucracy, the only cohesive and organized group in politics.

The Origins of the One-Party State in Kenya

At independence, Kenya was bequeathed a Westminster-type parliamentary system consisting of two main parties, KANU and KADU. KANU, under Jomo Kenyatta and Oginga Odinga, formed the first government, while KADU under Ronald Ngala, Masinde Muliro and Daniel Arap Moi, formed the opposition. However, the party system was relatively weak, the two parties having been formed only two years previously, in 1961. The lack of institutionalization of the party system was demonstrated when, after Kenya had become a Republic in December 1964 (with Kenyatta President and Odinga Vice-President), KADU disbanded, and its leaders joined the government, purportedly in the national interest. Within a year of independence, Kenya had become a de facto one-party state.

Underlying these changes was the legacy of the colonial state. First, the latter's form of accumulation and uneven economic development produced pronounced ethnic inequalities (Njonjo:1977). Second, the exclusion of Africans from the mainstream of the economy and politics ensured that indigenous classes remained weak and their productive capacity vastly underdeveloped, thereby providing a poor basis for the evolution of civil society. Third, in contrast, the colonial state, with the support of the economically dominant settler group, became central to the entire process of capital accumulation as it was the only institution capable of mobilizing resources, and organizing conditions for accumulation, and guaranteeing the reproduction of those conditions of accumulation.

In the absence of any revolutionary rupture in the transition to independence, the post-colonial state was destined to replicate the role previously performed by its colonial predecessor. Yet now it would be controlled by a new combination of interests: an intelligentsia from the labour movement, a peasant/working class alliance (then led by the left of KANU), and, most significantly, emergent indigenous classes of capital and property.

Precisely because of their weakness, these latter elements could not but share political power with the more numerous popular classes. Indigenous capital had its origins in pre-colonial and colonial primitive accumulation (Cowen & Kinyanjui, 1977), its central core being mainly located in Central Province, particularly within the Kiambu district. This dominant fraction has come to be identified as 'the Kiambu bourgeoisie' or 'the family' (Ajulu, 1992; Ngunyi, 1993).

For the new alliance in control of the post-colonial state, the significance of the transition to independence lay in the fact that it removed the racial fetters to personal accumulation, whilst access to state office secured its advantage relative to its historical rivals, local Asian commercial interests and sections of international capital. In Odinga's phrase

> ...the Luo Union and the Luo Thrift... were like heifers: they needed a bull to produce calves and milk. The bull was political power and a say in government... (Odinga, 1966:139).

As under colonialism, therefore, the main feature of politics became the struggle for access to, and control of, the resources and patronage afforded by the state. Furthermore, ethnic inequalities made the claims upon that state starkly conflictual. Consequently, control of the state or access to those who had it, became the main preoccupation of politicians. It was not for nothing that KADU's leaders so rapidly forsook opposition to join KANU in the cabinet. In the perception of a majority of politicians, there was nothing to be gained by remaining in opposition.

The explanation for the shift to single partyism must therefore be sought within the changing balance of class and social forces built around control of the independent state. KANU was initially an alliance of three distinct strata. The first was the embryonic bourgeoisie. Colonial policies of subsidizing and protecting settler capital had fettered its growth and, in frustration, sections of this class had fought alongside the landless peasantry in the armed struggle for independence (Mau Mau) in the 1950s. The second element was composed of the embryonic middle classes, particularly Nyanza traders-cum-teachers led by Odinga's Luo Thrift and Trading Corporation; and the third was made up of the mass of the trade union movement, the urban working class, the lumpen proletariat, peasants, and landless squatters (Spencer, 1985; Goldsworthy, 1982; Furedi, 1974; Kaggia, 1975; Odinga, 1966; and Lonsdale, 1977).

KADU was an alliance of similar but weaker sections of these classes but without the support of the urban working class. It was particularly strong in those areas least subject to capitalist penetration. As Njonjo (1977) shows, while the KADU-aligned middle class were predominantly primary school teachers, KANU could boast a handful of university lecturers, lawyers, and doctors. KADU's policy of *Majimboism* (regionalism) reflected this weakness and its associated inability to compete on an equal footing at the centre.

It was this character of KANU as the party of the urban working class, the peasantry and the radical middle classes, whose rallying cry was the return of lands expropriated under colonialism, which gave it its initial progressive image. In short, it was identified with the radical tradition of anti-colonialism which had been the trade mark of Mau Mau and so had an enormous advantage over KADU in the struggle for control of the independent state.

The Unsteady Alliance, 1963-66

The weakness of indigenous propertied classes bound them to other classes at independence. Consequently, radical middle-class groups and the urban working class and their allies could temporarily impose demands on an independent KANU government. However, soon after independence, this alliance began to disintegrate. At the same time, the KADU embryonic bourgeoisie, excluded from power, sought access to resources and patronage. The outcome was a realignment of social and class forces which was solidified by the merger of KADU and KANU in December 1964.

The emergence of a de facto one-party system strengthened the conservative elements within the ruling party. Odinga (1966) and Leys (1974) identify the emergence of two factions in KANU motivated by ideological considerations, one conservative, led by Kenyatta and Tom Mboya (Economic Planning minister, secretary-general of KANU, and a former leader of the Kenya Federation of Labour), the other radical, led by the vice-president Odinga. At the beginning of 1965, the struggle for control of the party and government began in earnest and, with it, began an erosion of civil rights and pluralism. For a start, Bildad Kaggia, a veteran of the trade union and anti-colonial struggle was dismissed from the government at the end of 1964. Kaggia had been imprisoned with Kenyatta in the 1950s, his political base being the landless Kikuyu squatters who had formed the striking force of the

Mau Mau movement. Not surprisingly, he became an unrelenting critic of the state's decision to leave the land question entirely to market forces and thereby lock the majority of squatters out of the agrarian dispensation. Then, in 1965, Pio Gama Pinto, a key underground activist in Mau Mau and by now a leading strategist among the radical middle class, was assassinated in Nairobi (Odinga, 1966).

By 1966, the conservatives were sufficiently confident to force a political confrontation. During the KANU 'annual' conference, the first in six years, Tom Mboya emerged as KANU's key strategist. The constitution of the party was changed and the position of vice-president replaced by seven provincial vice-presidents. In the ensuing elections, the left was routed: where they won, as when Kaggia won the Central Province vice-presidency, the vote was nullified and fresh elections held after extra delegates had been bussed in (Goldsworthy, 1982).

The left faction thereafter regrouped into the first post-independence opposition party, the Kenya Peoples Union (KPU) led by Odinga and Kaggia. KANU responded with a constitutional amendment to stem a tide of defections, this requiring that those who crossed the floor to the opposition were obliged to seek a fresh mandate from their constituents. This brought about the so-called 'Little General Election' of 1966. In the event, of the thirty or so MPs who had joined the KPU, only nine were re-elected, seven of them from Odinga's Luo group. This inevitably exposed KPU to the charge of being a tribal party, despite its substantial support in the urban areas. Nonetheless, despite KPU's reduced size, the country was once again a multi-party state.

Because of rising mass expectations, not least amongst the urban crowd, the new ruling class feared even a weak opposition which would require it to be accountable to a wider populace. Sections of this ruling group had already acquired large tracts of land through influence with government, which it was determined not to lose. The KPU's advocacy of an anti-imperialist policy, a thoroughgoing land reform, a safety net for the poor, free health and education, were consequently anathema to the new rulers, and the party was destined to be short-lived.

In July 1969, Tom Mboya, the only Luo of significance in Kenyatta's cabinet, was murdered in Nairobi by a Kikuyu. Coming at a time of growing resentment of Kikuyu political and economic domination, the assassination provoked riots in the capital and attacks against Kikuyu. Then, four months after Mboya's death, when Kenyatta visited the opposition Luo stronghold of Kisumu, he was confronted by an angry crowd demanding to know the 'big men' behind the Mboya assassination. In these circumstances, a clash between Kenyatta and Odinga was inevitable: a rally turned into a riot, and the police opened fire. This led to a state of emergency in Kisumu, the proscription of the KPU, and the arrest and detention of its MPs.

Kenyatta now called the first post-colonial general elections in which only KANU could participate, making the country once again a de facto one-party state and marking the end of radical opposition. In Leys' words,

> ... the political challenge of the petty-bourgeoisie, urban trade union, rural landless alliance led by Odinga and Kaggia was out-manoeuvred and finally destroyed in the banning of the Kenya Peoples Union in 1969. In the course of these struggles, the unionised working class was brought effectively under control of the state... (Leys, 1978:258).

Thus the 1969 general election ended a bitter struggle between the radical middle class and the embryonic capitalist bourgeoisie. At last the victors could now rule in their own name.

Kenyatta and the Kiambu Bourgeoisie, 1969-78

The banning of the opposition contained rather than ended conflict. The balance of forces within KANU, now predominantly an alliance of the Kikuyu bourgeoisie, particularly its Kiambu fraction, plus the old KADU interests of small property, ensured that politics after 1969 were structured by competition within the ruling party rather than outside it. This increasingly assumed the form of political rivalry between various provincial or regional barons for access to state resources which could be dispensed to clients further down the line. Hence patron-client relationships became the most important form of politics and in turn spawned a plethora of tribally-based power brokers.

Yet only a section of the bourgeoisie, the politically-dominant Kiambu faction, actually ruled. Its continued political and economic hegemony depended on its favourable access to, and the exclusion of other lesser members of the alliance from, the core of state power. That the government could still construct a stable political constituency based on patron-client co-optation owed much to relative economic buoyancy and growth. Keynesian policies dominant in much of post-colonial Africa during the first decade of independence initially registered encouraging growth. The government expanded expenditure in health, education and public services; Africanization created jobs in the public sector and the parastatals for the growing middle class; and the strategy of prising the Asian commercial classes from lucrative wholesale sectors created openings for indigenous trader classes. More significantly, as Njonjo (1977) argues, the support of the middle peasantry was secured through Kenyatta's ability to give priority to property rights in land (Atieno-Odhiambo, 1993: 11).

Finally the stature of Kenyatta as the leader of the pack, and the occasional beating of the drums of tribal chauvinism, as happened in 1969 in the aftermath of Tom Mboya's assassination (Karimi and Ochieng, 1980), bound these forces together in a semblance of political stability. This period thus helped to consolidate the position of the indigenous bourgeoisie; by the end of the first decade of independence, a powerful group had emerged which, although still heavily subordinated to foreign capital, straddled the heights of economy and politics. If the Kiambu faction constituted the inner circles, the rest were arranged in respective pecking order within the coalition, although Moi served as Kenyatta's constitutional deputy following a return to a single vice-presidency. This arrangement was not devoid of internal conflicts, and competition and factionalism continued within KANU. However, as long as factionalism did not threaten the stability of the pecking order, Kenyatta was content to allow a narrow space through which occasional anger could be channelled. Thus, the early 1970s witnessed a relatively vibrant 'opposition' within the ruling parliamentary group.

In 1976, however, a succession battle broke out into the open. Some members of the 'Kiambu bourgeoisie' launched the Change the Constitution Movement (CCM), which sought the repeal of section 6(1) of the constitution so that, in the event of the death of the President, the Vice-President did not automatically assume the presidency, a move clearly aimed at thwarting Moi's ambitions. As in the crisis after Mboya's assassination, the Kiambu faction appealed to narrow Kikuyu nationalism to retain control of the presidency. Unfortunately for the CCM, unlike in 1969, they could not count on undivided Kikuyu loyalty either within Kiambu or in the wider Kikuyu community. Two powerful figures, Charles Njonjo, then Attorney General, and Mwai Kibaki, then Minister of Finance, threw their weight and resources behind the beleaguered Moi and brought the campaign to a halt.

Moi and the Rise of a Kleptocratic Bourgeoisie

Kenyatta died in 1978 and was succeeded by Moi, who immediately indicated that he stood for continuity. In the longer term he was to change the alignment of dominant interests, displacing the Kiambu bourgeoisie in favour, not of his

Kalenjin group, but of a wider alliance of sections of the embryonic bourgeoisie and the middle-class traders who had occupied the periphery of Kenyatta's coalition. Initially, though, to gain the confidence of voters, President Moi adopted a populist stance. He released all political detainees, unbanned the University Students Union, and promised open government. This early posture must be understood as a response to the fact that the state remained largely under the control of the clique which had surrounded Kenyatta. Essentially Moi was not yet his own man and, preoccupied with survival, he sought to gain the confidence of other ethnic groups while he tried to dismantle the Kenyatta coalition.

For the first four years, Moi ruled through Kibaki, whom he made his Vice-President, and Charles Njonjo, the Attorney-General, who was seen or rather saw himself as the effective number two. However, these two came from different groups of the Kikuyu bourgeoisie and had occupied different positions in the Kenyatta coalition. There was also a rivalry going back half a century between the elites of the two districts from which they came (Spencer, 1985). Their moratorium was thus short-lived and they dissipated much energy doing battle over the supposed succession, as Moi was then still seen as 'a passing cloud' (Karim and Ochieng, 1980). Meanwhile, Moi was able to use this breathing space quietly assembling his own alliance.

The failure of a coup attempt in 1982 allowed Moi, firstly, to purge the army and air force and pack the military hierarchy with his loyalists and, secondly, to attack those political forces hitherto beyond his control. Njonjo, who had been instrumental in Moi's succession to power, and whose base was the judiciary and the old Kenyatta bureaucracy, was one of the first to go - publicly humiliated through a Commission of Inquiry appointed to investigate the circumstances of the coup attempt. Thereafter, Moi could construct his own ruling coalition.

As with the previous regime, a small clique, most notably of Kalenjin middle-level bureaucrats, university lecturers and second-tier army officers, formed the core of President Moi's kitchen cabinet (Atieno-Odhiambo, 1993). To this inner circle was cobbled a shifting alliance of the old KADU groups: the Masai were brought into the fold under Justus Ole Tipis and later William Ntimana, and one of their leaders, George Saitoti, later became vice-president; the Luhyia were recruited under the late Moses Mudavadi; and the coastal alliance was secured under Katana Ngala.

By the mid-1980s, Moi was using patronage and clientelism to construct and reconstruct his coalition. The centre however remained the same - the 'Karbanet Syndicate', as the dominant inner circle drawn from President Moi's tribal grouping was known.

This change in the composition of ruling groups coincided with a change in international market conditions which affected the country adversely. From earlier buoyancy, the late seventies and early eighties witnessed a deep economic crisis throughout Africa. More importantly, a decline in production and a fall in output led to indebtedness on an increasing scale. Between 1976-87, Sub-Saharan Africa's total indebtedness catapulted from US$21.1 billion to US$137.8 billion. Kenya was no exception and Moi, unlike Kenyatta, began to find it increasingly difficult to satisfy the expectations of either the masses or his core constituency, the middle classes.

Moreover, President Moi's new coalition comprised a relatively weak economic class compared to Kenyatta's, which had constituted the most prominent pre-colonial and colonial primitive capital accumulators (Cowen, 1981; Swainson, 1980; Kaplinsky, 1980; Spencer, 1985; Sorrenson, 1967). Thus, President Moi's most immediate task was to construct a capital base for his coalition. The absence of fresh areas of accumulation and the reduced size of the national cake meant that the new accumulators were compelled to do so at the expense of their predecessors, in other words, the capital base of the new coalition had to be constructed upon the dissolution of the already entrenched Kikuyu capital and later Indian commercial capital (Ngunyi, 1993).

The mechanisms of this accumulation were primarily rent-seeking activities: appropriation of public resources, enrichment through political and bureaucratic positions, allocations of business and trading premises, appropriation of land, contract inflation, kickbacks from multinational corporations and so on. It is not surprising that by the mid-1980s, prominent personalities within the Moi coalition were identified with corruption and fraud, including the appropriation of aid funds (Cheche Kenya, 1982). Thus, despite the rhetoric of continuity, qualitative shifts in economic and political power were indeed taking place. By the mid-1980s, Moi's alliance had succeeded in removing the old accumulators from centres of political power and, to some degree, key areas of the economy. These changes were bound to unsettle the balance of forces within the propertied and privileged classes, and by the later 1980s, the regime had marginalized important sectors of society - the Kiambu elite, the professional strata, university students, workers, and of course, the traditional opposition grouped around Odinga.

In this context it is not surprising that the regime was forced to rely increasingly on repression to maintain political stability. It centralized state power, obliterated that civil society which had survived the Kenyatta dictatorship, and gradually established a political culture of intolerance. As early as June 1982, an attempt to register a new political party, the Kenya African Socialist Alliance led to the detention of George Anyona, and the house restriction of Oginga Odinga. A constitutional amendment, clause 2(a), was hastily pushed through the National Assembly in just twenty minutes, turning the country, once more, into a de jure one-party state. From 1982, after the abortive coup, the university was closed several times and all political activity was increasingly suppressed. In 1986 the constitution was again amended to give the President the powers to dismiss the Attorney-General, the Judiciary and the Auditor-General.

This situation was further exacerbated by the introduction of queue voting for the 1988 general election. Ostensibly the equivalent of party electoral primaries at constituency level, the secret ballot was replaced by voters (who had to be party members) queuing behind the candidates of their choice. Any candidate who obtained more than 70 per cent at this stage of voting was returned to Parliament unopposed. The queuing system was open to all manner of abuse, especially as elections were run largely by provincial administrations under the Office of the President. It was widely interpreted as an attempt to circumvent the dwindling political base of the regime and consequently the 1988 general elections were widely regarded as having been 'rigged'. After 1988, even the most fertile imagination could not pretend that the Westminster model still obtained in Kenya or defend the Moi regime's democratic record.

The Re-emergence of Multi-Party Politics

In the aftermath of the Cold War, western pressure created a political space for popular forces on the ground in Africa to press for democratic reform and the restoration of multi-partyism. Osborne (1993) contends that external pressure provided a spark for mass discontent that had long existed in Africa. The combination of external and internal forces which propelled a number of African countries to multi-partyism are clearly visible in Kenya where, throughout the seventies and eighties, sections of the intelligentsia sought a space for the articulation of democratic demands. Yet ultimately it was the intervention of external forces which provided the pressure and political environment in which Moi found it difficult to resist demands for democratic change.

The internal dimension In 1986-87 a national campaign emerged for the restoration of multi-party politics. This developed gradually through a series of events. First, the *Mwakenya*[1] show trials beginning in 1986 and the government crackdown on its critics indicated that all was not well with the regime. Having put hundreds of political activists behind bars, the regime tried to implicate Odinga in the so-called *Mwakenya* activities in 1987. However, this attempt to tar Odinga misfired, enabling him to mount a counter-offensive, and in an open letter to Moi, the former Vice-President attacked the government for undemocratic practices. This not only caused the government considerable embarrassment, but marked the beginning of open comment on the nature of state repression.

Second, the 1988 elections held under the new queue-voting system was used to remove the remnants of KANU dissidents from Parliament, thus engendering a crisis within the ruling party. Third, a campaign waged by exiled opponents of the regime against human rights abuses in the country increasingly began to focus international attention on the country and to isolate the regime.

Finally, the assassination in February 1990 of the Minister for Foreign Affairs, Dr. Robert Ouko, was to prove the main catalyst for popular protest against the Moi regime. Ouko had been very popular, particularly in western circles, where he had been seen as a possible successor to Moi. The discovery of his burnt body near his home in Nyanza Province sparked off demonstrations reminiscent of the Mboya assassination in 1969 and, for the first time since Moi became President, there were public calls for his resignation and those of his closest lieutenants, Nicholas Biwott, Minister for Energy, and Hezekia Oyugi, Permanent Secretary in charge of internal security.

These developments produced a major shift in the balance of forces. From about 1989, the question was no longer whether Moi would concede political space but rather when he would do so. Indeed, over the next six months, the pace of political events was quickened by the emergence of a new coalition of opposition forces.

The Saba Saba demonstrations   An abortive pro-democracy rally, called by the unofficial opposition which emerged in the aftermath of the Ouko assassination, was held at the Kamkunji[2] grounds in Nairobi on 7 July, 1990. This opposition was led by Kenneth Matiba and Charles Rubia, former ministers in the Moi regime who had been expelled from KANU in 1988 following their complaints against the flawed elections. Representatives of the powerful Kikuyu class of capital (Matiba was a former Chief Executive of Kenya Breweries and Rubia the first African Mayor of Nairobi), they were already looking to a political dispensation beyond Moi. A third member of the leadership was Raila Odinga, the son of Oginga. This then was the beginning of a realignment of political forces which soon was to combine KANU dissidents and the traditional opposition into FORD. Predictably, however, Matiba, Rubia and the younger Odinga were detained on the eve of the rally, which was then banned.

In the absence of its leadership, the proposed rally disintegrated into widespread rioting and looting. Starting in Nairobi, moving to the Central Province, and spreading as far as Kisumu in Nyanza, thousands of people took to the streets protesting lack of democracy. Government sources held that 20 people were killed in the course of the demonstrations but journalists have claimed over 100 died in Nairobi alone (*Daily Nation*, 11 July 1991; *Africa Watch*, 1991:66-82).

The Saba Saba demonstrations marked the beginning of open demands for a democratic alternative, although a wave of detentions initially intimidated the opposition and, for a brief period, the government appeared to have regained the initiative. But at the beginning of 1991, the opposition forces were back at the forefront of developments, with their formation of the National Democratic Party.

The National Democratic Party With the KANU oppositionists and his son in detention, Oginga Odinga made a further return to the political stage. At the beginning of 1991 he sensed that he could recapture the political initiative from President Moi. With the backing of a younger generation, headed by James Orengo (a lawyer and former member of Parliament), Gitobu Imanyara (also a lawyer and publisher of the Nairobi Law Monthly) and Anyang' Nyong'o (an academic and former professor at the University of Nairobi), he founded the National Democratic Party (NDP) in March 1991.

The registration of opposition political parties had been prohibited since 1982. Consequently, Odinga and his lieutenants sought to get around this legal hurdle by seeking to register the NDP as a society. This strategy provoked a protracted legal wrangle before the NDP was refused registration. However, the opposition had won a victory in that the debate on single-party rule had now been brought out into the open.

The Forum for Restoration of Democracy In August 1991, Odinga and his associates found their way around the legal hurdle. Exploiting a loophole in the constitution, Odinga assembled 'notables' from various provinces to launch an opposition pressure group, the Forum for Restoration of Democracy. The group did not have much in common except that all had fallen out in the past with Moi. Masinde Muliro and Martin Shikuku had been leading lights in KADU, had subsequently joined KANU and had served under both Kenyatta and Moi until the late 1980s. Similarly, Philip Gachoka stood in for

Kenneth Matiba who had served in the cabinet until his resignation over the 1988 election controversy, whilst Ahmed Bamarhiz and George Nthenge owed their position in FORD as representatives of the Coastal and Eastern Provinces respectively. The Odinga camp, on the other hand, represented the mainstream of the traditional opposition, the left of KANU which had decamped in 1966 to found the KPU, and had since been in the political wilderness.

Thus from the very beginning, FORD was an alliance of personalities who represented different ethnic constituencies but whose only unifying platform was the desire to be rid of Moi. This fragile alliance partly echoed the tradition of political organization in the nationalist movement, the broad outlines of which represented the class forces of African nationalism.

The external dimension In the wake of the Cold War, the West was eager to initiate political reforms amongst the largely authoritarian developing countries held within its sway. In dealing with debtor regimes, in particular, there emerged a set of political conditionalities designed to foster 'good governance', defined in broad terms to include demands for political liberalization, public accountability, and respect for the rule of law and market principles.

In these circumstances, the Moi regime came under increasing pressure from several donor countries. In July 1991, the Nordic countries threatened to withdraw an $80 million aid agreement. In November, Norway broke off diplomatic relations and suspended new aid commitments after Koigi Wamwere, a former MP who was exiled in Norway, was allegedly kidnapped while visiting Uganda and charged with treason for illegally entering Kenya to plan Moi's overthrow. In the same month, the US Foreign Aid Appropriation Act specified four human rights conditions which Kenya had to meet before $15m in economic and military aid could be disbursed.

Finally, in November 1991, reacting to the government's continued repression, notably of FORD, the Kenya Consultative Group Meeting in Paris decided to withhold new aid commitments worth $1 billion pending political reforms and improvement in human rights conditions in the country. In December, the Moi regime finally succumbed to western pressure and repealed section 2(a) of the constitution, thereby once again legalizing multi-party politics.

The formation of new parties Odinga's FORD became the first to be registered as an opposition party, followed by the DP led by Mwai Kibaki. Then a fraction of FORD led by Kenneth Matiba broke away to become

FORD (A), leaving Odinga's FORD now known as FORD (K). The Kenya National Congress (KNC) was formed by Titus Mbathi, yet another former Minister. By the time of the 1992 general election, three other parties - KENDA, KSC and PICK - had also been officially registered. However, the major struggle for power was between the DP, FORD (A), FORD (K) and KANU.

Managing the transition From the onset, it was obvious that the government and the ruling party resented being pressured into accepting an open democratic system. President Moi himself consistently denounced the opposition as 'tribalists' and 'puppets of foreign masters' and pronounced himself (*Africa Events*, 8/2, 1992: 7-8) only a reluctant convert to multipartyism:

> ...I have not changed my mind - it is because of the Western media set against us, because of the economic setting today. ... we Kenyans have accepted [the multiparty system] not because we are influenced by anybody to jump on the wagon, but because of the attack from the West and all that. They tell you: do this... and they expect everybody to swallow what they say.

It is against this background that preparations for the December 1992 general election must be assessed. From the point of view of KANU, the transition and the democratic elections were a hurdle to be managed so as to secure victory. To this end it used the provocation of ethnic clashes, restrictions on freedom of movement and assembly, the packing of the Electoral Commission, manipulation of the media, and amendment of the constitution.

The provocation of ethnic clashes Even before the legalization of political parties, violent 'ethnic clashes' had erupted on a wide scale in the Rift Valley Province during September and October 1991. These followed a series of political rallies by a group of predominantly Kalenjin and Masai politicians close to or part of the President's 'inner cabinet' (Nicholas Biwott, Vice-President Saitoti, and William Ntimana, the Minister for Local Government). The main message of these rallies was that Rift Valley should be declared an exclusive zone of the ruling KANU and that those who were not Kalenjin or KANU supporters or who were, as they put it, 'outsiders in the Rift Valley Province would be required to go back to their motherland' (*Weekly Review*, 4 September 1992). This message was repeated at subsequent gatherings in the province. Thus, at a rally in September in Kericho District, the Kalenjin politicians present resolved to ban multi-party advocates from the province.

In October, fighting erupted between Kalenjin and non-Kalenjin residents throughout the province and continued well into 1992. Significantly, the government and its security apparatus appeared incapable of bringing the confrontations to an end. This, in turn, fuelled speculation of state involvement. By May 1992, the clashes, particularly in the Rift Valley, had escalated to an extent that suggested that this was no spontaneous outburst of anger and hatred between different ethnic groups, but rather was orchestrated by political forces seeking to derail the multiparty exercise.

In June 1992 an all-party Task Force, established by the National Council of Churches of Kenya (the Wanjau Report) to investigate the causes of the clashes, submitted a report which noted that in many of the affected areas 'tribes, namely Kalenjin, Kikuyu, Luo, Luhyia, Kisii and Masai had co-existed peacefully and intermarried since pre-independence days'. The Wanjau report observed:

> The prime cause of the clashes is political in the sense that it is geared at reducing the member (sic) of non-Kalenjin voters in the Rift Valley by evicting them from the Province and by disenfranchising those within the Province ... (Wanjau, 1992:17).

This political motive, it argued, was consistent with the hostile political speeches given at various places within the province late last year, and very recently in Narok District (Wanjau, 1992:17).

The report concluded by implicating senior government officials, cabinet ministers, Provincial Administration Officers and senior KANU officials in the organization of 'ethnic clashes' in the province and *inter alia* named Vice-President George Saitoti, Wilson Leitich, the KANU chairman in Nakuru, and KANU's Mt. Elgon MP, Wilson Kisiero, as being at the fore (Wanjau, 1992; *Africa Events*, 8/2, 1992: 7-8).

In October, a Parliamentary Select Committee Report on the clashes, the Kiliku Report, arrived at similar conclusions. It similarly named highly placed government ministers and party officials - notably Biwott, Saitoti, Ntimana and the Speaker of the House, Professor Ngeno - as being primarily responsible. The failure of the government to act on these findings only encouraged those involved and the 'clashes' continued well into the election period and beyond.

There is sufficient evidence to indicate that KANU was able to exclude opposition parties from large parts of the country - the bulk of the Rift Valley (where the 17 constituencies were uncontested), North Eastern Province and the remote sections of the Coast Province. The destruction of homes and subsequent dispersal of the homeless into other districts and provinces also inevitably disenfranchised a large number of potential voters.

As far as KANU was concerned, this type of punitive separatism was the only way out of democratic accountability. As Joseph Misoi, KANU MP for Eldoret South put it:

> We are saying that unless those clamouring for political pluralism stop, we must devise a protective mechanism by launching this *majimbo* or regionalism movement ... (*Africa Watch*, 1993: 12).

More recently, William Ntimana argued that with the introduction of a multi-party system, the survival of the smaller ethnic groups was threatened and that the only way to safeguard their interests was through this type of ethnic separatism (*Kenya Times*, 20 May 1993).

Freedom of movement and assembly   At the beginning of the election campaign, the Attorney-General announced the repeal of legislation which laid down that any meeting of more than nine people required a permit issued by the local provincial Administration, application for which had to be made not less than fourteen days in advance.   In practice, however, administrative officers continued as if nothing had changed, and frustrated attempts by opposition parties to stage meetings.

The electoral commission   Granted overall responsibility for administering the elections, the Electoral Commission had an image problem from the onset. The problem centred on the credentials and the credibility of its chairman, Justice Zachaeus Chesoni, who was widely deemed not to be independent of the Moi regime.   Opposition parties complained about the manner of the appointment and their lack of opportunity to propose alternative nominees (*Finance*, 15 September 1992).

Manipulation of the media   The media broadcasts by Kenya Broadcasting Corporation's two radio channels, in English, Swahili and vernacular languages, cater to some 80-85% of the population.   The Corporation also operates a television network, although the impact of this is largely limited to urban areas, where it reaches a little more than 2 million (although this audience represents the most educated and politically-conscious sectors of the population). The alternative Kenya Television Network (KTN) is owned by Kenya Times Media Trust in which KANU holds substantial shares. Its coverage is similarly restricted to the Nairobi area. Thus the electronic media continued to disseminate government propaganda during the election. A greater part of news chronicled the President's activities and visits to different parts of the country, his meetings with visiting dignitaries, and popular declarations and songs about him. During the transition period, anybody unfamiliar with the pattern of ownership could easily have mistaken the networks as the personal property of President Moi.

Amendment of the constitution In August 1992, the Government amended the constitutional rules governing presidential elections. As indicated earlier, this amendment stipulated that a successful presidential candidate required a simple plurality plus 25% of the votes cast in at least five of the eight Provinces. In the event that none of the candidates mustered 25% of the vote in five provinces, a run-off would be required between the two leading candidates. As further noted, this amendment also provided for the winning candidate to form a government from members of his own party even if that party did not have a majority in parliament. This provision for minority government suggests that KANU and Moi were more confident about the presidency than the parliamentary election. It also makes clear that the new multi-party system continued to entrench, rather than to challenge, executive power. The combination of all these strategies enabled Moi to conduct what Barkan (1993) has described as a 'C-minus' election. It was riddled with irregularities but none so blatant as to incur the wrath of international donors.

A divided opposition In the final analysis, however, it was the division of the opposition which delivered the election to the government. Why could the opposition not hold together until after the elections? Once again, this question can be answered only by understanding the nature of the opposition parties and politics that emerged out of 30 years of one-party rule.

As indicated earlier, FORD (K) initially represented a fragile alliance of the Kikuyu bourgeoisie represented by Matiba, Rubia, and their followers, petty-bourgeois professional and intellectual strata instrumental in the struggle for political liberalization throughout the 1980s (the mainstream opposition of the Odinga camp), and a motley collection of small capitalists and regional (tribal) notables who had either been expelled from KANU, 'queued' out of parliament during the 1988 election, or simply defected from KANU at the beginning of the multi-party process. At this early stage, therefore, the opposition had mass support within the four main ethnic groups and looked to be a government in waiting.

But this alliance was always going to be difficult to hold together and so it proved. The formation of Kibaki's DP in January 1992 began to complicate the picture. Kibaki was not only a former Vice-President but, more importantly, he was able to pull together the old Kenyatta coalition. Unashamedly a Kikuyu party, DP brought together the old Kiambu bourgeoisie and its Nyeri counterparts to represent the leadership of the Kikuyu ethnic group, thus denying Matiba that role as long as he remained under Odinga's fold in FORD. And with Kibaki as the only obvious presidential candidate from DP, it meant that Matiba, the other contending Kikuyu leader had very little chance if he remained in FORD.

Matiba therefore needed to win the FORD leadership from Odinga or form his own party. This led to the subsequent split and the emergence of FORD (A). In constructing his coalition, Matiba had to appeal beyond the Kikuyu vote. This he did by offering the vice-presidency to Shikuku, the self-appointed leader of the Luhyia, in the hope that he could deliver the Luhyia and thus forge an alliance of the two of the largest ethnic groups.

This picture was further complicated by traditional rivalries between different factions of the Kikuyu elite. While Kibaki's DP now constituted the political home of the old Kenyatta kitchen cabinet, FORD (A) comprised the former second-tier of the Kenyatta coalition, which had resented Kiambu domination, and saw themselves as the true representatives of the Kikuyu rank and file. Moreover, because he had resigned from KANU earlier, Matiba could pose as the true champion of the Kikuyu rank and file beyond Kiambu. This accounts for the ferocity of Matiba's attack on Kibaki at an election rally weeks before the election:

> ... Even today, these people (Kibaki and Moi) are together. Let him not cheat you that he (Kibaki) has the welfare of the common man at heart. We always thought and considered him our (Kikuyu) leader... Who is he? Did he not come out recently after we fought the battle and won... (*Society*, 28 December 1992).

On the other hand, FORD (K) was a coalition which was centred very much around Odinga and the Luo as its power base. From the point of view of the Luo, there was a feeling of having been betrayed and marginalized by the Kenyatta regime despite their importance in KANU's victory over KADU in 1963. Thus, while they were prepared to enter a coalition with any of the representatives of the Kikuyu vote, it was on condition that FORD (K) retained the presidency. More importantly, the Luo presidential candidacy was non-negotiable precisely because control of the state, it was believed, would enable them to redress the developmental imbalances and marginalization suffered under the two previous regimes. Thus, at the core of these considerations was the presidency and control of state power. The two Kikuyu factions wanted it in order to resume the old patterns of accumulation, FORD (K) to redress the deprivation of the past, and Moi's KANU to protect the gains of the previous 14 years. The centrality of the state thus remained at the heart of the new multi-party process and shaped its outcome.

Such considerations ruled out any possibilities of temporary coalition between the three main opposition parties. If Kibaki went with Odinga, he was likely to lose the Kikuyu vote to Matiba and vice-versa. In such circumstances, politics was reduced to elite pacts and complicated horse-trading to determine which of the regional (tribal) barons was capable of delivering their constituencies. Politicians who only a few months earlier had been vocal in denouncing multi-partyism from within KANU, now sought respectability in different opposition camps.

Table 6.5   1992 Kenya general elections - combined opposition presidential percentage vote compared to KANU

Province	Opposition	KANU
Nairobi	84	16
Central	98	2
Coast	39	61
North Eastern	27	73
Eastern	63	37
Rift Valley	29	71
Western	61	39
Nyanza	85	15

And it was clear even before the first vote was cast that the deals stitched together by the different opposition parties could not deliver the presidency. FORD (A)'s alliance of Matiba and Shikuku could at least deliver the required 25 per cent in Central, Western and Nairobi provinces, but was still two provinces short even if it won a majority presidential vote. FORD (K) was assured of Nyanza, and had some chance in Nairobi, Western, and Coast but seemed to have little chance of a fifth. And the same problem afflicted the DP,which secured only two provinces, Central and Eastern. Ironically, the joint opposition presidential vote did pretty well in all the provinces, and secured the required 25% even in KANU's strongholds, as Table 6.5 shows.

The Survival of the Old Order

The most significant outcome of the 1992 election was its confirmation of the status quo. The result legitimated the Moi regime in a manner that had not been possible during the three previous elections held under a one-party system. As indicated, Moi was not a convert to the multi-party system. In fact, he was compelled by internal pressure and western conditionalities to open up democratic space. It is not surprising therefore that having survived the process, he should seek to consolidate the old order. His first target after the elections was the press, particularly the alternative press which had emerged during the democratic struggle and had been instrumental in exposing corruption and scandals within government circles. This was soon followed by the resumption of 'ethnic clashes' in the Rift Valley, with overwhelming evidence of government complicity.

The next target were organizations in civil society, particularly those active in exposing state involvement in 'ethnic clashes' and providing support for the victims. One example will suffice. In the last week of February 1993 some 65 hooded police officers stormed the premises of Kilimanjaro Pharmacy in the Hilton Hotel. The proprietor, John Makanga, a member of a group in the forefront of the campaign against ethnic clashes in the Burnt Forest area of Rift Valley was brutally assaulted in public and taken off to an unknown police station (*Weekly Review*, March 1993).

At the same time, the regime harassed the opposition in order to force defections, demoralize critics and ensure a comfortable majority in the House. Early in March 1993 there were allegations of government bribes to encourage opposition MPs to cross the floor. Initially the Mboya Amendment stemmed the predicted haemorrhage from the opposition within the Assembly but only for a time. The first defection took place in Lugari constituency in Western Province where FORD (A) was forced to defend a 13,000 margin. In the subsequent by-election KANU took the seat with a narrow margin over FORD (K), but not before, it was alleged, KANU had 'produced' an extra polling station. That notwithstanding, this one by-election stimulated a wave of defections to KANU. Of the 9 seats that FORD (A) had won at the general election, it lost all but two to KANU. FORD (K) suffered three defections (but successfully defended the seats in its Luo heartland), and DP, too, suffered a number of desertions, including that of its deputy-leader in February 1995.

Within three years of the election, it was business as usual for President Moi and KANU. The press had returned to self-censorship, whilst the wave of by-elections caused by opposition members returning to KANU saw the politicians re-adopting their old habits of patronage. Worse, despite rigid conditionalities imposed and supervised by the IFIs, corruption remained rife - a report by the auditor-general in 1995, for instance, indicating that some £178.6 million sterling was missing from the treasury (*Mail & Guardian*, 13-19 October 1995). In addition, Moi continued to weaken the opposition with an eye to the general election in 1997. Most notably, in September 1995, there were moves to amend the constitution to compel every party to field a presidential candidate (thus preventing a united opposition candidate).

The emergence of authoritarianism in Kenya under colonialism and during the post-independence period is not some fortuitous accident. The form of primitive capitalist accumulation with which it has been associated has precluded any notion of liberal democracy. Experience in the whole of Sub-Saharan Africa has, in the opinion of many scholars, demonstrated that authoritarianism, not democracy, is the accompaniment of IMF/ World Bank market reforms. Ongoing economic reform and enforced broadening of the political space therefore have a contradictory relationship: for one to succeed, the other must give way. The lesson of December 1992 is that formal political reform did not alter the authoritarian order. In Kenya, the more things have changed, the more they have remained the same.

Notes

1. *Mwakenya*, an underground political movement, surfaced in the mid-1980s when a number of opposition figures were arrested and charged with subversive activities. According to UMOJA, the London-based United Movement for Democracy in Kenya, Mwakenya had its origins in the December 12 Movement, a broad left grouping active prior to the 1982 coup attempt. In the 1986-88 crackdown, hundreds of trialists charged with sedition were forced to plead guilty without legal representation and were jailed for terms ranging from 4 to 6 years (*Africa Watch* 1991: 129-44 and Amnesty International 1987).

2. Kamkunji is an open field in Nairobi's Eastlands - the segregated African residential area during the colonial period. It is famous as the rallying point of anti-colonial struggle and is therefore synonymous with anti-establishment political activity. Saba is Swahili for seven, hence Saba Saba.

7 Settling Old Scores: from authoritarianism to dependent democracy in Lesotho

ROGER SOUTHALL

The first free general election to be held in Lesotho since independence in 1966 took place on 27 March 1993. The result was an astounding clean sweep of all 65 parliamentary seats by the Basutoland Congress Party (BCP), and a subsequent handing over of power by the military regime, latterly led by Colonel Elias Ramaema, to a civilian government headed by Ntsu Mokhehle, the leader of the BCP since its foundation in 1952. The scale of its defeat not only plunged the formerly ruling Basotho National Party (BNP) into crisis, but posed awkward questions concerning the wisdom of the retention of the plurality electoral system for relaunching democracy following a long period of (both civilian and military) authoritarian rule. Indeed, democracy was to be directly imperilled by a military-backed monarchical coup which temporarily displaced the newly-elected government in mid-1994 until it was restored following direct intervention by neighbouring states, most notably South Africa. If it was previously a dependent authoritarian state, Lesotho has now become a dependent democracy.

The Post-Colonial State: Authoritarianism and Dependence

Lesotho - a tiny, mountainous country which is completely surrounded by South Africa - proceeded to independence under the BNP which, led by Chief Leabua Jonathan, had secured a narrow victory in the pre-independence election of 1965 with 31 seats (and 41.6% of the vote) compared to the 25 seats (and 39.7% of the vote) won by the BCP. The balance of 4 seats in the then 60-seat National Assembly was won by the Marematlou Freedom Party (MFP), which advocated executive authority for the recently installed King, Moshoeshoe II. The state which the BNP inherited from the colonial administration was extremely fragile. Only about 13% of its land was suitable for cultivation, the country possessed few natural resources other than small deposits of diamonds and the hydroelectric potential of its rivers, and, since the turn of the century, it had become increasingly dependent upon the export of (mainly male) migrant workers to South Africa. Erected on neither a manufacturing, nor a commercial, nor a secure agricultural base, and financed principally from revenue derived from the South African-dominated Southern African Customs Union, Lesotho was a dependent state *par excellence.*

The BCP had mobilized an emergent intelligentsia, largely educated in the Protestant missions, together with a stratum of traders whose economic expansion had been stifled by the chiefs and the colonial state, around a radical nationalist and anti-apartheid programme. This had alienated conservative forces, notably the influential Roman Catholic hierarchy and the majority of lesser chiefs, who had responded with the formation of the BNP in 1958 as a bulwark against communism and a guarantor of good neighbourliness with South Africa. It was by harping upon the threat which a BCP victory represented to rural household incomes, which were heavily dependent upon migrant remittances, that the BNP initially obtained the support of the majority of women voters and clinched its victory in 1965 (Bardill and Cobbe, 1985).

However, because it represented social forces which in a free market would not have been able to compete on an equal footing with their opponents in the BCP, the BNP used its control of the state to move initially into a highly collaborative relationship with Pretoria (Ajulu, 1995).

The BNP was supremely confident of retaining power in the election of 27 January 1970. However, whilst its collaborationist strategy had done nothing to counter a deeply-based anti-Boer sentiment amongst ordinary Basotho, it had not yet yielded sufficient economic returns to enable the party to extend its social base. Furthermore, it had alienated key segments of its support by its neglect of rural areas. Consequently, as the results came in, it became clear that it was the BCP which had now secured a majority. Subsequent analysis indicated the BCP to have received 49.8% of the 306, 529 votes polled and to have won 36 seats, in contrast to 42.2% and 23 seats for the BNP, and 7.3% and one seat for the MFP. However, rather than relinquishing power, Prime Minister Jonathan overrode the elections on the alleged grounds that they had been marred by violence. Backed by South African advisers and the security forces, he declared a state of emergency and suspended the constitution (Macartney, 1973).

The next 'election', held only in 1985, saw the return of 65 BNP members to an expanded House of Assembly following a boycott of the polls by all the parties of opposition. The intervening years had seen a comprehensive breakdown of the Basotho body politic. Following the 1970 election, some hundreds of opposition supporters had been dismissed from the civil service; the BCP had split over whether to participate in an appointed National Interim Assembly; a bungled 1974 attempted counter-coup had been followed by the flight of key BCP leaders (including Mokhehle) into exile in Botswana; and Jonathan, having encouraged a considerable inflow of South African commercial capital, now sought to offset the limitations of his collaborationist strategy by projecting Lesotho as a haven of racial harmony, and as increasingly strongly identified with the struggle against apartheid.

Jonathan's shift attracted substantial foreign aid to replace the South African support that was lost. On the other hand, it turned the international alignments of Lesotho's parties upside down. In short, by refusing to acknowledge Transkeian 'independence' in 1976, by establishing diplomatic contacts with Eastern Bloc regimes, by building low-key relations with the ANC, and by providing sanctuary for a substantial number of refugees, the BNP now claimed the anti-apartheid mantle. In contrast, in the late 1970s, the BCP launched a Lesotho Liberation Army (LLA) which depended upon covert South African goodwill to undertake destabilizing operations against the BNP government. The latter responded by strengthening the military, and stressing its role as apartheid victim following South African Defence Force (SADF) strikes into Maseru, the capital, in 1982 and 1985.

However, Jonathan's political somersault reaped an inevitable cost. Within his own government, his anti-apartheid stance alienated a right-wing faction, led by Planning Minister Retselitsoe Sekhonyana, which enjoyed close business links with South Africa and close political links with the army (the latter already embarrassed by its failure to rebuff both the SADF and the LLA). In contrast, a more radical faction, which supported Jonathan in distancing Lesotho from Pretoria and reaping the consequent benefits of foreign aid, responded by attempting to transform the BNP Youth League into an alternative military force. The resultant strife between the BNP right and the BNP radicals culminated in bitter struggles between rivals for constituency candidate nominations in the 1985 'election', and registered a shift of power within the ruling party in favour of the radicals. Under the leadership of Vincent Makhele (Minister of Foreign Affairs) and Desmond Sixishe (BNP Secretary-General), the radicals now assumed control of key areas of decision-making as authority began to slip away from Jonathan.

Apart from threatening the right, the new predominance of the radicals also challenged leading elements within the army (then known as the Lesotho Paramilitary Force, or LPF). Headed by Major-General Justin Lekhanya, the LPF had provided the major prop for the BNP since the coup of 1970, it had put down the attempted BCP counter-coup of 1974, and had provided the main line of defence against guerrilla incursions by the LLA. It was also almost certainly responsible for a number of killings of government opponents by shadowy death squads that dogged Jonathan's last years. Yet more damaging to the integrity of the LPF was its invasion by BNP factionalism, notably after Jonathan had demoted Sekhonyana from Foreign Affairs to the Ministry of Planning. Sekhonyana, who had recently attempted to forge a non-aggression pact with Pretoria, was rumoured to have business links with Lekhanya, himself the recent victim of an attempted demotion by Jonathan, which he had only survived because of his broad support amongst the officer corps. It was their failure to secure his dismissal which propelled the radicals into building up the BNP Youth League as an alternative military force.

The result was the right-wing coup of January 1986. This was precipitated by an extended border closure by South Africa, which was concerned to secure both the expulsion of ANC refugees and final agreement (delayed by the radicals) to Lesotho's collaboration in the long-proposed Lesotho Highlands Water Project, a massive construction project whereby Lesotho would facilitate the supply of water to the Witwatersrand (Southall, 1995a).

Contest and Collaboration under the Military

The new Military Council, led by Lekhanya, formally vested executive and legislative power in the King, appointed a Council of Ministers which drew upon a mix of officers, politicians (notably Sekhonyana), technocrats and senior civil servants, and re-packaged the LPF as the Royal Lesotho Defence Force (RLDF). It moved swiftly to disarm the BNP Youth League and to eliminate radical supporters from within the army; elements within it were likely responsible for the assassination of both Desmond Sixishe and Vincent Makhele; and it worked hand-in-hand (despite disclaimers) with South African security forces in expelling ANC personnel and South African refugees in return for Pretoria clamping down upon the LLA. Meanwhile, it encouraged the return of BCP exiles from Botswana, although it simultaneously proclaimed an official suspension of politics.

However, all this began to unravel as the King, who was wont to present himself as a progressive, soon clashed with the military when he attempted to assert his authority. This culminated in Lekhanya purging the government of the King's supporters and his forcing Moshoeshoe to leave the country 'on sabbatical' in early 1990. He then sought to legitimize his actions by setting a timetable for the reintroduction of democracy by 1992. By this latter move,

Lekhanya recognized that, whilst he yet retained the support of the soldiery, his regime had otherwise almost wholly lost credibility. Church leaders had complained publicly about the lack of democracy; *The Mirror* newspaper had launched a campaign against high-level corruption, which had become particularly visible under the military, focusing in particular on alleged misappropriations by Sekhonyana (who had returned to the Finance Ministry) dating back to 1981; reports issued by Amnesty International were highly critical of the government; and related protests against human rights abuses by academics had provoked a clampdown on university autonomy. Meanwhile, a massive increase in the budget deficit since 1986 highlighted gross mismanagement of the economy and necessitated the imposition of major cutbacks in public expenditure. Additional to this, the return of Mokhehle to Maseru saw the initiation of talks between the BCP and BNP with a view to their pressing jointly for a restoration of parliamentary rule.

Lekhanya's battle with the King emphasized the fragility of his position, not least because Moshoeshoe himself launched a voluble rearguard action from exile in Britain, alleging corruption in high places and a reluctance by the military to return the country to democracy. The General therefore sought to quieten Moshoeshoe by inviting his return to Lesotho under unpublished, but clearly restrictive, conditions. By now, however, the King had called for the replacement of the military regime by an interim civilian government, and declined to come back to Lesotho unless the army stepped down. This particular intervention cost him his crown.

Proclaiming that he had exceeded constitutional bounds, the Military Council announced in November 1990 that the King had been dethroned, and was to be replaced by his son as Letsie III. This marked the end to the era of dual power inaugurated by the coup of 1986 (Southall, 1995a).

The Military: Containing the Transition

The military's chosen instrument for steering the country back to democracy was a National Constituent Assembly (NCA). This was appointed from army officers, civil servants, chiefs and recognized politicians. The NCA was charged with devising a new constitution as a prelude to the holding of a general election.

Arguing that the 1966 Westminster-style constitution had failed, Lekhanya proposed that it should be amended by provision for a custodian to protect it from the executive, for a watchdog body to supervise elections and the subsequent formation of a government, and for a code of conduct for political parties. He also insisted that members of an outgoing administration should be guaranteed against retrospective prosecution to facilitate a free transfer of power.

The NCA endorsed the 1966 constitution as the basis upon which to work, and proceeded to accept, too, the thrust of amendments suggested by the military. By far the most ambitious of these was the suggestion that the Commanding Officer of the Defence Force should be an *ex officio* member of any cabinet, but Lekhanya also fully intended that henceforth both a prime minister and the King would be ultimately subject to the authority of a Council of State upon which the heads of the defence and police forces would both be major influences.

Apart from these recommendations, the NCA proposed that the 1966 constitution should remain substantially unchanged. This meant, in particular, the restoration of a Senate which would be primarily representative of the chieftaincy. Importantly, however, the nature of the electoral system was barely broached, with the idea of proportional representation being barely discussed.

Following the swearing in of the new King, Lekhanya announced that the new constitution would be complete by early 1991 and elections held by June 1992. However, what he reckoned without was that an underlying stream of discontent would burst its banks and sweep him summarily back into civilian life much earlier than he had intended.

On 30 April 1991, Lekhanya was forced to resign by junior and non-commissioned officers after having refused to dismiss Foreign Minister Tom Thabane and Finance Minister Sekhonyana. These latter immediately fled the country, leaving rumours of corruption behind them. Colonel Elias Ramaema was subsequently sworn in as head of government. He stressed that the military remained committed to returning to the barracks in 1992, and thereupon lifted Order No. 4 of 1986, clearing the way for a resumption of free political activity. He also promised immediate attention to the holding of a census and a delimitation of constituencies. The soldiers' revolt had been precipitated by their dissatisfaction with a 22% pay rise they had been awarded in the recent budget, which they contrasted adversely with the supposedly fabulous financial gains being reaped by those at the centre of power.

These resentments had severely compromised Lekhanya's hold upon the army rank and file, but he was also, in part, a victim of a popular storm unleashed by the announcement by South African President F.W. De Klerk on 2 February 1990 that he was unbanning the ANC and other such organizations as a first major step towards the dismantling of apartheid. Indeed, Lekhanya's own inauguration of a democratization process only weeks later was clearly viewed within Lesotho as evidence that the military could no longer hold its line. The consequence was an upsurge in popular and trade union activity which extended well beyond the ambit of the established political parties. Central to this was a strike by teachers which ran for three months from 30 May 1991. It was eventually crushed following police disruption of a demonstration, and a swoop upon various trade union leaders who were organizing a more general stay away. However, it had constituted a major challenge to the government in that it had defied the ban on political activities, and had activated wider community support.

Apart from confronting the military, the teachers' and other strikes had also alarmed established politicians, some of whom linked the unrest to supposed ANC ambitions to incorporate Lesotho into a post-apartheid South Africa. Such fears were subsequently amplified by an official ANC meeting with the 'Solidarity Movement', a grouping which included a local Mandela Reception Committee, the Basotho Mine Labour Workers' Cooperative, the University Staff Association and various student organizations. However, what really advertised the government's loss of control was the abrupt cancellation of a visit to Maseru by Nelson Mandela, scheduled for 28 March 1991, following protests from the Solidarity Committee that he should not even be considering meeting with a discredited junta whilst the ANC itself was campaigning for an elected Constituent Assembly in South Africa (Southall, 1995a).

The displacement of Lekhanya by Ramaema owed not a little to the humiliation of the regime by the cancellation of Mandela's visit. However, the change in figurehead did nothing to prepare the regime for a further wave of industrial turbulence. Precipitated by a full-scale riot against foreign (notably Taiwanese) businesses, which left 34 people dead and much damage in its wake, this involved some 70 strikes during the last six months of 1991. The brutality with which the authorities responded - by assaulting workers, detaining a host of union leaders, and extending various controls over the labour movement - undoubtedly contributed to the determination of Lesotho's major aid donors that the military government should hand over to a civilian regime as soon as possible (Tangri, 1993). Delays in the registration of voters and delimitation of constituencies were to result in the election being postponed, first to November 1992 and later to March 1993.

All this inevitably provoked suspicion of the military's agenda. Ramaema therefore, faced the simultaneous challenge of assuaging such misgivings whilst protecting the military's interests throughout a protracted transition to civilian rule. Moshoeshoe had declared from London that one of the major reasons for his exile was the pressure he had exerted for a Commission of Inquiry into corruption in the public service (*Mirror*, 6 March 1992). Lekhanya's administration had responded by attempting to secure political immunity for past wrongs by aggressively building an effective military veto into a new constitution. In contrast, Ramaema's reformist administration projected itself as a cleansing regime whilst in practice resisting the growing pressures for open government.

The demand for cleaner government came in part from international donors (*Mirror*, 13 December 1991; 6 March 1992). In contrast, statements by the BCP that the army and police would be indemnified, and left to eradicate irregularities by their own methods, suggested that the party had done a deal with the military so as not to endanger a transition (*Mirror*, 12 June 1992). Most of the domestic pressure upon the government, therefore, came from the non-government press which provided a continuous mix of fact, rumour and speculation, and from the churches and various NGOs, which became increasingly active in highlighting a host of other developmental and human rights' abuses. Elements of the BNP which resented the army for usurping their rule also at times joined in the chorus. Meanwhile, the NGOs also established a forum to monitor human rights, with an immediate view to playing an educational role in the run up to the elections (*Mirror*, 13 December 1991).[1]

Pressure upon the army to come clean on its abuses of power increased as the election drew near. Consequently, late in the day, it slipped an anti-democratic provision into the draft constitution whose effect would be to empower the Defence Commission to restrict enquiries into matters concerning national security (LG, 1993a: section 145). It also proclaimed immunity for members of the various security services with respect to all their doings 'in good faith' since the last coup (LG, 1993b). NGOs responded by insisting that the constitution should be duly re-amended by a democratic government. However, the more popular concern was that the military was trying to influence the election in favour of the BNP.

Establishing the Electoral Framework

The contested nature of Lesotho's electoral history required that the administration and outcome of any election be externally endorsed if it were to be accepted domestically. This was to result in an extensive international monitoring exercise and considerable foreign input of finance and expertise by the Commonwealth, United Nations and various human rights groups

(Daniel, 1995). The most particular contribution was the arrival in May 1992 of Noel Lee, Director of Elections in Jamaica, as Chief Electoral Officer. In the event, a four-month postponement of the election necessitated Lee's return to Jamaica, and his replacement by Jocelyn Lucas, Chief Election Officer of Trinidad and Tobago. Meanwhile, the retention of the plurality electoral system required a fresh delimitation of boundaries (last conducted in 1985), which subsequently provided for the addition of five extra constituencies to the sixty seats competed for in previous elections (Lucas, 1993: 4-12).

The registration of voters began in December 1991.[2] From the beginning it proved a contentious process, with all parties, but most notably those which most feared defeat, evincing distrust of the procedures at one time or another. To overcome such suspicions, Lee was at pains to render the registration process transparent. To this end, he established an Electoral Advisory Committee, composed of representatives of political parties, and published two provisional lists of voters, to allow corrections to be made. In short, although both the BNP and the MFP in particular were highly vocal in their complaints, its supervision by a Commonwealth-provided Chief Electoral Officer meant that the administration of the electoral process could be less effectively contested than in 1970, when it had been conducted under the auspices of the BNP government with South African assistance (Khaketla, 1971: 193-206). The final list was published on 10 March 1993, showing the number of persons registered as 737,930, perhaps as many as 90 per cent of the potential electorate (Lucas, 1993: 7-10).

Campaigning began the moment the military lifted the ban on political activity in May 1991. A code of conduct for the political parties, introduced by the military, was ostensibly designed to provide for free and fair elections. This imposed restrictions upon the carrying of weapons at rallies, the use of inflammatory language, the disruption of other parties' meetings and so on. The military also sought to insist that political debate be restricted to party platforms and future policy options, and that all reference to past happenings should be avoided. Politicians were also required to refrain from criticizing the government (*Lesotho Today*, 6 August 1992).

Provisions like these inevitably fed rumours that the military was attempting to impose its will upon the outcome of the election. Such fears were fuelled not only by the army's presumed antipathy to the BCP, but also by the election in December 1991 of Sekhonyana as leader of the BNP, and that party's subsequent adoption of Lekhanya as a parliamentary candidate.

The Political Parties

The election was contested by a total of 242 candidates drawn from the BCP, BNP, MFP and ten smaller political parties. Only the BCP and BNP ran candidates in each of the 65 constituencies, although the MFP, which fielded 51 contenders, alleged that 14 of its would-be candidates had been denied registration on trumped-up technical grounds. Otherwise, only the Patriotic Front for Democracy (PFD) and *Ha Re Een Basotho* (HB) put up a significant number of candidates (17 and 13 respectively).

Despite its bluster, and the drama surrounding its cause provided by the military's clash with the monarchy, the MFP remained a marginal force, caught in the classic squeeze often faced by third parties under the plurality electoral system. As in 1965 and 1970, the election revolved around an essentially two- way fight between the BCP and BNP.

In 1993, however, for all that the official rhetoric associated the democratization process with a new beginning, the election proved to be much more about the past than the present. Too much bloodied water had passed under the bridge for Lesotho's recent bitter history to be forgotten, with the campaign providing the opportunity for the electorate to pass its verdict upon the consequences of the aborted election of 1970.

The BCP - claiming its inheritance

The democratization exercise was recognized by the BCP as an unprecedented opportunity to capture the levers of power. In 1965 the party's radical nationalism had been countered by institutional support extended to the BNP by the chiefs, the colonial administration and the powerful Catholic Church. In 1970 the BNP's control of state security, backed by South Africa, had enabled it to overturn the result and subsequently to defeat the BCP's attempted counter-coup in 1974. In 1985 the BCP had, unsurprisingly, dismissed the merits of yet another BNP-administered election.

By 1993, however, even though it retained close ties to the military, the BNP had lost state power and was reduced to competing with the BCP on more or less equal electoral terms. To Mokhehle, the frustrated contemporary of first generation post-independence leaders such as Nkrumah, Nyerere and Kaunda, it must have seemed that the wheel of fortune had completely turned in his favour.

From the moment in 1988 that BCP exiles began to return to Lesotho, they were in no doubt that their destiny was to inherit the state. Once the election campaign was in full swing, Molapo Qhobela, the new Deputy Leader of the party, went on record as predicting that the BCP would win all 65 constituencies (*Mirror*, 21 June 1992; 20 February 1993). As he admitted after the election, such bold assertions were simply electioneering, and the party leadership had fully expected to lose between ten and fifteen seats (*Interview*, 29 March 1993). Nonetheless, it had every conviction that it would win a sweeping victory. 'Basotho' declared Qhobela, 'did not support what happened in the 1970 election' (*Mirror*, 20 February 1993), and that was enough to guarantee the BCP a convincing majority. Yet before that moment of triumph there were important internal battles to tackle, plus the task of mobilizing the vote for a party that had for so long been bitterly divided.

Chief Jonathan's appointment of an Interim National Assembly in 1973 had split the BCP when a faction led by Gerard Ramoreboli had disobeyed the party leadership by participating in what the government trumpeted as an exercise in national reconciliation. These internal differences had then become entrenched when, after the BCP's failed uprising in 1974 (which the rebel wing had opposed), Mokhehle and his most immediate followers had fled the country, and Ramoreboli, still claiming his party allegiance, had joined the government as Minister of Justice.

Ramoreboli never enjoyed more than a small minority following. Indeed, the internal BCP had by the early 1980s become even more divided between those who remained committed to Mokhehle and those who had repudiated the LLA, whilst even in exile there were those who opposed the launch of the armed struggle and the incipient collaboration with South African security that it implied. Factional struggles within the LLA, over which Mokhehle rarely enjoyed undisputed command, further fragmented the party (ACR, 1982 - 85).

The return of Mokhehle and the exiles allowed for the healing of many wounds, but reconciliation did not extend as far as Ramoreboli, who together with two close associates (Khauta Khasu and Phoka Chaolane) was excluded from the party's national executive committee. An action in the High Court, initiated by the trio, resulted in the party being ordered to include them (*Mirror*, 5 July 1991). However, their triumph was short-lived, for they were voted off the national executive when, in January 1992, the party held its first Annual Conference for 21 years. They subsequently broke away to form *Ha Re Een Basotho* (HB) (*Mirror*, 6 March 1992).

A major feature of the BCP's new executive was the emergence of Qhobela, who even from its earliest days had worked for the party outside the country (in South Africa, Africa and England), as deputy leader (*Mphatlatsane*, 1 February 1992). Qhobela, who had a large following amongst former and current members of the LLA (which was rumoured to have retained a significant armed presence in South Africa), thereafter appeared as the party's most vigorous spokesman and strategist, charged with holding its various contentious elements together. Party unity was otherwise reconstructed around Mokhehle, whose embodiment of the BCP's struggle against colonialism and subsequent injustice ensured that his leadership was automatic.

Qhobela, working closely with Mokhehle, had already played a key role in laying the groundwork for victory. From the moment that the prohibition on political activity had been rescinded, party structures had been put in place in every constituency, this linked to a major effort to assess the level of support right down to village level. The large majority of candidates were elected at constituency level many months before the election, well before those of the BNP, with local sentiment only occasionally bruised by the interference of the national leadership. Numerous meetings were held at local level, in urban and both lowland and mountainous rural constituencies, and Mokhehle himself, despite the visible infirmities of old age, held mass meetings in each of the country's ten administrative districts throughout the course of the campaign.

Although the BCP local selection procedure was greatly exercised by the social status of its representatives (Quinlan, 1995), its candidates were characterized by a far higher level of political commitment than those of the BNP. Whereas even in rural areas, the BNP campaigned in vehicles, BCP activists walked or travelled by pony; and whereas BNP candidates seem to have assumed categories of support (Catholics and women), their BCP opponents actively mobilized around a cause they fiercely believed in. Indeed, many BCP candidates would seem to have had long histories of personal involvement in community projects or political struggle, seventeen of them had stood for the party in previous elections, and most of them had been directly involved in the party's travails since the early 1970s (Southall, 1995b). This culminated in a sense of conviction which readily transmitted itself to the voters.

Importantly, too, BCP campaigning focused heavily around two major themes. The first concerned explication of the whole process of voting (how to register, how to actually vote, and its symbolic meaning) - an astute approach amongst an electorate which had not only been denied free choice since 1965, but whose size had more than doubled since 1970, and a substantial majority of whom had never voted before. The second involved stress upon the historical right of the BCP to rule, and the concomitant need for repudiation of the BNP, whose corruption and incompetence was highlighted as having ruined the country. For its part, the BNP failed to impress by its obvious state of division.

The BNP - fighting against history

The BNP faced the electorate in 1993 as the bad loser of 1970, and as the focus of popular discontent for Lesotho's unhappy history since independence. Worse, the close involvement with the RLDF of the right wing of the party, led by Sekhonyana, meant that it was also identified with the excesses of military rule. All this inevitably meant that the former ruling party was on the defensive throughout the campaign, its difficulties compounded by its unresolved internal tensions and the need to elect a new leader to succeed Jonathan, who had died in 1986.

The military's clampdown on the Youth League and the assassination of Sixishe and Makhele had decimated the radicals, and left the right as the predominant force in the former ruling party. However, following the coup, the right itself split between those who favoured collaboration with Lekhanya, and those who had favoured defeat of the radicals yet never the military's actual displacement of the BNP from power. This divide now culminated in an open struggle for the party leadership between Sekhonyana, and Peete Peete, formerly Minister of Agriculture and the widely-deemed heir apparent to Leabua.

Assurances of amnesty allowed Sekhonyana's free return to Lesotho, some four months after his ouster from government, and the launch of his campaign for the leadership. Yet his absence from the country meant that organizationally he was well behind his rival. Peete Peete enjoyed much greater constituency support, for Sekhonyana's limited rural following had, in any case, been crushed by the radicals in the pre-election battles of 1985. This enabled Peete's faction to arrange an early vote on the leadership, only to be outwitted by Sekhonyana who, as Party Chairman, managed to get the required National Conference postponed until December (*Mirror*, 1 November 1991). By that time, Sekhonyana's financial resources and the key support of party Secretary-General, Chief Lekhoana Jonathan, enabled him to rally a majority (*Lesotho Today*, 12 December 1991). In a show of public unity, Peete accepted the deputy leadership, but the reverberations of the struggle ran deep, as in numerous constituencies the party remained divided and lost the support of local notables. Indeed, with only seven candidates who had stood for the party in 1970 being renominated in 1993, the BNP evinced far less continuity at the constituency level than did its major rival.

Sekhonyana's proved a pyrrhic victory, as throughout the rest of the campaign he was contesting perpetual allegations of corruption. His troubles began when Paul 'Mabathoana, a leading member of the Peete Peete faction, alleged irregularities in the leadership election, and appealed to Ramaema to enquire into Sekhonyana's involvement in misappropriation of funds under Lekhanya. His name thereafter featured prominently in various unsavoury legal cases, particularly damaging being his enforced removal by the High Court from the position of executor of the estate of the late Chief 'Maseribane, former deputy to Chief Jonathan (*Mirror*, 17 July 1992). Then, just prior to the election, newspaper reports suggested he was deeply implicated in the disappearance of a US$4 million grant made to Lesotho by Taiwan in 1990 (*Mirror*, 8 January 1993; 29 January 1993; *Mphatlatsane*, 30 January 1993). Although Sekhonyana weighed in with defamation proceedings to stem the bad tidings, much mud inevitably stuck to the BNP.

The public reappearance of Lekhanya as BNP candidate in the Thaba-Moea constituency did nothing to improve the party's image; nor indeed, did its heavy reliance upon the provision of transport, food and drink to swell the ranks of its public meetings, which contrasted poorly with the well attended rallies of the BCP.

Sekhonyana maintained his bravado throughout the campaign, yet it becomes clear in retrospect that he appreciated that he would not win a free election. This explains the numerous complaints that he made about supposed inadequacies and irregularities in the electoral registration procedure, which first came to a head in April 1992. Such protestations were designed to serve two purposes: first, they sought to distance Sekhonyana from the military government; and second, they prepared the way for the BNP to challenge its defeat.

The MFP - a right royal cause

The military's dethronement of Moshoeshoe II provided the MFP with what it deemed a major opportunity to make an impact upon the election. This presumed that the electorate was absorbed with the fate of the monarchy and, by implication, in shoring up the declining powers of the senior chiefs. However, although the MFP linked its royalist platform to strident attacks upon both the military and its major rivals, it fared no better than in 1970. Nor was the party assisted by a wrangle which saw the displacement of its long-time leader, B.M. Khaketla, by Vincent Malebo (its former assistant general secretary), a Minister of Information and Broadcasting under Jonathan (*Mirror*, 2 October 1992).

The MFP had won only four seats in 1965 and one in 1970. It had no organization to speak of, only five of its candidates had stood for election before (two of these for the BNP in 1970) and its campaigning was centred heavily around Malebo, who was based in Maseru. Nonetheless, the MFP's role was not insignificant. First, its launch in early 1992 of a highly sensationalist newspaper, *Mphatlatsane*, did much to keep the issue of corruption alive, to the particular detriment of the BNP. Second, its noisy focus upon the monarchy fuelled fears that the election might boil over into violence, not least because the former king had become embroiled in a highly public dispute with Ramaema about the timing and conditions of his return to the country. In the event, he had arrived home in July 1992, and kept conspicuously quiet about the military and whether he should be allowed to regain his throne. But in early 1983 Letsie had declared he had been forced on to the throne, and called for the nation to be allowed to decide who should be king. It was this which led Ramaema to cancel a royalists' 'National Conference' on Moshoeshoe Day (12 March) 1993. Yet in so doing he had almost certainly overestimated the willingness of Basotho to be distracted by a sideshow. Only 500 of them had previously turned out to welcome the former king home, and in retrospect this was as good a guide to the MFP's marginalized status as any.

The minor parties - runners and radicals

In 1970, the three established political parties were challenged by only twelve other candidates: three representing the small right-wing United Democratic Party (UDP), one representing the Lesotho Communist Party (LCP) and eight independents (Macartney, 1973: 482). In 1993, in contrast, there were a total of 53 candidates drawn from nine minor parties, as well as 7 independents. These we may identify as 'runners' and 'radicals'.

The runners (so-called because they ran without serious hope of election or distinctive political agendas) were made up of mavericks, spoilers and rebels. The first category was represented by the UDP (4 candidates) and National Independence Party (1), which were principally the personal vehicles of established right-wing critics of the BNP who had long favoured closer relations with South Africa. Meanwhile, both the Lesotho Liberal Party (1) and the Lesotho Educational Party (1) ran on rather quirky populist platforms, as did the Kopanang Basotho Party, a party formed by and led by women.

More interesting were the spoilers and rebels. These were composed on the one hand, of independents who sought to damage those they deemed to have stolen their nomination for one of the major parties (as in Thaba-Moea constituency, where C. B. Maketha was incensed by Lekhanya's representation of the BNP); and on the other, by HB and the United Party, which embodied organized responses by party rebels against the BCP (the ousted Ramoreboli tendency) and the BNP respectively.

The radicals, composed of the Lesotho Labour Party (LLP) and the Patriotic Front for Democracy (PFD), were no better placed than the runners to make an impact at the polls, yet they were distinguished by their left-leaning concerns. The LLP proclaimed itself a social democratic party committed to working closely with the trade union movement and condemned both the major parties for having failed Lesotho. However, although the LLP claimed to want the break the established mould of party politics, it was constrained by its origins. These lay in a stream of trade unionism born out of the BCP's populism, yet which had after 1970 become entangled in the BNP dominated trade union federation (Southall, 1984). Having also been repudiated by a wave of new, independent unions which developed in the 1980s, this labourist tendency had lost a political home, and had now proceeded to create one. Yet its leaders were far more attuned to trade union in-fighting than serious mobilization, and the LLP never became more than a token force.

The PFD, in contrast, presented a more sophisticated image, both strategically and ideologically. It was formed in May 1991 as a result of consultations between various popular forces in Lesotho (notably the new trade unions, local NGOs, ecumenical organizations and left academics) which sought to develop a common platform on which to elaborate a strategy for democratization and 'comprehensive social transformation' (*Mirror*, 5 July 1991). Identifying Lesotho's crisis as the consequence of acute dependence on external forces, apartheid, and a grossly inequitable distribution of internal resources, the PFD dismissed the existing major parties as sectarian, corrupt, undemocratic and non-accountable, and aspired to forming a broad front of popular forces to challenge them. In the event, only one party - the minuscule LCP - threw in its lot with the PFD, which became closely identified with a group of university intellectuals and never managed to develop a mass base, despite a rudimentary structure of regional branches around the country. However, its importance lay in the challenge it posed to the major parties to state their position concerning Lesotho's status with regard to a democratic South Africa. In short, the PFD - albeit never in so many words - raised the fundamental issue of Lesotho's separate existence as a state.

The Election Campaign and Result

On January 29, 1970, a broadcast by Leabua Jonathan declared the recently concluded general election to have been conducted 'in an atmosphere of peace and quiet' (Khaketla, 1971: 207). His satisfaction was endorsed by newspaper, radio and police reports which agreed that there had been no serious disturbances (Macartney, 1973: 484). The election campaign, noted one press account, had been 'bitterly fought but dull .... notable for its lack of violence and controversy'. For all that rival politicians had tried to make South Africa a bone of contention, they had made little impact, as the electorate knew that Lesotho had precious little choice but to accept the constraints of its encirclement by the Republic (*The Friend*, 22 January 1970).

The outward peacefulness of the campaign fooled many external observers, who were inclined to accept Jonathan's prediction of a comfortable victory as valid. But as it turned out, well over 300,000 voters (81.9% of those registered) went to the polls, and a 5.8% swing (between the major parties) in the vote should have seen the convincing defeat of the BNP (Macartney, 1973). Instead, on 30 January, the Prime Minister declared a state of emergency, and denounced his opponents for having created an atmosphere of fear and violence. Khaketla (1971: 262-91) has eloquently described the 'reign of terror' which followed.

Table 7.1 Lesotho's election results - 1993 compared with 1970

Parties	Seats Won		Votes Cast		Share of Votes	
	1970	1993	1970	1993	1970	1993
BCP	36	65	152,907	398,355	49.8	74.7
BNP	23	0	108,162	120,686	42.2	22.6
MFP	1	0	22,279	7,650	7.3	1.4
Others	0	0	1,909	6,287	0.7	1.2
Total	60	65	285,257	532,978		

Sources: Macartney, 1973: 485; Lucas, 1993: 26-27.

Some twenty three years later, a casual visitor to Maseru, just days prior to the poll, could be forgiven for not noticing that an election was in progress. There were scarcely any election posters, and little visible party activity. There was most certainly little excitement, and the prevailing atmosphere was one of apprehension: would polling go peacefully and smoothly? Would the military accept the result? Would the election be free and fair? Fears were also enhanced by a widespread view that the margin of victory for any party would be narrow, and hence open to contestation (*Weekly Mail*, 26 March - 1 April 1993). But the result was a BCP landslide, as Table 7.1 indicates.

For Macartney (1973: 473, 485-86) the 1970 result demonstrated that the deep political divisions in Lesotho were primarily 'ideological, with religion, the monarchy, and economic factors playing a significant role; lines of division, in short, more reminiscent of Europe than most African countries'. The collapse of the MFP in that election (down from 16.5% of the vote in 1965), together with the squeezing of the other minor parties, indicated a definite polarization: 'radical versus conservative, BCP versus BNP'. This was reflected in the two issues which dominated the campaign: relations with South Africa; and the government's record, notably with regard to economic development and the allocation of benefits.

The polarization of the electorate was amply confirmed by the results of the 1993 election, with the smaller parties taking an even smaller proportion of the vote (2.6%) than they had in 1970 (8%). By now, however, it was no longer clear that the divide between BCP and BNP was simultaneously radical versus conservative. In 1970, cooperation with South Africa had been promoted by the narrowly nationalist, capitalist BNP as fostering the material development of Lesotho. In contrast, the pan-African, socialist message of the BCP, with its overt hostility to Pretoria, was pilloried as risking economic devastation. However, in 1993, the manifestos of the major parties exhibited little difference. Both favoured a mixed economy, cooperation with a new South Africa, and the extension of social welfare and security packages (Keketso, 1993). Further, both by then had an established record of collaboration with South Africa. In short, the ideological gap between the parties had closed, thereby concentrating voters' minds upon the clear-cut issue of historical justice. Aided by the withdrawal of the Catholic Church from the party political arena, as well as the collapse of the 'communist threat', this facilitated the massive shift of voters away from the BNP towards the BCP.

Meanwhile, with both major parties asserting the continuing national integrity of the country as a sovereign state, it had fallen to the PFD - the new radicals - to link the prospect of prosperity to the option of Lesotho's future integration with South Africa. Yet even the PFD did not predict that the neighbouring country, which had done so much to undermine Basotho democracy in the past, would be called upon to play a major role in restoring it as early as 1994.

The Fragility and Dependence of Lesotho's Democracy

Democratic government was now formally restored, yet politics in Lesotho continued to revolve around contested claims to the state. Challenges to the BCP's rule came from three sources - the BNP, the military and the monarchy - whose diverse discontents were to culminate in an uneasy alliance which saw the King depose Mokhehle's government just sixteen months after the election. To the BNP the 65-0 clean sweep by the BCP signalled more than humiliation: it also suggested fraud on a massive scale. It immediately rejected the election results as 'robotic', by which it meant that the swing to the BCP was far too uniform to be believed. It therefore filed an application to the High Court to prevent the results being gazetted, arguing that the seating of an effective one-party government would prevent proper investigation of alleged electoral irregularities. However, given acceptance of the results by every other party, together with the unqualified endorsement of the election as free, fair and transparent by every local and international monitoring group, the Court rejected the BNP's case. Rather belatedly, therefore, the BNP came to argue that the constitution was deficient, proposing in particular the need for PR (Sekatle, 1994, 1995).

To the military, the return to civilian rule implied an end to its untrammelled ability to plunder the state. The terms of its retreat, notably its retention of various veto powers under the constitution, signified a most reluctant withdrawal rather than any commitment to democracy. Meanwhile, the BCP inherited a state machinery which had lost all capacity to exert control over the armed forces during more than two decades of authoritarian rule. The result was an inevitable crisis.

Mokhehle had effectively conceded reserve power to the military when, during the election campaign, he pronounced that the LLA had been disbanded. This signalled the BCP's recognition that its demand for integration of the LLA with the RLDF, which for years had recruited solely from those who professed support for the BNP, would endanger the transition. Nonetheless, suspicions remained after the election that the BCP was planning to parachute LLA personnel into key positions in the security forces, fears which were encouraged by the recruitment of former members of the LLA into a private security firm hired to guard key installations. The tension was then heightened when, in early November 1993, Sekhonyana alleged that the LLA was arming itself, and called on the BNP to prepare itself to fight to the death. Later that month, with Mokhehle unwilling to risk disciplining them, mutinous junior officers forced four of their superiors to resign on grounds of their alleged connections with the LLA.

Emboldened by the government's powerlessness, soldiers in Maseru demanded a 100% pay rise from Mokhehle (now Prime Minister). When this was denied, in January 1994, they agreed that the government should be toppled - but differed over whether it should be replaced by the BNP or by a return to power by the military (Matlosa 1995). A collapse of order which followed saw two weeks of heavy fighting between soldiers of the Makoanyane and Ratjomotse barracks which was only brought to an end after mediation by officials from the OAU and Commonwealth, and (following an appeal from Mokhehle) a meeting in Gaberone between Presidents Masire of Botswana, Mugabe of Zimbabwe, De Klerk of South Africa and Mandela (of the ANC) in which it was agreed to appoint a ministerial taskforce to investigate the causes of the mutiny. Before this, South Africa's Foreign Minister Pik Botha had made it clear in talks with Mokhehle and Sehkonyana that whilst South Africa would not intervene militarily, it would close the border and deny customs revenue to any undemocratic government.

The reluctance of the army to collaborate with the taskforce led the latter to recommend that Mugabe and Masire involve themselves directly. Their report, completed by mid-February, went well beyond the immediate crisis, and concluded that the political malaise in Lesotho required that the RLDF be reduced and restructured to include members of the LLA, and steps be taken to 'confirm, or possibly restore' the legitimacy of the monarchy, implying that Moshoeshoe be restored to his throne.

Mokhehle's problem remained his inability to impose change upon a fragmented and resentful army. Consequently, he played for time, apparently reckoning to do nothing until the April election in South Africa which would see a democratic government there which could be presumed upon to lend him moral and, even, substantive support. Rebellious soldiers responded by temporarily capturing members of his cabinet, and assassinating the Deputy Prime Minister, Frances Baholi, who, as Minister of Finance, was holding out against their pay demands. Again, the government did nothing to confront the rebels and opted rather to concede a substantial (66%) pay rise.

It was only after the South African election that Mokhehle felt emboldened to confront the political crisis in Lesotho head on. Yet remarkably, he then did so in a manner which was calculated to maximize the threat to his government's stability. First, in June, he announced appointment of a Commission of Inquiry into the Defence Force which, *inter alia*, was charged with recommending the means of integration of LLA and redeployment of existing personnel. Then, in July, he followed up by establishing a further Commission of Inquiry into the former King's past role in Lesotho and the more immediate events surrounding his dethronement.

Relations between the BCP and Moshoeshoe were soured by the alliance between the monarchy, the military and the BNP right during 1986-90. Thus, although the Commission might have led to Moshoeshoe's reinstatement, it was bitterly opposed by the former King, not only because it might focus on his past unconstitutional actions, but also because it threatened to investigate his financial dealings, notably his failure to repay substantial debts to an agricultural cooperative which had gone bankrupt (Sekatle, 1994: 71).

The scene was now set for the remaking of the alliance which had broken down with the dethronement of the King in 1990. On 16 August 1994, BNP supporters joined the MFP in petitioning Letsie for the dissolution of parliament and the restoration of Moshoeshoe. The following day, the King announced the deposition of the government and the appointment of a six-person Provisional Council, headed by Hae Phoofolo (a former Deputy Governor of the Central Bank previously imprisoned for fraud) and including Sekhonyana as Foreign Minister. The Council was to administer the country and establish an Independent Electoral Commission to prepare for a new election based on proportional representation - so as to end 'elective dictatorship'. The quiescence of the army signalled its assent.

The King's government lasted less than a month. On 14 September the BCP was reinstated following the signing of an agreement between Letsie and Mokhehle which, *inter alia*, offered immunity from prosecution for all those involved in the coup and, crucially, provided both for cancellation of the Commission on the monarchy and the restoration of Moshoeshoe. Following the necessary legislation, he subsequently reclaimed his throne in March 1995.

Letsie's intervention had aroused much popular protest. BCP supporters staged a mass rally outside the Royal Palace, only to be beaten back by the police and RLDF; and, significantly, the Lesotho Council of NGOs, which had been critical of the high-handedness of the BCP during its tenure of office, spearheaded widely-supported stayaways from work and demanded a national conference. Yet the security forces remained firm, and maintained an effective night-time curfew throughout the crisis.

However, if the government could face down internal opposition, it proved unable to resist external pressures. These included warnings by the US, Britain and the European Union that they would cut all economic assistance unless democracy was restored. Yet more crucial was the close involvement of the three governments which had previously been engaged in attempting to resolve the problems of the military. The difference now was that whereas South African involvement had been restricted prior to that country's April election, the new government led by President Mandela felt obliged to intervene. Mandela issued an early warning that South Africa might be forced to despatch a peace-keeping force. Acting jointly with Masire, Mugabe and OAU General Secretary Salim Salim, he urged the various actors in Lesotho to negotiate their own solution. When negotiations stalled, troops from the South African National Defence Force conducted manoeuvres on the border, and South African planes flew over Maseru. Finally, it was the threat of sanctions by the three Presidents which produced the agreement by Letsie that the Provisional Council would stand down in exchange for the concession by Mokhehle that the inquiry into the monarchy would be dropped. But the BCP leader refused to concede changing the electoral system to PR (Matlosa, 1995). The Provisional Council had learned swiftly, and to its cost, how much dictatorship in Lesotho, from 1970 under Jonathan, and from 1986 under the military, had depended upon the compliance of apartheid South Africa. But similarly, Mokhehle's government had also discovered that, notwithstanding its popular legitimacy, its ability to control the state was ultimately dependent upon support from the new democracy next door.

The extent of distrust between the contending forces in Lesotho rendered the survival, let alone the deepening of democracy, highly problematic, even if the demilitarization of the country's politics might now be achieved by virtue of foreign limitations placed upon the army's freedom of action. Indeed, the disinclination of the BCP to contemplate introducing PR, which at a future election would offer greater prospect of inclusion to the BNP as well as to the smaller parties in opposition, suggested that it was reluctant to view the state as little more than its historically deserved preserve. However, unless any government in Lesotho adheres to reasonably democratic norms in the future, the country's pretensions to maintaining a polity separate from South Africa will become progressively less convincing, both to popular forces domestically and to regional and global powers.

Notes

1. The Lesotho Human Rights Alert Group (LHRAG) was officially launched in mid-1992, following the publication of a particularly critical report by Amnesty International (*Mirror* 12 June 1992; *Work for Justice* 13 June 1992).
2. To qualify for registration, persons needed to be 21 years of age and resident, or to have retained a residence, in a particular registration area. Migrant workers were required to return home to vote, the government turning down a request that Basotho miners should be able to cast their votes at their place of work.

8 Blocked Transition in Nigeria: democracy and the power of oligarchy

CHUDI OKOYE

Nigeria's current difficulties with democratic transition, culminating in the aborted presidential elections in 1993, illustrates the fragility of current transitions in Africa. It may be tempting, initially, to seek to explain the Nigerian crisis in terms of a powerful military oligarchy refusing to relinquish power. Yet reality is more complex than that, for rather we have a situation where a seemingly progressive faction of the military elite (led by General Ibrahim Babangida) took power promising an early democratic restoration. In keeping with that promise, a detailed transition programme was initiated which, though much-troubled and constantly assailed by military interference, nonetheless produced civilian structures at national and sub-national levels of government. Then came preparations for a presidential poll in June 1993 and, despite several crises, an election between two contenders endorsed by the military. At this point, a truly bizarre drama began to unfold. In what seemed at first an incomprehensible turn of events, the ruling junta simply refused to declare the winner. The military eventually annulled the election, despite intense local agitation, and in time nullified the entire transition programme.

It might seem that the military's unwillingness to disengage from power is at the core of the Nigerian debacle. However, left there, it begs the question of why and how the military could have orchestrated a detailed and even innovative transition programme, galvanizing civil society in the process, only in the end to terminate it abruptly while the votes were being counted.

The search for an answer to this question leads us to a broader analysis which looks to the interlocking impact of environment, design and agency: an environment characterized by ethnic and class tensions fed by economic crisis; a design problem, emanating from the flawed perception and muddled methodology of those promoting the transition; and the agency of a military regime whose authoritarianism and self-interest further complicated the fragile process of transition.

Taking all these together, this paper argues that the military's final veto of its programme arose not only out of some instinct of self-perpetuation, but also because its outcome threatened the hegemonic position of a wider elite coalition which the military represented. Political engineering produced unintended consequences, compelling a last minute veto by the military to reassert the status quo.

The Instability of Democratic Politics in Nigeria

Post-colonial Nigeria has had eight military administrations. In over three and a half decades of independence there have been only three civilian governments, lasting just 10 years between them. It is tempting to conclude that democracy is not feasible under contemporary conditions in Nigeria. The forces unleashed by democracy have often brought the country dangerously close to disintegration. They exploded into civil war in the First Republic (1960-66) and produced agitation for a looser federation during the Second Republic (1979-83). Then as we shall see, the Babangida transition programme, which gave brief hope of a Third Republic, came to grief partly due to civilian discord.

The instability of democratic politics seems somewhat surprising, considering the continuing appeal of democracy in the country. Leaders of the early nationalist movement, for example, mostly espoused democratic government. They affirmed not just the ideal of liberalism and popular participation but also the value of federalism in Nigeria's complex multi-national setting (Azikiwe, 1961 and 1974; Awolowo, 1968 and 1970; and Epelle, 1964).

Such sentiments continued to be held by succeeding leaders and have persisted despite instability and prolonged military rule. Such is the appeal of democracy in Nigeria that military rule, though far more the norm than civilian, continues to be considered an aberration. Successive military rulers have felt a need on acceding to power to proclaim their commitment to a restoration of democratic rule. Indeed, although military regimes emerge for reasons of democratic breakdown, their fortunes have nonetheless largely depended on demonstrated democratic commitment. Regimes shy of such commitment, such as those of Ironsi, Gowon and Buhari, have encountered much political peril.

Why, then, has democracy failed to flower in Nigeria? One explanation of democratic disorder is the impact of behavioural factors such as the corrupt, undemocratic and conflictual conduct of major political actors. Such conduct culminated, for instance, in the political and constitutional crises which undermined the First Republic.[1] The lack of elite consensus about the distribution of power and resources was evident even in the colonial period but, after independence, without the glue of anti-colonial nationalism, it became worse. The result was a heightening of ethnic chauvinism, regional polarization, and the intensification of political violence, all of which led to the collapse of the First Republic.

Much the same and more was evident in the Second Republic: the inordinate corruption of party rule, the abuse of power manifested as much in the repression of political opponents as in unbridled misappropriation of public resources. The excesses of the politicians created severe stress in the economy and the political system, providing the justification for the return of the military in December 1983.

A number of factors have been highlighted to explain this dysfunctional political behaviour. One is the diversity of Nigerian society and its component nationalities. Another is the unbalanced federal structure which makes for a perennial domination by the North over other regions (Sklar, 1965; Dudley, 1966). A third is the enormous size of the central state which makes the competition for power (and the resources it brings) particularly intense. Writers who adopt a radical political economy perspective explain the massive size of the state in terms of the legacy of imperialism in distorting the process of accumulation and class formation in Nigeria. They argue that colonial subjugation retarded the growth of local dominant classes, forcing the post-colonial state to provide leadership in many sectors of social life. The result has been to make the state central to political ambitions and so hideously oversized that it has inevitably become the object of struggles between communities and elite factions. Furthermore, the situation has been aggravated by the rise of oil as the dominant element of accumulation in Nigeria. State control of the oil economy has bloated the public sector and made the struggle to capture state power all the more ferocious (Oyovbaire, 1983; Nnoli, 1981; Osoba, 1977; Williams, 1976; Ake, 1985; Falola and Ihonvbere, 1985; and Forrest, 1986). Such conflict has resulted in repeated military interventions, most recently under Major-General Buhari in 1983-84, and then under General Babangida in 1985-93.

The Babangida Regime and Liberal Reformism

When Babangida and his colleagues displaced Buhari in 1985, they seemed particularly concerned with the problem of Nigeria's over-sized state sector.

Thus, in his Address to the Nation on the Assumption of Office on 27 August 1985, Babangida decried 'the large role played by the public sector in economic activity with hardly any concrete results...'.[2] In a subsequent speech during the inauguration of the Technical Committee on Privatization and Commercialization (TCPC) he repeated those sentiments, urging members of the committee to 're-examine with a view to revising the direct and wasteful over-commitment of government in the economy'.

Babangida's principal criticism of the Buhari regime (in which he had been Chief of the General Staff) was that it had not been sufficiently radical to provide a 'solution to (Nigeria's) economic predicament'. Insisting that there was not merely a need for austerity policies, as Buhari had offered, but a 'comprehensive strategy of economic reforms' (ibid.), Babangida sought (unlike any of his predecessors) a radical re-ordering of the system of state-based accumulation. Subsequently, the regime instituted micro- and macro-economic changes designed to reduce the role of the state in the economy, including fiscal controls, reduction in state subsidies, liberalization of the financial sector, deregulation of the foreign-exchange market and devaluation of the Naira, the abolition of state commodity boards, trade liberalization and export diversification, and privatization and commercialization of state enterprises. These measures were designed first, to reverse the state interventionist thrust of the early military reforms, thereby possibly minimizing the political premium placed on the control of state power; and second, to promote a new ethos to eventually permeate the realm of partisan politics.

The other concern of the Babangida administration was to manage a process of democratic transition in such a way as to control the fissiparous tendencies of civilian politics. This concern arose from a presumption that previous democratic dispensations had been undermined by a failure to control political mobilization, with the result that electoral politics had become acutely overloaded. The Babangida government sought to design the new democracy in such a way as to control the dynamic of partisan competition. Clearly a product of the military's regimentary ethos, it led to the adoption of a number of controversial measures. For instance, the government attempted, by legislation and coercion, to exclude certain specific groups from participating in the democratic transition, as in the case of a ban on so-called 'old-breed' politicians and former holders of public office. According to Babangida, they were to be excluded because their actions when in office had been 'detrimental to the evolution of... good government and the assurance of the welfare of the people' (Oyediran and Agbaje, 1991: 223). The (increasingly punitive) sanctions against the old political class was matched only by the unrelenting repression of so-called 'extremist' groups, including labour and student unions, radical academics, sections of the independent press, and various professional, civil rights and pro-democracy groups. Though widely divergent in their objectives, these groups had one thing in common: they rejected the more unpopular aspects of Babangida's economic and political reforms.

For Babangida and his colleagues, their agitation was sufficient reason to exclude them from the transition process. They were quite explicit about this. For instance, in 1988 the President declared that, while the ruling junta were not interested in choosing their successors, they were resolved that, in addition to the former politicians and public office holders affected by statutory prohibition, they were not going to be succeeded by 'extremists'.[3] These were defined as those

> uncompromising, fanatical or immoderate in their views; who go beyond the limits of reason, necessity or propriety to advance their cause.... Such zealots do not tolerate the views of others, and need to be put in check for the protection of the rights and freedoms of others.[4]

True to this perception, there were repeated instances of suppression of opposition groups, involving harassment, arrest, detention and torture, closure of media houses, and attacks on professional and other organizations. This brings us to another feature of the government's attempt to control the transition - its role in the process of political party formation.

The Regimentation of Politics: Political Party Formation

The lifting of the official ban on organized politics on 3 May 1989 produced an eruption of political activity. Within weeks more than fifty political associations had sprung up across the country. The effect was to create, for the pathologically order-conscious Babangida regime, an immediate concern about control, one heightened by the nature of the emerging organizations. Some trumpeted radical alternatives to the liberal economic reforms of the government. Others espoused primordial political tendencies disavowed by the incumbent regime (Oyediran and Agbaje, 1991: 224). In the light of these tendencies, the Babangida government felt constrained to regulate the process of party formation, falling on the proposals of the Political Bureau, an apparatus established in 1986, to produce a blueprint for transition. This had endorsed what was widely known to be the military's preference: the institutionalization of a *de jure* two-party system, with both parties hedged around by 'some degree of regimentation'.[5]

The initial manifestation of the military's regimentation of the process of party formation was a set of restrictive guidelines governing registration. The major ones were as follows:

- associations had to disavow 'political extremism'; there were to be no women's or youth wings; and banned politicians and public office holders were not to hold any executive positions or contest elections within the associations;
- each association had to provide a list of registered members with passport photos and addresses;
- aspirant associations had to show evidence of physical and organizational presence, including full-time staff, in at least two thirds of the states and local government areas of the federation;
- associations and their executive members had to submit statements of their assets and liabilities;
- associations had to submit 10 printed copies of their proposed constitutions, detailing name, symbol, emblem and motto, as well as electoral and financial procedures, and of their manifestos, wherein they had to state how they intended to tackle the country's socio-political and economic problems. In this regard, they were required to indicate their position on a number of issues, including strategies for economic development; rural and community development; women, youth and labour; the armed forces in politics; human rights; revenue allocation; and group interests and ethnicity.

The registration application required a non-refundable fee of N50,000, and the deadline for submission was 15 July 1989 (Economist Intelligence Unit, 1989:8; Madunagu, 1992:17). It is easy to identify the military's concern, in stipulating these conditions, to free the transition from the acrimonious politics of the past. This concern seems justified given the resurgence of the old political networks. It is also understandable that the government should want prospective parties to be properly organized and resourced, given the poor organizational structure, the lack of proper internal accountability, the programmatic poverty and the predominantly sectionalist appeal of previous political parties in Nigeria. That said, however, the registration guidelines are remarkable for their complexity and stringency and, more critically, the internal inconsistencies which ultimately made them problematic.

Too little time was allowed for the emergent associations to mobilize for registration. The charge was also made that, by demanding so much in so little time, the guidelines were weighted in favour of the 'rich' associations

(Oyediran and Agbaje, 1991: 224). Given that some of them were close to the Babangida administration, it was only to be expected that there would be complaints about military partiality, despite Babangida's assertion that his 'administration has no vested interest in the registration of any particular political association as a political party' (Akinola, 1989:313).

Yet there is some justification for the view that the guidelines were framed to exclude both less affluent associations (on the grounds that they might not be viable) and radical groups which sought to replace the ongoing economic reforms with avowedly socialist or welfarist programmes. Thus, the guidelines specified sanctions against 'extremism' and required associations to indicate their stand on certain national issues. It is instructive that, during the run-up to registration, many associations felt compelled to try to enhance their prospects by proclaiming that they had no links with either 'socialists' or the old, discredited politicians, and moreover that they were prepared to preserve the administration's economic reform programme (Akinola, 1989:314). Both the programmatic and resource stipulations imposed by the guidelines essentially weighed against the same categories of groups. In many cases radical groups were also those with the leanest resource base. But the issue goes beyond apparent bias of the conditions.

One of the unintended effects of the guidelines was to jeopardize the stability of the transition process by making it possible for some groups excluded by the military, namely the heavyweights of the old political order, to hijack the party-formation process. Although the guidelines specifically precluded the discredited political class, the stringency of the conditions they imposed made it inevitable that emerging parties would try to avail themselves of the material and political resources accumulated by the old guard. Faced with the need to meet an unrealistic deadline for applications, aspiring associations often fell back on existing political allegiances.

This served two purposes. First, by providing instant access to existing political constituencies it facilitated the mobilization of supporters to meet the military's rules on the size of party membership. Second, it gave the emerging politicians access to ready funds, thus enhancing prospects for organizational consolidation. In this way, then, the new associations were infiltrated by influential Nigerians who had been banned for holding public office in the past. Babangida and his associates were subsequently to offer this as a reason for not registering any of the associations but such groups were simply responding to the internally contradictory nature of the guidelines.

Because of this, it was ultimately impossible for the electoral commission to register any of the aspiring associations. Non-registration marked a watershed in the evolution of the transition process. The electoral commission found none of the thirteen existing associations to have fully satisfied the requirements for prospective political parties - although it unenthusiastically recommended six of them to the Armed Forces Ruling Council (AFRC) for recognition. This paved the way for deeper military intervention in the process of party formation. In a broadcast on 7 October 1989, Babangida announced that the government had decided not to register any of the existing associations. He cited the electoral commission's findings, particularly the incidence of factionalism, malpractice and a recrudescence of the old forms of politics. He noted that 'healthy debates over policies and programmes (had given) way to conflicts over the sharing of party offices and government posts' and that ethnic, geo-political and religious conflicts had resurfaced in 'these "new breed" associations which were expected to transcend those lines of cleavage and promote issue-based politics...'. For these reasons then, the President said, the AFRC felt compelled to reject all the associations.

The military believed that the aspiring politicians lacked the creativity to organize credible political movements. As Babangida saw it, this was part of an ongoing problem. Nigeria's 'history as a nation... has been such that (it has) not had enough exposure to party politics - its culture, its organization, its challenge...'. Nigerians, he said, 'have had much more experience in running governments than in running political parties (and thus their) capacity to organize people in political movements is quite modest'. Therefore, he proposed that the military would take over the process of party formation; the government had 'no choice but to give leadership in the form of the provision of the needed technical expertise for political party construction and management'.

The government intervened in party formation in two main ways. The first involved the creation of a 'corrective' mechanism to rectify the presumed technical and organizational deficiencies of the political class. This was to lead to the establishment of a Centre for Democratic Studies whose main task was to 'identify sources and types of anti-democratic attitudes, beliefs and behaviour in Nigerians and devise measures to correct them through educational, bureaucratic and political institutions'.

The second component of intervention was more audacious. The military regime decided itself to create and fund two 'grassroots' political parties which Nigerians would then be invited to join. The two parties, to be known as the Social Democratic Party (SDP) and the National Republican Convention (NRC), were to depend in their formative period on state funding and administration; they were to adopt emblems and constitutions designed by the government; and, above all, they were to adopt centrist manifestos, also designed by the government, one of which would veer 'a little to the left' and the other 'a little to the right'. Babangida sought to dispel concerns about the strategy of parties evolving through government diktat, not least about freedom of association and programmatic autonomy. But, he argued, principles of associational rights were 'not violated so long as a one-party state is not decreed' while the manifestos bequeathed were only for guidance and the parties had the right, subject to approval by the military council, to revise them (EIU, 1990:9).

In the event, the manifestos of the two parties which evolved did show some significant differences. For instance, for the SDP progressive taxation was a means of enhancing disposable state revenue and redistributing incomes, while the NRC preferred a policy of low taxation to encourage savings and investment. Again, where the NRC accepted the need to work within the international political economy, the SDP employed the radical language of 'resist(ing) imperialism, neocolonialism... and all forms of external intervention and domination'. The Economist Intelligence Unit (1990:10), for one, considered that the SDP's manifesto leaned more towards socialism while that of the NRC embodied a more conservative, pro-market agenda and concluded, on this basis, that neither the AFRC nor the international financial community would view 'with particular favour' an SDP election victory.

The EIU's reference to the preferences of the AFRC and its global sponsors underscores some of the arguments deployed later to explain the cancellation of the 1993 presidential election. Nevertheless, the point remains that whilst the differences between the programme were real, they were also 'minor' (EIU, 1991:8). The fact is that both the SDP and the NRC endorsed the liberal economic reforms of the Babangida regime; both, to varying degrees, aimed to promote private capital; and both countenanced a significant level of state participation in the economy. These positions defined the essential character of the two parties, at least as they were *initially* conceived, as centrist. Accordingly, it could even be asked if, in its search for political harmony and ideological homogeneity, the military had not created a virtual one-party system (Oyediran and Agbaje, 1991: 228).

However, this initial lack of distinction between the parties proved inimical to the stability of the transition. In the absence of clearly distinguishable programmes, other, more disruptive forms of differentiation became salient, particularly religious and ethnic factors. Having minimal objective appeal for the electorate, the political class tended to fall back to the old, problematic patterns of politics. This generated intense conflicts within and between the two parties, leading in turn to impulsive and arbitrary interventions by the military and ultimately to further uncertainties in the transition programme.

Progress and Crisis: The Development of the SDP and NRC

The factionalism within the two parties had a critical effect on the entire transition. It also indicated a failure to achieve one of the key objectives set by the military, namely a two-party structure in which each party would serve as an inclusive entity embracing a diversity of interests and forces united by a common platform and allowing for greater accommodation of interests. In the event, the development of the two parties revealed two distinct, superficially contradictory, processes. While diverse forces did enter the parties and some measure of ideological difference did develop, the lack of a distinct programmatic character in either party resulted in frequent crises as forces within each struggled for ascendancy.

These internal conflicts were rapidly appropriated by regionalist interests. In this connection, Akinola (1989: 322) observes, shortly after the creation of the NRC and the SDP, Babangida's ideological designation of them came to be parodied as 'a little to the North' and 'a little to the South', whilst the parties themselves came to be referred to as the 'Northern Republican Convention' and the 'Southern Democratic Party'. These jibes had some basis in fact. Again, as noted by Akinola (1989: 321-3), there was an observable 'lineal connection of past political alliances with the imposed new political parties'; the NRC could be traced back to the old Northern-based alliances and the SDP to those of the South.

Yet we must not take this argument too far. Although the capacity of the parties to transcend regional divisions was gradually eroded, a North-South demarcation never completely materialized. One reason was that ideology did play some role in determining the membership of the parties. Thus, factions of more 'progressive' associations gravitated towards the SDP, while more conservative elements found the NRC a more natural habitat. These migrations did transcend the old divisions and enabled the parties to make electoral inroads in states across the entire federation. Some sections of the Nigerian left, for instance, threatened by marginalization under the imposed two-party framework, sought to re-enter the political arena by joining the SDP. This considerably widened its ideological base and further crystallized the NRC as the preferred party of conservative interests.

Paradoxically, however, this reinforced public perceptions of the parties in regionalist terms. Given the historical association of the South with progressive politics, the entry of radicals into the SDP seemed to confirm its perceived southern bias. In turn, the conservative interests in the NRC were dominated by the traditional religious, military, and commercial interests that characterized the dominant classes of the North, a consequence of the way religion, class and the pattern of imperialist penetration of Nigeria had shaped these interests. Region and ideology were not coterminous, but the perception persisted and the SDP-NRC dichotomy came to be seen in geo-political terms, especially as each party was stronger in one region than in the other.[6]

The perception was strengthened by the first party-based local elections, in December 1990, when the NRC had 1,406 councillors elected in the North, compared with 1,156 in the South, while the SDP won 1,384 seats in the North and 1,570 in the South. This trend continued in State elections held in 1991, with the NRC securing 306 seats in the North compared with 211 in the South, while the SDP picked up 280 and 329 respectively. In the federal House of Representatives election of 1992, the NRC obtained 168 seats in the North and 107 in the South, while the SDP secured 150 and 164 respectively (*Nigerian Tribune*, 22 July 1993). In every case, the NRC performed best in the North and the SDP best in the South.

The regional pattern of internal competition was reinforced during the parties' first national conventions in August 1990, when northern and southern interests in both the SDP and NRC manoeuvred to make the coveted post of presidential flag-bearer their own.[7] Thus, attempts were made to foist other posts, say the party chairmanship, on contenders from the opposing region, thereby enhancing the prospects of securing the presidential candidacy. The North's pitch for the presidency was particularly concerted in the NRC, and the same was true for the South in the SDP. The strategy seemed to work: the NRC got a southerner, Tom Ikimi, as chairman, while a northerner, Baba Gana Kingibe, became chairman of the SDP; and eventually, a northerner, Bashir Tofa, emerged as NRC presidential candidate, while a southerner, Moshood Abiola, stood for the SDP.

Despite having a trans-regional membership structure and an inclusive ideology, therefore, both the SDP and the NRC were captives of the intense regional and factional conflict long present in Nigerian politics. Most party-based elections were characterized by violence, acrimony and allegations of malpractice. In turn, they elicited authoritarian interventions by the military, with candidates summarily disqualified, results invalidated or elections rescheduled. These patterns emerged also in the run-up to the presidential election.

Transition and Deepening Crisis: The 1993 Presidential Election

The military envisaged the presidential contest as the terminal event in the progressive transfer of power to civilians. However, events leading up to the election reflected the increasing instability of the transition process. For instance, a succession of presidential primary elections (held from May through September 1992) had to be cancelled because of violence and electoral misconduct; only in March 1993 did primaries finally produce the candidates for the June election. The two candidates, Abiola for the SDP and Tofa for the NRC, emerged only after a cast of previous contenders had been disqualified by the military. Again, the 12 June 1993 date for the presidential election was chosen only after a series of postponements and was itself threatened by a spate of litigation aimed at preventing its being held. And when the election did go ahead, it was cancelled by the military, due partly, so it was claimed, to a spiral of post-election judicial challenges.

Years later, it is still not entirely clear what lay behind the concerted legal confrontations that attended the 1993 election. One argument is that these contestations were orchestrated by the military who were cynically seeking to abort the election and thereby defer their departure from power. Another is that the SDP's electoral ticket, which featured two Moslems (the westerner, Abiola, and his running mate, the northerner, Kingibe), ignored prevailing regionalist traditions by excluding someone from the mainly Christian Ibo East in the distribution of positions, including the party chair. On the other hand, although the NRC had embraced the conventional Moslem-North/Christian-East formula, with the powerful post of party chairman allocated to the West, prospects for electoral victory were not certain. Thus, goes the argument, the run-up to the June 1993 election was such that major regional-political blocs felt their interests threatened, and resorted to judicial challenges to the election.

It is significant that the critical move in ensuing legal manoeuvres was initiated by a murky group, the Association for a Better Nigeria (ABN), headed by a previously disqualified SDP presidential aspirant, Arthur Nzeribe, an Ibo easterner. A few weeks prior to the election, the ABN instituted high court proceedings in the North for the results of the SDP's March convention to be quashed on the grounds of irregularity. The suit also adjured the court to suspend the imminent presidential election because it was based on the 'undemocratic' outcome of the March convention, and to empower the Babangida regime to remain in office until democratic primaries had been held. Two days before the election, the court granted an injunction restraining the NEC from conducting the election until the case filed by the ABN had been determined.

In its response to the ABN's suit, the electoral commission pointed to Section 19(1) of Decree 13, promulgated in February by the military government, which stated categorically that no interim or interlocutory order or ruling, judgement or decision made by any court or tribunal before or after the commencement of this Decree, in respect of any intra-party or inter-party dispute or any other matter before it shall affect the date or time of the holding of the election, or the performance by the (National Electoral) Commission of any of its functions under this Decree or any guidelines issued by it in pursuance of the election.

That was not the end of the matter, however, for Section 19(2) of the decree made clear that this did not extend to the *outcome* of an election, including challenges lodged before the elections. It stated that 'a court or tribunal... may *continue* with any proceeding before it after such election and make any decision as is reasonable in the circumstance'. The electoral commission thus went ahead with the election despite the court ruling,[8] and by common observation it passed off reasonably well. There was a low voter turnout, only 36.5% of the 39.1 million registered voting. There were also certain logistical problems and minor procedural irregularities, although only some 24 persons were arrested nationwide for electoral offences (*Guardian Express*, 14 June 1993). Yet overall, there was little of the familiar violence and malpractice associated with elections in Nigeria.

Table 8.1 suggests that the SDP's Moslem-West/Moslem-North ticket worked well at the polls. Thus, of the total 14,293,396 votes cast, the party secured some 8,341,309, a clear majority of 58.36%. A breakdown shows that the party had secured a plurality in 19 of the 30 states as well as in the Federal Capital Territory, Abuja. For its part, the NRC's conventional Moslem-North/Christian-East ticket led by Bashir Tofa and his running mate, Sylvester Ugoh from the East, obtained 5,952,087 votes, 41.64%. With these results, the SDP's candidate clearly satisfied the statutory requirement that the winner of the presidential election must secure a simple majority of the total votes cast. Section 132 (1) of the 1989 Constitution of Nigeria also demanded that the winner, in addition to gaining a simple majority of votes, had to secure a minimum of one-third of votes cast in each of at least two-thirds of the states of the federation. This condition too the SDP easily met, obtaining over 30% in all but one of the 30 states.

It was a historic performance by the SDP's candidate. This was the first time in Nigeria's history that a southerner had won an election for civilian head of state. Further, the SDP's performance was even more impressive because Abiola's support cut across the traditional ethno-regional and religious boundaries of Nigeria. Abiola secured large majorities in all five western and in two mid-western states, these being his primary constituency. The NRC held the south-eastern states where it had gained most of the seats in the elections of 1991. Even here, however, Abiola obtained the majority vote in three of the seven states. Of the 16 northern states, he won a plurality in nine (four in the middle belt and the rest in the northern core territory, including Kano, his opponent's home state).

The decisive electoral victory achieved by the SDP left little room for any partisan disputes about the outcome. Soon after the voting, however, the ABN returned to the courts to stop the NEC announcing the results. This time the ABN was successful since the law no longer protected the NEC. On 15 June, with half the election results already released, a northern high court issued an injunction restraining the NEC from announcing the results. There followed a torrent of countervailing injunctions from courts of comparable competence in the south ordering the commission to declare them, yet on 16 June the NEC chairman announced that the commission had no choice but to suspend the announcement of the election results.

The NEC's decision invited intervention by the military. On 23 June the government announced that, to prevent 'judicial anarchy', it had decided that 'all court proceedings pending... in respect of any matter... relating (to) the Presidential Election', should stop. This was necessary in order 'to rescue the judiciary from intra-wrangling, (and) to protect (Nigeria's) legal system and judiciary from being ridiculed and politicised'. The government also announced the suspension of the NEC; the abrogation of the two decrees upon which the June 12 election was based (the Transition to Civil Rule (Political Programme) (Amendment) Decree 52 of 1992 and the Presidential Election (Basic Constitutional and Transitional Provision) Decree 13 of 1993); and that all acts executed under the auspices of these decrees were no longer valid (*Guardian Express*, 23 June 1993). Abiola's election had thus been set aside.

Events in Nigeria after the annulment of the election produced severe social dislocation, growing disharmony and economic crisis, with investment and production plummeting and unemployment and inflation rising to unprecedented levels. Deepening instability made the position of the Babangida regime untenable and forced the exit of the general in August 1993. The institution of a new, largely civilian 'Interim National Government' was followed after less than three months by the reinstatement of military rule under General Sani Abacha, a leading figure of the Babangida regime. The new junta abrogated the transition programme and dissolved all democratic institutions created under the programme. Widespread repression of pro-June 12 activists and the imprisonment of Abiola became part of a descent into a dispensation of atavistic and brutal authoritarianism. The Abacha regime initiated a new transition process leading to civil rule in 1998, measures as susceptible to the underlying contradictions as was the Babangida transition.

Table 8.1   Unofficial results of the 12 June 1993 presidential election

State	Registered voters	NRC vote / %	SDP vote / %	Total valid votes / % reg voters
Abia	991,569	151,227 58.96	105,273 41.04	256,500 25.87
Adamawa*	954,680	167,239 54.28	140,875 45.72	308,114 32.27
Akwa-Ibom	1,032,955	199,342 48.14	214,787 51.86	414,129 40.09
Anambra	1,248,226	159,258 42.89	212,024 57.11	371,282 29.75
Bauchi*	2,048,627	524,836 60.73	339,339 39.27	864,175 42.18
Benue*	1,297,072	186,302 43.06	246,830 56.94	433,132 33.39
Borno	1,222,533	128,684 45.60	153,496 54.40	282,180 23.08
C' River*	876,599	153,452 44.77	189,303 55.23	342,755 39.10
Delta*	1,155,182	145,001 30.70	327,277 69.30	472,278 40.88
Edo	912,680	103,527 33.52	205,407 66.48	308,979 33.85
Enugu*	1,291,750	284,050 51.91	263,101 48.09	547,151 42.36
Imo*	1,141,630	195,836 55.14	159,350 44.86	355,186 31.11
Jigawa*	1,130,215	89,836 39.33	138,552 60.67	228,388 18.56

State	Registered voters	NRC vote / %	SDP vote / %	Total valid votes / % reg voters
Kaduna	1,614,258	356,860 47.80	389,713 52.20	746,573 46.29
Kano	2,583,057	154,809 47.72	169,619 52.28	324,428 12.56
Katsina*	1,661,132	271,077 61.30	171,162 38.70	442,239 26.62
Kebbi*	824,254	144,808 67.34	70,219 32.66	215,027 26.06
Kogi	978,019	265,732 54.40	222,760 45.60	488,492 49.95
Kwara	669,625	80,209 22.76	272,270 77.24	352,470 52.64
Lagos	2,397,421	149,432 14.46	883,965 85.54	1,033,397 43.10
Niger	1,002,173	221,437 61.90	136,350 38.10	357,787 35.70
Ogun	941,889	59,246 12.22	425,725 87.78	484,971 51.49
Ondo*	1,767,896	162,994 15.58	883,024 84.42	1,046,018 59.17
Osun*	1,056,690	72,068 16.49	365,266 83.52	437,334 41.39
Oyo	1,579,280	105,788 16.48	536,011 83.52	641,799 40.64
Plateau	1,513,186	259,394 38.32	417,565 61.68	676,959 44.74
Rivers*	1,908,878	640,973 63.37	370,578 36.63	1,011,551 52.99

State	Registered voters	NRC vote / %	SDP vote / %	Total valid votes / % reg voters
Sokoto*	1,636,119	372,250 79.21	97,726 20.79	469,976 28.73
Taraba*	769,912	64,001 38.58	101,887 61.42	165,888 21.55
Yobe*	665,299	64,061 38.41	111,887 63.59	175,948 24.45
Abuja FCT	152,686	18,313 47.84	19,968 52.16	38,281 25.07
Totals	39,025,492	5,952,042 41.64	8,341,309 58.36	14,293,387 36.53

Sources: NEC Scoreboard, Abuja, The News, Newswatch, Tell, African Concord, Citizen, Nigerian Link.
*Not released by NEC, but correspond in all sources.

Explaining the Failure of the Babangida Transition

There is substantial circumstantial evidence to support the claim of self-perpetuating designs on the part of the military regime. Numerous events and comments during the transition provide indications of such manoeuvring. The frequent intervention of the regime in the process produced much cynicism, particularly on the part of pro-democracy activists, about the motives of the military reformers. The argument was frequently made, in the face of innumerable alterations to the transition programme, that the military were enacting a hidden agenda to derail their own transition programme. In the aftermath of the presidential election, an ostensibly contrite former director of the ABN, one Abimbola Davies, alleged that the association's goal, orchestrated by the military, had been to create 'an organized confusion' to justify aborting the transition (*Guardian*, Nigeria, 17 July 1993: *Guardian on Sunday*, 18 July 1993). The claims produced a torrent of denials but, in a later interview, the man at the centre of it all, Nzeribe, confirmed the allegations (*Newswatch*, 20 December 1993: 8-18 and 27 December 1993: 30-35).

Nzeribe claimed that the objective of the ABN had been to block the presidential election so as pave the way for the extension of Babangida's incumbency, though it seems all to have been rather obliquely communicated:

> Babangida would very rarely tell you I want you to do this or do that. I used to have an expression with him that used to say 'Am I reading your lips right'... and then I'll take the answer from his demeanour... Unfortunately for him, ... not many of his close aides or associates could read his lips as effectively as I could. So that even when he didn't want to go, he will continue telling his closest aides, of course I'm going, of course I'm going, and they will believe him and they will be doing things in good faith to further his departure, believing that's what he wants because that's what he said ... I read his lips well. I offered ABN to do the job (*Newswatch*, 20 December 1993: 10-11).

It is also possible that Babangida was being manipulated by people around him. Such people, Wole Soyinka has argued, might indeed have 'had a greater stake in Babangida staying in power than Babangida himself' (*Newswatch*, 27 September 1993). Whatever the reason, he hung on to office until his support within the military had almost completely dissipated and he was forced to make his exit in August 1993. In keeping with Soyinka's view, the Babangida government itself subsequently claimed that it could not uphold the outcome of the election because there existed within the armed forces a powerful group opposed to an Abiola presidency - a view given credence later by Babangida himself when he stated that his administration could not 'hand over to anybody who [did] not command the respect of the military' (*New African*, September 1993: 13).

There is good reason to believe that an anti-Abiola group did exist within the military which was unwilling to permit him to become president (despite his close links with the regime) and which Babangida may have been too weak to dispel. Such antipathy was on occasion expressed quite publicly, as in the vehement outburst of Brigadier Halilu Akilu, co-ordinator of national security (and so of the three intelligence services - State Security Service, Defence Intelligence Agency and National Intelligence Agency), who swore that Abiola would be president only over his dead body (*New African*, September 1993: 13; *The Guardian*, London, 24 June 1993). Abiola himself subsequently came to believe that invalidating the election had been forced on Babangida by 'the Abacha boys' (*The Week*, 23 May 1994: 14). This view is reinforced by the fact that those who succeeded Babangida went on to abrogate the entire transition programme.

Why was there such vehement opposition in the military to the prospect of an Abiola presidency? Part of the answer may be provided by the vast commercial and financial holdings of the SDP candidate. Abiola, a British-trained accountant who became vice-president of ITT for Africa and the Middle East, was one of the wealthiest men in Nigeria, with interests in shipping, banking, publishing, agriculture, aviation, oil exploration, communications and confectionery. He reportedly had business interests in more than 2,000 companies in over sixty countries, his overseas investments ran into tens of millions of pounds and his wealth was described as being 'in the stratospheric category' (*The Guardian*, London, 14 May 1993). Significantly, his commercial ascendance depended largely on his long-standing, intimate and mutually-rewarding relationship with the military hierarchy. Published figures show, for instance, that from the early 1970s, when Abiola's relationship with the military began to blossom, the value of government contracts awarded to companies with which he was associated amounted to some N43.7 billion. It is claimed that in the eight-year reign of Babangida alone, companies in which Abiola had interests secured government contracts worth some $845 million (*The Independent*, Nigeria, 4-10 July 1993; *Newswatch*, 12 July 1993: 9-13; *New African*, September 1993).

Two crucial points illuminate anti-Abiola sentiment in the military. The first is that Abiola's vast financial holdings, if added to the powers of an executive president, held the prospect of a presidency largely autonomous of a military class long used to being in power or to controlling those in office. Added to this was the second, related, fact - that Abiola knew intimately the dynamics of military accumulation. Given the acquisitive and often corrupt behaviour of the military when in power (Othman, 1989), it could have been extremely awkward for the military to have a populist politician with an inner knowledge of the workings of the system as president. Furthermore, the prominence of radical forces in the SDP would undoubtedly worry the military hierarchy.

There are at least two perspectives from which we may explain the anti-radical concerns of the military hierarchy: self-preservation and system preservation. A crude expression of the former emerged in the days after the cancellation of the election, with talk of officer concern that Abiola might contemplate investigations of human rights abuses and misuse of public funds (*New African*, September 1993: 12). Such open anxieties by the military clearly concerned Abiola and had led him to try to cool the situation during the election campaign; he stated that he had no intention of investigating the military. Despite his assurances, key officers were said not to trust his ability to fend off radical pressure. The argument of system preservation is even more important. If Abiola were indeed beholden to radical elements, much wider interests would be threatened: the entire structure of societal power relations long preserved under military rule could be in danger.

Geo-Politics and Class: The SDP, the Election and Power Relations

Shortly after the presidential election was cancelled, a former head of state, Gen. Obasanjo, stated publicly that the election had been invalidated because it 'didn't go the way (the military) wanted'. It had 'been an open secret that... Babangida and his advisers had hoped that Bashir Tofa ... would win' (*The Guardian*, London, 24 June 1993). These remarks was echoed later by a commentary which argued that 'a small but powerful clique of officers and religious leaders from the north rejected Chief Abiola because, although a Muslim, he is from the south and a Yoruba' (ibid. 1 July 1993). *New African* (September 1993:13) similarly proposed that

> it was not Babangida, but a northern military coterie that was determined to stop civilian rule at all costs....behind (them) the northern power brokers who have chosen every president bar one... since Nigeria's independence. (They) simply could not face the prospect of Abiola becoming president. ... Babangida has ultimately been proved to be a weak and spineless man who could not stand up to the pressures of the military and the northern power brokers.

The foregoing suggests that there is a geo-political dimension to the cancellation of the election, even if it is unhelpful to construe the crisis in the primordial terms of North-South rivalry. Yet a broader geo-political construction is unavoidable. As already mentioned, the SDP emerged as a party with a diverse membership in which liberal and radical elements had considerable influence. It also gained considerable support. It secured a majority of local government councillorships (2934 to the NRC's 2562), a majority of state assembly seats (609 to 517, though NRC had more governorships); a majority in both houses of the National Assembly (House of Representatives 314 to 275; Senate 52 to 39); and in June 1993, it won the presidential election. For the conservative forces which had dominated Nigerian politics since independence, this was a situation with ominous portents. A coalition of opposing forces had 'suddenly won a decisive victory under the leadership of a man too wealthy, too astute and too confident to be easily overawed...' (*The Guardian*, Nigeria, 18 August 1993). Thus, Odugbemi

(*The African Guardian*, 19 July 1993) suggests that the decision to cancel the election was a project undertaken on behalf of all Nigerian conservatives:

> There has been a small but potent coalition of elite factions in power for years under one guise or another, whether during or outside military rule, and it has not been defeated by main force. This coalition has at its core the (conservative Sokoto) Caliphate but it has partners, naturally, nation-wide. The members have constituted the governing class... Against this governing elite has been ranged (a) hitherto incoherent counter-elite (who) came together in the SDP (and) pulled off an electoral victory ... June 12 delivered a mandate that (brought) with it the possibility of fundamental change. To the old governing class, June 12 mean(t) disaster... For what characterized the old governing class is that all its members... are wards of the Nigerian state (dependent) on their access to the patronage system. June 12 (brought) the barbarians to the gates ... the radicals, the agitators, the no-nonsense technocrats and so on who would have manned by sheer insistence an SDP presidency. All the forces opposed to fundamental change (we)re trying to prevent that from happening.

In short, the military regime's decision to nullify the election had a distinct class dimension which, given the intricate connection between class and ethnicity, also had a discernible regional flavour, clearly demonstrated in the pattern of civilian responses to the military's manoeuvres. For example, the NRC leadership was badly divided about how to respond to the changing situation. While the western leaders in the party, including the chairman, argued that Abiola had won fairly, others, mostly the northern and eastern leaders, warned that any attempt to instal him would be violently resisted. In the SDP, which was even more deeply split, confrontation was between a western and middle belt axis revolving around Abiola, on the one hand, and a northern faction dominant in the National Assembly, over which Shehu Yar'Adua held sway, on the other. These internal regional clashes made it difficult for the parties to join in a common front against the military.[9]

But the problem of regional polarization was not exclusive to the two parties. It also permeated other sectors of civil society, as seen in the chauvinistic interventions of traditional rulers,[10] the judiciary,[11] the press[12] and even the supposedly radical pro-democracy movement.[13] The important question to ask then is this: how could the presidential election have engendered so blatant a return to the old patterns of politics? Any proper answer must, in our view, refer to the perceived consequence of Abiola's victory for the 'traditional' balance of power in Nigeria.

The Election and North-South Power Relations

For a host of reasons, there is a considerable gap in the comparative levels of aggregate socio-economic development in the north and south of Nigeria. The south, longer in contact with the currents of cosmopolitan culture and with relatively less stratified and more permissive social systems, has had the edge in terms of gross material attainment. Even though the development gap has greatly narrowed in recent time, thanks to momentous catch-up initiatives by successive northern leaders, the perception of massive northern disadvantage has persisted, even in policy thinking. Consequently, a certain unspoken balance has existed wherein the south's economic power is compensated for by the retention of political power in the north. True to this formula, southerners have hardly risen to the pinnacle of political power, and even when they have, they have rarely remained there for long. Although resentment in the south at what is deemed 'imperial' domination by the northern oligarchy has simmered over the years (Okeke, 1993; Takaya and Toyden, 1987) the north has clung stubbornly to power.

The hegemonic agenda of some northern leaders, often stated with remarkable clarity and sometimes backed by threats that the north would rather secede than allow a southward shift of political power (*Quality*, October 1987; *The News*, 14 June 1993), arises from the calculation of using state power to reduce the development gap between north and south. Analysis of regional allocation of state resources invariably shows a disproportionate share going to the north. For example, an early study by Dudley (1966) showed that in the 1962-68 Development Plan the bulk of federal development spending (was) concentrated in the north. More recently, Okeke (1993: 140) has indicated that the disproportionate flow of federal resources to the north continues. He shows, for instance, that of the total federal allocation for river basin development in 1983, the approximate sum of N325.2m went to the north, while the south received only about N102.1m.

My own calculations confirm this trend. For example, while it is true that, of the total N16,472.8 million federal grant to the states in 1991, southern states (with a popular minority) received N8,367.8 (50.8%) to the north's N8,105 million (49.2%), a closer analysis reveals that northern states actually benefited more. This becomes clear when we analyse the ratio between federal allocations and revenues internally generated by the state governments. Of the total N3,322.2 million generated by the 21 states in 1991, N2,336 million, or 70.3%, came from the southern states and only 29.7% (N986.2 million) from their counterparts in the north. Yet the difference is even starker than this for, in the total budget for the south (that is federal allocation plus internal revenues), which came to N10,703.8 million, the proportion of federal funds to that internally generated was 78.2 to 21.8. The corresponding ratio for the north was 89.2 to 10.8. In 1991, therefore, the federal grant was over eight times the size of internal revenues in the north, whereas in the south it was only three and a half times.

Setting aside questions of distributive equity, the North is far more dependent than the south on federal finance. To this extent it has been more concerned than the south with control of federal power. It is also true that atavistic anxieties in the north were aroused by the structural adjustment programme launched by the Babangida regime. Statistical data is scant, but the available evidence suggests that certain adjustment measures including the deregulation of the financial sector, trade liberalization and the privatization of public sector enterprises had differential regional effects, with the south seemingly benefiting the more. Financial deregulation, for one, led to a disproportionate increase in the number of financial institutions operating in the south, with the result that the enhanced opportunities for financial flows and financial sector employment greatly energized the southern economy. Again, trade liberalization, involving a repudiation of the old import licensing system hitherto dominated by the northerners who held the levers of governmental power, tended to liberate the southerners' fabled commercial energy. Similarly, it appears that even the privatization programme, like the indigenization exercise of the 1970s before it, worked to the greater advantage of southern elements.

As the privatization exercise unfolded, an explicit northern perception emerged that northerners were disadvantaged by the exercise. In 1991 for instance, two northern industrialists cautioned the government on the pace of the privatization programme, particularly the privatization of banks, since people from the north were not participating fully. One of them, Aliko Mohammed, pointedly stated that owing to the economic imbalance in the country, particularly the imbalance in the ownership of banks, the privatization of federal banks ought to be suspended. He further explained that there were three basic levers of power in Nigeria: control of the economy, control of the bureaucracy and dominance in the political sphere. He contended that the north controlled political power, whereas the economy and the bureaucracy have been historically within the south's control. He insisted therefore that the north must retain the control of political power. 'If that slips away, then God help us' (*New Nigerian*, 19 February 1991).

At a more general level, the north's apparent unease about privatization reflected deeper misgivings about the overall direction of economic restructuring, for it feared that a freer economy might shift economic (and therefore political) power to the south (International Forum for Democratic Studies, 1995:9). It is indicative of these concerns that under the reassertive pro-northern regime of Gen. Abacha steps were taken towards reacquisition of some of the privatized enterprises, especially banks, by the state (*Newswatch*, 30 October 1995).

In short, the Babangida regime's invalidation of the June 1993 presidential election and the Abacha government's final blow to the transition programme itself were pre-emptive strikes to scuttle any potential upset of the existing geo-political power relations within the country.

Conclusion

It was noted at the start of this essay that an examination of the problems of transition in Nigeria could help to illuminate the complex issues of democratization in contemporary Africa. It was argued in particular that the Nigerian experience underscores the interaction between the forces of socio-economic interests and environment, on the one hand, and questions of method and agency involved in the process of change, on the other, as critical to the outcome of democratic transition. We have seen in this case that specific elements of the Babangida transition, especially the regimentational disposition of the executors of the programme, had the effect of exacerbating the contradictions of Nigerian politics, such that in the end the transition programme could not be sustained.

In the final analysis, the Nigerian case indicates that a broad-based elite pact on issues of power sharing, the distribution of national resources and, indeed, the modality of the transition itself, is a necessary pre-condition for any sustainable democratization. It points up the necessity of holding an exhaustive and inclusive pre-transition sovereign national conference. Equally importantly, the Nigerian experience also underlines the point that, given the delicate nature of any democratization process in so divided a society, military rule is not an auspicious sponsor of a successful transition. This is because, as was dramatically demonstrated in this case, military authoritarianism may prevent the fluid interplay of political forces necessary in the period of democratization. A transition away from military rule may be required before any subsequent transition to democracy is possible. Even after Abacha's death, these problems remain unresolved in Nigeria.

Notes

1. For the crises that engulfed the First Republic, see Coleman (1958); Sklar (1963); Mackintosh et al. (1966); Post and Vickers (1973); and Dudley (1973).

2. *Portrait of a New Nigeria: Selected speeches of IBB* (Lagos: Precision Press, n.d.).

3. Babangida, Speech to the 10th Graduation Ceremony of the National Institute for Policy and Strategic Studies, Kuru, 22 October 1988, in *Portrait of a New Nigeria: Selected speeches of IBB*.

4. Ibid: 204.

5. Ibid: 221.

6. Ibid: 3-9, 15-16.

7. The membership figures are hardly conclusive. By August 1990, although the NRC had fewer members from the north than from the south (2,322,528 to 2,634,291), it had more members in the north than the SDP (2,322,528 to 2,063,024). And while the SDP had slightly fewer southern members than the NRC (2,633,032 to 2,634,291), more of its members were in the south than in the north (2,633,032 to 2,063,024). Calculated from Oyediran and Agbaje (1991: 215).

8. I observed the parties' national conventions as a news reporter. But observations made here are confirmed in *EIU* (1990:9).

9. NEC officials were probably also encouraged by the 11 June ruling of a Lagos high court ordering the commission to proceed with the election because any postponement would lead to turmoil.

10. For detailed reports on the conflicts and positions, see *The Guardian*, Nigeria, 17 and 18 June 1993; *Newswatch*, 11 October 1993 and 1 November 1993; *Africa Confidential*, 2 July 1993 and 30 July 1993.

11. For example, the *Ooni* of Ife, an important Yoruba chief, was strident about the 'inviolability' of the 12 June verdict (*The Guardian*, Nigeria, 7 July 1993) while the Sultan of Sokoto, the 'symbol of northern power', seemed more inclined, after being initially supportive (*The Independent*, 12 July 1993) to advise Abiola to resign himself to the nullification of the election (*The Guardian*, Nigeria, 9 September 1993).

12. As *The Guardian*, London, 19 July 1993, pointed out, it became clear after a time that amid the 'conflicting court decisions on the legality of blocking the presidential election, the judiciary (was indeed) dividing along regional political lines', with southern and northern courts camped more or less neatly on opposite sides.

13. While a majority of the media houses in the south, particularly the Lagos-Ibadan press, ranged themselves against the cancellation, the bulk of the northern media, led by the *New Nigerian* newspaper and Radio Nigeria Kaduna, continually supported it. The various pro-democracy groups campaigning for the restoration of the 12 June election seemed predominantly southern movements, with the scope of their activities geographically limited. Wole Soyinka lamented this state of affairs, saddened 'that most of our actions took place in the western parts and certain parts of the east... and one or two places in the north' (*Newswatch*, 27 September 1993).

9 The Democratic Transition in Malawi: from single-party rule to a multi-party state

DIANA CAMMACK

Malawi was applauded by the international community for its comparatively peaceful and orderly transition from a single-party state to a multi-party democracy through the agency of elections. Even President Hastings Kamuzu Banda, who presided over thirty years of brutal repression exercised by his Malawi Congress Party (MCP), was commended by international observers and Malawians for his graceful acceptance of electoral defeat. Indeed, the euphoria that accompanied what was seen as the finale to a successful transition caused many to overlook past abuses as well as some of the more fundamental weaknesses within Malawian society that might ultimately undermine the fledgling democracy.

The Banda Years

Even people who knew little about Africa recognized the eccentric old president who dressed like a London banker, established an 'Eton in the Bush', and promoted congenial relations with apartheid South Africa. Western donors and South Africans who sought to denigrate the socialist development model followed by Malawi's neighbours, propagated Dr Banda's international reputation for successfully developing Malawi's capitalist economy. His human rights' abuses were conveniently ignored by cold warriors who needed an ally to fight communism on the subcontinent. Thought by many to be pragmatic, prudent and effective, Banda's reputation as a successful African leader survived in some quarters until the 1990s.

But inside the country Dr Banda and his close associates, John Tembo and Tembo's niece (and Banda's 'official hostess') Cecilia Kadzamira, were feared. During three decades senior party and government officials sometimes disappeared after making ill-considered remarks; some were found dead,

183

others never emerged from prison alive. Various intelligence services, as well as the Malawi Young Pioneers, everywhere eavesdropped and arrested those who criticized the regime or ignored its rules. Villagers far from the cities were not spared: land was confiscated and peasants relocated to make way for tobacco estates, military training camps, and national parks. Jehovah's Witnesses were rounded-up, killed or detained, and their property expropriated. So-called 'traditional courts', manned by untrained chiefs, tried offenders, including political opponents, who were denied access to legal representation and rights. Bureaucrats survived in government by following orders. Citizens were safest if they attended party meetings, if they sent their women to dance for Banda, if they lined the streets to cheer his passage, and if they bought and produced their party cards as ordered. Opponents kept their mouths shut, or fled the country.

Malawi's economic miracle was also an illusion (Mhone, 1992: 1-33). Built on 'relations of domination and exploitation', Banda's policies left Malawi one of the poorest countries in the world.[1] Using parastatals and his own group of companies, Press Holdings, Banda sought from the mid-1960s to raise foreign exchange earnings by expanding primary exports (tobacco and tea especially), to increase production of inputs for local industry, to indigenize ownership of agriculture and commerce, and to boost local food production. A differentiated agricultural sector was to be the basis of economic growth, and the government used regulation, credit, and extension services to foster the production of export crops by the estates and domestic cash crops by the top group of smallholders. The peasant majority was left to grow subsistence crops. Senior civil service and party officials were encouraged to open tobacco estates, and state-owned banks and parastatal provided them with credit and technical advice. The implications were obvious: 'this policy appeared to be an attempt to create a new class of wealthy Malawians, who not only would aid the country by their development efforts but also would owe the president an important political debt' (Pryor, 1990: 81).

This strategy turned customary land into estates for Banda's favourites and reduced the amount of land under cultivation by small farmers, thus compelling dispossessed peasants to seek waged labour. The government's minimum-wage policy discouraged urban migration (still home to only 10% of the population) and ensured cheap labour for the estates. Economic expectations were intentionally discouraged by limiting the availability of education, while labour was tightly regulated. The differential marketing policy of the agricultural parastatal, ADMARC, provided no incentive to expand smallholder production and kept producer prices low compared with final domestic and export prices. While it subsidized peasant consumption (which had political benefits), ADMARC accumulated profits and holdings which - like estates, overseas trips, and loans - became a major source of patronage.

Except for the new emphasis on estates, the economic policies implemented until 1979 were much the same as those of the late colonial era. With average economic growth of 5% per year and a real per capita annual income increase of 2.5%, Banda's early policies appeared successful partly because growth started from such a low level (Pryor, 1990: 45-7). Importantly, food output kept pace with population growth, although smallholder production declined and was off-set by the output from the estate sector (Chipande, 1987). Also, formal sector employment tripled between 1968 and 1989, yet total average real wages declined by 38% between 1969 and 1980, a decline that continued into the 1990s.

The major economic slump at the end of the 1970s was precipitated by deteriorating international terms of trade, transport problems arising from the war in Mozambique, the rising cost of oil, and poor weather. Manufacturing, monopolized by parastatals, Press Holdings and a few multinational companies, stagnated; parastatals began to run heavy losses; and the profits of estates, from upwards of 25% per annum in the mid-1970s, now fell significantly. Many estates went bankrupt as politicians and civil servants lost their land; the 'new rural bourgeoisie' had by the mid-1980s, become a 'disappointed class' (Pryor, 1990: 83-5).

Although a structural adjustment programme in the early 1980s temporarily halted the decline in GDP, inflation, the budget deficit and the public debt service ratio continued to climb. Meanwhile, both per capita GDP and per capita expenditure on economic and social services fell. As Mhone has explained (1992: 29-31), the failure to diversify the domestic economy and exports, and to reduce import and aid dependency, combined with Banda's policy of maximizing 'state and private entrepreneurial interests at the absolute expense of the majority', created a pool of cheap and under-skilled labour, a 'crisis of underconsumption', and ultimately enormous poverty and discontent. It was this group of impoverished Malawians who gave weight to the reform movement, though its leadership came from quite a different class.

The Rise of Opposition

The reform movement was led by relatively well-educated bourgeois men (and very few women), most of whom were employed in the liberal professions, the church, business, the university, or civil service. The army, fashioned by the British, kept its distance from politics, though generally sympathized with the multi-party movement and contributed to it in not insignificant ways. Its leadership largely excluded the police and traditional rural elite (chiefs and headmen had been the basis of Banda's support). The movement was given voice by an underground opposition, which faxed and hand-carried newsletters around the country, and later by the emerging independent press, run mostly by people trained in the party- and government-controlled media. Importantly, many of the movement's (and especially the UDF's) leaders had been senior MCP officials, though many had at one time or another been imprisoned by Banda and Tembo.[2] Those who had not been arrested had seen their friends and colleagues taken away.

The democratic transition is generally supposed to have begun on the first Sunday of Lent, 8 March 1992, when the local Catholic Bishops issued a pastoral letter, entitled *Living our Faith*, read from pulpits all over the country. It called for better wages, education and health care, freedom of expression, justice and rights protection, a climate of trust and openness, a more just distribution of wealth, and an end to corruption. It was written by churchmen who had no political ambitions and had not been critical of the regime for decades. Yet the letter was momentous because the Bishops 'opened the throats' of Malawians, giving expression to the unvoiced resentments of millions (Cullen, 1994).

The Bishops were interrogated by the police, while several hundred parish councillors and lay leaders were 'invited to lunch' at police headquarters, where they were warned about being misled by the Bishops. The letter was declared seditious and hundreds of Malawians were arrested for possessing it. The MCP used the government-controlled media to denounce the Bishops for destroying the tranquillity of the nation. Meanwhile, the MCP executive met in extraordinary session, where they decided that 'to make things easier we just have to kill these Bishops'. A tape recording of the meeting was leaked to embassies and the BBC and the plot collapsed. Yet the MCP's frenzied response was to have important consequences in Europe, when donors met in May to consider further aid to Malawi.

Events unfolded quickly. In the following week, students at Chancellor College (singing 'we want multi-party') and then at the Polytechnic, marched in support of the Bishops; many were arrested. Meanwhile the movement continued to take shape, as the internal opposition kept up pressure by printing and circulating broadsheets denouncing Banda's regime; thousands of people were arrested in the coming months for possessing this literature. Two weeks after the pastoral letter was published, Chakufwa Chihana,[3] the Lilongwe-based secretary general of the Southern Africa Trade Union Co-ordination Council, and scores of exiles (including the United Front for Multiparty Democracy founded in July 1991 in Zambia) joined together in Lusaka to form the Interim Committee for a Democratic Alliance. Chihana returned to Malawi to organize a national conference to press for reform. But when he flew into Lilongwe in early April 1992 he was met by supporters and western diplomats, and by security men who arrested him (Nkhwazi: 1995).

Strikes, unprecedented in independent Malawi, raised the level of tension in early May, starting first at the Chancellor College in Zomba and then moving to factories near Blantyre. Vandalism and then rioting ensued; the President's chain of grocery stores was a principal target. Unrest spread to Lilongwe, where a battle ensued between tobacco workers and the police. Roadblocks were thrown up by workers on a major industrial estate. Bank, railway and airline employees marched for more pay. Workers on the tea, tobacco and sugar estates joined in, demanding higher wages in the face of devaluation and inflation. Before peace was restored in Blantyre at least 20 people were killed by police who fired into the crowds. But on 7 May 1992 President Banda stated that all genuine grievances should be looked into expeditiously and, a week later, the minimum wage for manual workers was raised by 20 per cent (to less than 70 US cents a day) while civil servants received an increase of between 40 and 50 per cent.

Banda's unpopularity and the regime's growing inability to control the unrest were evident in early May when Chihana was not brought to court as scheduled and some three thousand angry people marched through Lilongwe to old town, where looting and stone-throwing ensued. On 14 May an organized boycott resulted in only a modest crowd materializing at the normally well-attended Kamuzu Day celebrations in Blantyre and the single-party election held in late June had the lowest turn-out ever. At the same time, tension in the townships persisted, as several people were shot dead for breaking the night curfew. Policemen were attacked by unarmed youth in Blantyre, and Banda's motorcade was stoned in July. Between March and July some two thousand people were detained for a variety of offences having to do with advocating democracy.

Outside pressure on Malawi also increased. A report by Amnesty International (6 March 1992) was scathing about prison conditions, punishment and detention in Malawi and would influence the donors. Western governments also took note of Chihana's detention, the plan to kill the Bishops, and recent shootings and mass arrests. These incidents, together with the West's post-Cold War emphasis on rights' protection and democratization meant Banda's human rights record was closely scrutinized at the donors' meeting in Paris. Before this meeting, John Tembo visited both Britain and the United States, where he was confronted by Herman Cohen, US Assistant Secretary of State for Africa, with a list of detainees' names. Banda's choice was simple: political 'pluralism and Western aid or totalitarianism and ... isolation'. The Malawi government refused to bend and in Paris the donors suspended all non-humanitarian aid for six months (some US$74m).

By mid-1992 a combination of factors had given birth to sweeping demands for reform. Business people and estate owners, early beneficiaries of Banda's policies, were now troubled, while widening impoverishment, landlessness and drought fuelled popular discontent. Devaluation and inflation forced workers onto the streets, while corruption in government frustrated entrepreneurs. Ordinary people were tired of being forced by party youth to purchase MCP cards, and many resented Banda's preferential treatment of his Chewa tribal group and of his, Tembo's and Kadzamira's conspicuous accumulation of wealth. The army quietly complained that it was asked to fight and die in Mozambique while protecting the Nacala railway from RENAMO, who at the same time were being trained and aided by Banda, Tembo and the police. Lawyers highlighted the injustice of traditional courts, the poor conditions of the prisons, and the repressive laws used to detain and dispossess Banda's enemies. Journalists condemned broadcasting, literary and press censorship, and especially the statute that prescribed life imprisonment for filing stories 'damaging to Malawi'. The unresolved murder at Mwanza, back in 1983, of four prominent politicians who had criticized Banda and advocated financial accountability, became a focus of resentment.

The reform movement succeeded in 1992 because of its volatile nature (popular violence had not been seen in Malawi since colonial times) and because defiance of the regime was so widespread, making it difficult for the security forces to subdue. No doubt the militant struggle was useful to reform leaders. Yet this militancy was short-lived because it was contained, first by the MCP, by agreeing piecemeal reforms, and then by the opposition leadership.

None of the leaders of the two largest parties, the United Democratic Front (UDF) and the Alliance for Democracy (AFORD), was radical. They did not want 'anarchy' or to be 'overtaken by events' (*Africa Information Afrique*, 2 November 1992). Nor were the Protestant churchmen, who took the multi-party effort forward from mid-1992, revolutionary: they preached social justice, held peaceful demonstrations, distributed literature, and advocated the creation of a commission to study political reform. Ecumenicalism, new to Malawi, culminated in August in the formation of the Public Affairs Committee (PAC), an umbrella group of secular reformers and churchmen who pressed for the creation of democratic structures and an end to human rights abuse. (The UDF and AFORD 'pressure groups' had joined PAC by 1993.) PAC was in the forefront of the reform movement, and entered into negotiations with government through the newly formed President's Committee on Dialogue.

After the Paris meeting, Banda made concessions to please donors while trying to check the reform movement at home. For instance, a Detention Review Tribunal was established and in June and July 1992 17 political detainees were released, including Aleke Banda and (after 27 years) Machipisa Munthali. Their release and the temporary liberation of Chihana raised the level of political excitement. For the first time since 1969, the International Red Cross was allowed to visit prisons. Yet, at the same time, thousands of ordinary people were detained for possessing opposition leaflets and attending meetings. A bill was tabled in parliament reducing the maximum term from life to five years imprisonment for writing damaging reports about the country, but the editor of the independent *Financial Post* was threatened with 'deep trouble' if he returned from Namibia. The government entered into a dialogue with the World Alliance of Reformed Churches, yet refused to hold joint discussions with local Catholics and Anglicans.

If Banda expected his reforms to mollify the donors, he was to be disappointed. In early September 1992 Chihana was finally charged with five counts of sedition and two counts of acting to undermine confidence in the government. While on bail, he met with British human rights lawyers, who concluded that he 'had not committed any act which could reasonably be regarded as a criminal offence in accordance with basic human rights standards applicable to freedom of expression'. The same week, Baroness Lynda Chalker, for the British government, said that she thought western donors should not resume aid; its suspension was vital to bringing about democratic change (Radio Botswana, 16 September 1992; British House of Lords, 1993).

The Referendum

In mid-October, Malawi's most famous political prisoner, Orton Chirwa, who had been abducted from Zambia and detained for eleven years, died in prison. That same week Banda stunned the nation by announcing that a referendum would be held to decide whether to keep the single-party system of government. Banda, seemingly unable to judge the public mood, felt that it would be a public vote of confidence in himself. What he did not count on was that the referendum, and later the election, would be run under very different conditions than in the past (Snead, 1995). On New Year's Eve he announced the polling date as 15 March 1993, placing it during the rainy season when travel is difficult and giving reformers little time to spread their message. He rejected a postponement and other recommendations made the previous month by a UN technical team. Especially contentious was the issue of whether to use one or two ballot boxes: while the MCP insisted on two boxes placed out of sight of polling officers, the UN and multi-party advocates felt that such a system would lead to intimidation and fraud and recommended that voters make their selection and place their ballot in a single box in public view.

As the campaign began, the government restricted the access of multi-party advocates to radio, journalists were harassed and detained, and rallies could only be held with the approval of the police. Multi-party advocates became the main target of detention and of attacks by MCP supporters, the police and Young Pioneers. Crowds attending multi-party rallies were dispersed, marches halted, and leaders arrested. Yet the combined pressure of the reformers (including threats to boycott the polls), human rights campaigners and donors (who voiced not-so-subtle threats) forced Banda to modify his stance. Contributing to the strain on government was a deteriorating economy, resulting from the suspension of aid, drought and labour unrest. Other than instituting stark and widespread repression, Banda had no choice but to go on with reform. Consequently, in February 1993 he agreed to a request from the United Nations' Secretary General, Boutros Boutros-Ghali, to postpone the referendum until mid-June. The registration period was also extended, which was expected to help the multi-party cause.

The MCP now went on the offensive. First, the party's candidates throughout the country condemned the 'chaos of multi-partyism', a refrain started by Banda: multi-partyism was not a remedy for Africa's economic or social ills and would result, as in Kenya most recently, in ethnic violence and war. Second, abductions and beatings by MCP youth of 'confusionists' (the name given by the MCP to multi-party campaigners) escalated, while both AFORD's *Malawi Democrat* and the *UDF News* were banned (with only partial success). As part of the effort to maintain rural support for the MCP, villagers were told that the drought-relief maize given to them by government was in fact, provided by the President. Banda also made his own personal plea for their support.

On polling day (14 June 1993) Banda's call for peace and calm had a salutary effect on the nation, including the party youth and the Young Pioneers (MYP). Religious groups joined together to pray for peace as millions of people rose before dawn to join the queues. Two-thirds (3.1 million) of registered voters (4.7 million), or over three-quarters of the adult population, went to the polling stations. There they had to cast one of two ballots, either a black cock (the MCP symbol) or a lantern, to decide the question: 'Do you wish that Malawi remains with the one-party system of government with the Malawi Congress Party (MCP) as the sole political party or do you wish that Malawi changes to the multiparty system of government?' 63% of the voters (nearly 2 million people) 'voted for change', though in the central region (Dr Banda's home and the Chewa area) people voted heavily (66%) in favour of a single-party government. As for the fairness of the referendum, West European observers expressed the views of many: 'the government showed that it was not able to conduct an unbiased referendum, so any election must be run by a neutral body' (*Guardian*, 19 June 1993).

Unfortunately, it had not been made clear exactly what was to happen if the referendum were to favour multi-party rule. No schedule of measures to effect change had been laid down. Hence, when Banda acknowledged defeat on radio he promised that a constitutional amendment would be passed to legalize multi-party politics within a month, and he held out hope for elections within the year. Yet this did not satisfy those in the opposition who wanted Banda to become a 'figurehead' and who argued for real power to be shared between the MCP, AFORD and the UDF in a 'government of national unity'. 'What we're worried about', said Harry Thomson of the UDF, is 'if they are going to change the constitution, how can they change it without the (input of the) democratic parties?' One member of PAC, the Rev. Chande Mhone, went so far as to threaten a 'call to civil disobedience, to stay away from work (and to) tell the donors to continue to withhold aid' if the opposition's demands were not met (*Guardian*, 19 June 1993).

The Transition

Before any serious negotiations took place, the MCP reorganized itself for the coming battle. Heading the new effort was Hetherwick Ntaba, a medical doctor married to a Banda niece. Already publicity secretary for the MCP, he was appointed Minister of External Affairs in the cabinet reshuffle following the elections. The civil service, which went on strike over wages in early September, was placated with a pay hike of 9.3 per cent. Within weeks of the referendum, the Presidential Committee on Dialogue and PAC agreed to form a National Consultative Committee (NCC) and a National Executive Committee (NEC) to negotiate the transition. These were formalized by parliament in mid-November. The NEC, supposedly a shadow cabinet, was never very effective, but the NCC, comprising representatives of seven political parties[4] with a rotating chair, played a more important and contentious role. Mandated to oversee the transition to a multi-party state, it was considered by some to be only a consultative group advising parliament, while others thought it should be the supreme body whose decisions were final. Time and events would establish the limits of its power, though these and its credibility continued to vacillate under different chairmen.

At a roundtable meeting soon after the referendum it was decided to set up an independent Electoral Commission to organize and oversee a free and fair election. The Electoral Commission, chaired by Justice Anastasia Msosa and in place by mid-December, delimited constituency boundaries, and formed committees on civic education, the media, and violence. The first of these worked closely with PAC to establish a civic education programme, while the media committee helped the government-owned radio station, the Malawi Broadcasting Company (MBC), prepare and present civic education and political programmes. The violence sub-committee moved around the country, as needed, to investigate and report on cases of electoral fraud and intimidation.

Soon after the referendum, section 4 of the old constitution was repealed, allowing opposition political parties to form. An amnesty was declared for exiles to allow them to return and start their own parties. Other long overdue reforms were undertaken, including repeal of the Decency in Dress Act, reduction of the voting age from 21 to 18 and passage of a limited Bill of Rights. In addition, the ban on Jehovah's Witnesses and other sects was lifted, the Forfeiture Act repealed, and the Life Presidency abolished. Work on the new constitution was started by a sub-committee of the NCC in January 1994, with technical advice provided by the UN (Micaletti, n.d.). It was hoped that if the drafting took place before the election, the process would be relatively apolitical. While this was not wholly the case (van Donge, 1995), it is true that changes to the new constitution made after the election were more obviously politically motivated.

In October, in the midst of a struggle between the MCP and the opposition over how much power the NCC should have during the transition, the President was rushed to South Africa for urgent medical treatment. Members of the NCC saw this as their opportunity to transfer executive power to the NCC, though their divisiveness and indecision left the MCP room to create a triumvirate to rule as a Presidential Council. It consisted of Gwanda Chakuamba, a senior MCP member recently released from 22 years imprisonment for sedition and, amazingly, appointed General Secretary of the party; John Tembo and Robson Chirwa, Minister of Transport, MCP Regional Chairman for the North, and a Tembo ally. It continued to govern the country until the enfeebled President reassumed office in early December.

Dr Banda was forced to return prematurely in order to regain control of the government after 'Operation Bwezani'. For months there had been a move afoot to disarm and disband the Young Pioneers, the hated MCP youth. Indeed, the NCC had agreed in mid-September that the MYP would be disarmed immediately but this had not happened. Instead there were reports that they were stockpiling weapons to ensure a Banda victory or to overthrow the opposition if it were to win. Trouble erupted in Mzuzu, after a quarrel in which MYP members killed two soldiers.

Within days the army, instigated by middle-rank officers who may have acted with the approval of members of the NCC (*Africa Confidential*, 17 December 1993), attacked MYP bases and the homes of its leaders in an effort to disarm them. Over the next two days, MYP headquarters in Lilongwe was shelled and burned to the ground, as members hid in a nearby forest. MYP bases throughout the country were attacked and destroyed by the army, shops were looted, and the MCP headquarters in Lilongwe was stripped of all furnishings and files as private cars were commandeered by soldiers to cart away the booty. Significant stores of arms and ammunition were captured while members of the MYP removed their uniforms and fled to villages and across the border into neighbouring states. As many as 8,000 (though the estimate soon dropped to 2,000) were supposed to have taken refuge with RENAMO in central Mozambique.

Instead of overthrowing the government (as some observers had predicted), the soldiers returned to their barracks, demanding the removal of the senior army command. One of Banda's first acts after resuming power was to appoint a new commander and deputy commander of the army, and a new Minister of Defence. In his remaining months as President, he tried to mollify the soldiers by offering them better wages, conditions and housing.

The Election

A new register of voters 18 years old and above was opened in late February, with the election set for 17 May. At first people were reluctant to register, partly due to confusion about why they were to vote: had there not been an election last year? Why was another needed? Did not the various parties already have 'presidents'? Others were discouraged by the need to bring identification to registration officials to prove age, especially as such documentation was difficult to obtain and birth dates were not always known. Many were too preoccupied with the erratic rains, the breakdown of the agricultural credit scheme and the impending crop disaster to think seriously about politics. People were also increasingly apathetic because the parties addressed few issues relevant to rural voters, and because they felt betrayed when opposition politicians failed to carry through on promises they made during the referendum. People were also reluctant to register because they were unsure of voting procedures and unwilling to make fools of themselves on election day. For these reasons civic education was vital, yet the Electoral Commission was slow in getting it started (Article 19, 1994b,c; UNEAS, 1994a).

Violence and intimidation also affected registration and, after registration closed on 26 March, the campaign. It began with panga-wielding mobs attacking opposition leaders in the central region and the dismissal of employees favouring multi-partyism from their jobs in the south. Soon, violent acts of intimidation were being reported from all over the country. Some chiefs and headmen barred opposition parties from holding meetings in their areas. In more than one district, MCP local officials moved door-to-door, collecting the names of people and their political affiliation in a book, an act which intimidated many citizens. Some officials promised food and clothing to those who supported the MCP, while food aid was being provided in some villages to only those who supported Dr Banda. The MCP also used the Chewa dance cult, the *Gule Wamkulu*, to intimidate people. They forced people 'to join campaign rallies or to disturb meetings of other parties', according to the Electoral Commission (1994d; UNEAS, 1994a; Article 19, 1994a,b and c).

In mid-March, the Electoral Commission (1994b) summarized the situation. There were, it reported

> flagrant abuses of the Electoral Law and the Code of Conduct by some Party officials and Chiefs. The commission has examples of Chiefs being bribed.... (and) Chiefs intimidating voters and acting themselves as Monitors and in other places keeping their own bogus registers. Some chiefs are taking away certificates from registered voters.... Party officials have, in some places, instigated violence..., attempted to register under-age school children..., (and are) allowing their monitors (sometimes ten to a Registration Station) to frighten away people of different parties.

After being censured by several organizations, the MCP inundated the Joint International Observer Group (JIOG) and the Electoral Commission with reports of attacks on its rallies and members. Some reports investigated by observers were clearly fabrications (UNEAS 1994b), but it is also true that the nature of intimidation changed, as tit-for-tat disruptions of campaign rallies and attacks on politicians of all parties became more common. There was a noticeable decrease in the level of intimidation of voters, particularly after Justice Msosa and District Commissioners explained to chiefs and headmen that they must remain impartial, allow all parties to campaign freely in their areas, and permit their villagers to participate in multi-party politics.

Nonetheless, complaints continued to be received by observers and the violence committee up until the election. These included reports that

> people in some areas were not being allowed to hold opposition party meetings; certain chiefs were still intimidating voters; party functionaries were buying registration certificates; party officials were manhandling journalists; members of the... MYP were threatening villagers; guns were hidden in locked rooms (and) insurrectionists lurked in forests and across the border; party flags were burnt; rallies disrupted; and various politicians were marked for assassination. Many of these reports were inaccurate and others were either unproven or unprovable... (Article 19, 1994c).

The Electoral Commission also fought a rearguard action against the police. First, it tried to register the police, but the Inspector General, an MCP appointee, objected because he considered voting a political activity and not allowed by police regulations. The Commission, on the other hand, argued that voting was a basic human right, and the Attorney General and the Minister of Home Affairs agreed. In the end, registration was re-opened for the police, but only half of them and their families took advantage of the opportunity, apparently afraid to act against the implicit wishes of their superior (JIOG, 1994; Electoral Commission, n.d.).

The Electoral Commission also had trouble getting the police to take action against those who contravened the Electoral Law. It felt that in order to halt further violence and intimidation, cases had to be exposed and perpetrators tried: justice had to be seen to be done. This was difficult to do because the Commission's lawyer (the Attorney General) was also Minister of Justice in the MCP government. Therefore, the Electoral Act had to be amended so the Commission could hire independent counsel. Even after this was done, it remained difficult for the Commission to obtain a conviction. As Justice Msosa explained, some of the cases it prepared and handed over to the police were 'straightforward (and) could have been prosecuted before the election', but were not. The Commission 'watch(ed) helplessly, waiting for a police response'. There was, as one commissioner stated, a lot of 'foot dragging'. The Commission also felt that during the election 'many Malawians lacked the courage to report incidents in writing because of cultural, political, social or economic reasons' (Electoral Commission, n.d.: 23 and Appendix VI; *Malawi News*, 14-20 May 1994; *The Monitor*, 11 May 1994).

Civic education was initiated by the Electoral Commission, and undertaken by various NGOs, including PAC, and by MBC radio. The Electoral Commission's civic education committee co-opted outside members to assist it, hired a public relations firm to do some of its work, organized workshops for civic educationalists, and scheduled its programmes so that people were taught, first, how and why to register, and later, how and why to vote. Information was passed on through newspapers and posters, and by radio - where drama, music, discussion, poetry and prayer were used to convey these and other messages about the democratic process. A small human rights network, relying heavily upon rural clerics, did civic education work in the countryside (and reported abuses to PAC in Lilongwe). While civic education was incomplete, the staff at polling stations made up for it on election day by explaining to people how to vote. As a result, only just over 2% of votes cast were null and void (Electoral Commission, n.d.: Appendix XI).

Radio is the primary medium for disseminating information in Malawi (there is no television and illiteracy runs at 61%), and MBC's political programming was central to the campaign effort. Guidelines were established for MBC by the Electoral Commission (1994b) to ensure equal access and editorial impartiality, and these were, by and large, followed. Nonetheless, bias crept into MBC. For instance, MCP ministers' speeches were broadcast as news, as were parliamentary 'debates', which were, in reality, MCP campaign speeches. One major breach of the media guidelines occurred when Dr Banda gave an unscheduled campaign speech on radio, four days before the election. The breach was rectified when the Electoral Commission (to the consternation of MCP officials) offered equal airtime to the other presidential candidates, an offer that the UDF candidate, Mr Muluzi, accepted the following night.

Bias was also introduced, in part, through the government-owned news agency (MANA), which provided news stories to the radio station. For instance, MANA produced approximately 170 party-political stories over the seven weeks preceding the election and, of these, 130 dealt with MCP meetings and candidates, while the remaining 40 covered the other parties' leaders and rallies. MBC's main failing during the campaign (and before and, unfortunately, since) was its inability to critically analyse, contextualize and present news in depth. None of the parties' policies or campaign speeches was thoroughly discussed or assessed. Substantive domestic issues (e.g., the political implications of devaluing the kwacha, or the deteriorating security situation) were often under- or un-reported. News conferences run by the army, the NCC, the Electoral Commission and its committees, which were frequently broadcast in their entirety, were the best (and sometimes the only) means by which the public learned of important events. Attempts to hold political debates were only partially successful; for instance, Dr Banda refused to participate. But coverage on election day, during the vote count, of Banda's acknowledgement of defeat and Muluzi's inauguration demonstrated that the MBC had the capacity to report hard news critically (Article 19, 1994c).

Though it was mid-winter and cold, by the time the polls opened at 6 a.m. on 17 May, voting queues were hours' long. Rumours of MYP moving into Malawi from Mozambique to attack polling stations raised the level of tension in some areas, but the army patrolled the border to guarantee the peace. In the event, the day was calm and the polling went relatively well, even though the process was complex, with strips of ballots presented to voters, who chose their presidential and National Assembly candidates and placed their ballots in two separate envelopes and boxes, and put the rejected ballot stubs into discard boxes. This complicated procedure slowed the voting (though officials helped the voters through the process), and the counting of votes that night in dark buildings and tents lighted only by lanterns was a lengthy process. Only on the morning of the 19 May did Banda concede defeat. But as he did, people poured onto the streets singing and dancing with joy, amidst cars with blaring horns.

The following month the election was re-run in two southern constituencies due to 'irregularities' (Electoral Commission, n.d.: Appendix VIII) and a by-election was held because Muluzi gave up his National Assembly seat to become president.

Multi-partyism and the Quest for Unity

During the campaign there was little open dissension between the various opposition candidates and parties, partly because the ideological distance between them was minimal, partly because few issues were debated in any case, and partly because of the spectre of the electoral disaster in Kenya which resulted from a disunited opposition. The socialist alternative was largely discredited in southern Africa by 1994 and the right was represented by their common enemy, the MCP. That left the electorate with little to choose from other than candidates' personalities, tribal affiliations and histories. Indeed, the candidate's first task was to explain his role during the Banda years to the satisfaction of constituents. Tribalism remained a political force at the local level because regional and ethnic differentiation and exclusion had been part of Banda's way of dispensing patronage and maintaining power (Africa Watch, 1990; Posner, 1995; van Donge, 1995) and because most citizens had little attachment to Malawians outside their district. The election results seemed to prove Banda right: multi-partyism would result in ethnic division, while genocide in Rwanda, underway and reported hourly by MBC during the election, underscored the fears of some that the ethnic and regional split evident in the electoral result (Table 9.2) could be dangerous.

Table 9.1 Malawi election results 1994 - percentage distribution of votes

A. Presidential Election

Candidate	National	North	Central	South
B Muluzi (UDF)	47.2	4.5	27.8	78.0
H K Banda (MCP)	33.4	7.3	64.3	16.1
C Chihana (AFORD)	18.9	87.8	7.5	5.2
K Kalua	0.5	0.4	0.4	0.6

B. National Assembly Elections

Party	National	North	Central	South
UDF	46.36	5.31	27.69	76.02
AFORD	18.99	84.91	7.22	6.74
MCP	33.68	8.23	64.40	16.23
Other parties	0.76	1.53	0.48	0.71

Table 9.2   1994 Malawi election results - National Assembly seats won by region

Party	National	North	Central	South
UDF	85	0	14	71
MCP	56	0	51	5
AFORD	36	33	3	0

A very unstable political situation resulted: of the 177 National Assembly seats contested, UDF won 85, AFORD 36 and MCP 56. Looking strictly at numbers, Muluzi needed a coalition to get legislation through the assembly or to change the constitution (some amendments to which required a two-thirds majority). Moreover, each major party and presidential candidate was particularly strong in only one region, which made it difficult for Muluzi to talk about a national mandate to rule. Seeking stability, many people concluded that the best way forward was to form a government of national unity, in which Muluzi would include members of AFORD, or even the MCP, in his cabinet.

In the days following the election, efforts were made by Muluzi to persuade AFORD to join the UDF in government. It was reported that Chihana wanted the vice presidency and insisted that several cabinet seats be given to AFORD members, but that Muluzi thought Chihana's demands were too steep. So talks collapsed. Meanwhile, Muluzi steadfastly refused to consider including the MCP in a cabinet: he said a year later it was because he felt a multi-party democracy needed a viable opposition (*The Nation*, 7 April 1995). However, he left a few minor cabinet posts vacant in case Chihana changed his mind. Consequently, when parliament opened, the UDF MPs took their seats as a minority bloc.

Muluzi turned to governing, first releasing all remaining political prisoners, visiting neighbouring states to re-establish ties and obtain relief maize, organizing free primary education for all Malawian children for the first time, appointing a commission of inquiry to investigate the death of the four senior politicians at Mwanza in 1983, and initiating a national Poverty Alleviation Programme. The country was facing another year of drought and people were hungry, the MCP had set the currency to float the previous February and the rate of inflation was beginning to climb, the civil service was still restive, and donors were demanding fiscal reform. These and other problems faced the new administration, while the public, having voted for change, had no real understanding of the problems facing Muluzi, but had great expectations.

The MCP and AFORD were busy discussing options. In mid-June their 'Memorandum of Understanding' was made public and soon their joint shadow cabinet was announced. The aim in forming a pact was, they said, to ensure national unity and security in the face of dangerous regional and tribal divisions within the country. Commentators and the UDF saw the pact as a ploy to undermine the government - which it was clearly capable of doing. For instance, the opposition was able in July to dictate the composition and leadership of seven parliamentary committees formed to undertake house business. The opposition also challenged the right of non-elected UDF cabinet ministers to sit in the house, making it clear that it would be able to hinder the passage of legislation when presented to the National Assembly by Muluzi later (*Southscan*, 4 August 1994).

Muluzi found that the MCP was, even in defeat, a force to be reckoned with as long as Chihana was willing to conspire with them. At the same time, many democrats (including some in the AFORD executive) felt betrayed by Chihana, questioning his motives for signing the unity pact. Not surprisingly, Muluzi took the offensive and by late September he had managed to entice Chihana away from the MCP by giving him a second vice presidency, a post that had to be specially created (and in so doing caused a furore), and by including several AFORD members in an enlarged cabinet. At first, Chihana claimed that their new positions would not wreck the MCP-AFORD pact or change the role of the united opposition: it would continue to scrutinize the performance of the government, he insisted. But very soon it was clear that the alliance was finished. Unity within a multi-party government became a fact on 27 July when AFORD and UDF signed a coalition document to 'broaden and place on a sound and sustainable footing' the relationship between the two parties and to 'form a coalition government'. Not all AFORD members were pleased, and in the ensuing months Chihana faced a revolt within his party, weakening his bargaining position with Muluzi, who counted on Chihana being able to deliver the parliamentary vote.

The MCP then began to disintegrate. Banda had already retired from active politics in August 1994 as his physical and psychological condition deteriorated, leaving the enigmatic Chakuamba as effective party leader. In October, Ntaba was arrested for ordering the burning of three houses as part of a domestic dispute with political overtones. In January 1995, the commission investigating the death of the four politicians at Mwanza in 1983 submitted its report to Muluzi. Then, soon after the report was serialized in the press, Dr Banda, John Tembo and four policemen were arrested and within weeks, another six policemen and Cecilia Kadzamira were indicted for conspiracy to murder. Chakuamba tried to distance the MCP from the case, but as the horrific details of their murder unfolded in the press, senior politicians left the party. Meanwhile, the prosecution of several senior MCP officials, including Tembo, for conspiring to murder the Bishops in 1992 further weakened the party. In an effort to give the MCP new life, Chakuamba shunned Tembo as he languished in prison, and made a bid in mid-1995 to oust Banda from the MCP presidency.

The new government's attempts to undermine Press Holdings' control of the Malawian economy were also less obviously underway. By mid-1995 Banda's pet project, Kamuzu Academy, was suffering from a cash crisis, indicating that Banda and the party were divorced from their traditional source of funding, the public treasury. Soon the name 'Kamuzu', which had graced virtually every large dam, bridge and road in the country, was removed from the international airport, only the start of a trend that MCP supporters saw as a vicious attempt to deny Dr Banda his standing as father of the nation. Within a year of the election, close observers were beginning to wonder if there existed a functioning opposition within Malawi at all.

The Sustainability of Multi-Party Democracy in Malawi

Most African states need legal reform and new institutions rather than exceptional men and women to guarantee a successful and sustainable transition to democracy. Yet a year after its first multi-party election and three years into its democratic transition, Malawi had affected few changes that would ensure, if necessary, that a new dictatorship would not arise. This is particularly important in Malawi because pacificity, tradition and history, along with certain strong personalities, have tended to sustain a closed and repressive society.

Inhibiting the completion of the democratic transition was the relatively poorly developed political consciousness of the mass of people in Malawi (compared, say, to other SADC nationals). Having missed the consciousness-raising experience of a protracted colonial liberation struggle, the people were relatively politically uninformed. With little industry, the working class was small, the trade union movement weak, and radicalism confined mostly to the university. Because Malawi was cut off for decades from even its closest neighbours, innovative ideas - about socialism and alternative development strategies, for instance - passed the country by. The whites whom Banda depended on to run the estates, the civil service and Press, many of whom were South Africans, along with the conservative Asian community that dominated commerce, did little to radicalize the population either. Illiteracy and poverty contributed further to the ignorance of the majority. In the government, party, and related institutions, a strict hierarchy of authority developed, which was dangerous to defy. And by using traditional leaders and customary authority to govern, Banda did nothing to foster modern ways of thinking or alternative socio-political structures in the countryside. Together, these factors mean that the majority, excluding most of the urban and a few of the rural elite, were both hesitant and ill-informed politically and economically.

Nonetheless, their expectations were high. From the referendum onward, many people believed that voting for change meant that with a new government, they would be able to seek work in South Africa again, reclaim estate land, and obtain free seeds and fertilizer and better prices for their produce, more security, better health care, and a free education for their children. Prices would stabilize and wages would increase.

During the referendum and election campaigns, politicians exacerbated the problem by promising these and other things. Neither they, civic educationalists nor the media did much to explain to the populace why these were difficult goals to achieve or why, after thirty years of MCP rule, larger social and economic reform was nearly impossible to implement. It was not an issue-based campaign, and the media and parties focused on personalities, rather than analysing platforms and manifestos or discussing relevant concerns.

Since the elections, as economic crisis deepened, many people, especially those in the rural areas, did not understand what was happening. Prices rose, retrenchment began, government spending was curtailed, and crime and corruption mounted. People blamed the UDF and compared the problems with an earlier time of seeming prosperity and order, a view which, naturally, the MCP encouraged. Many multi-party advocates became disillusioned with the machinations of the new political leadership and with reports of corruption. Meanwhile, government wrestled with how best to deal with impending strikes and possible social unrest.

In the midst of this, the institutions that might foster human rights and the rule of law were largely missing. First, the parliamentary committee charged with re-drafting the constitution was under enormous pressure as the whole process became politicized after the election. The resulting constitution was unknown to the majority of Malawians and its legitimacy questioned by many of the elite. Civic education was virtually non-existent, and the vast majority of people remained as ignorant of their rights as before. The structures provided for in the Constitution that might nurture the democratic transition - for instance, local elections, an independent ombudsman, a law commission, a human rights committee, a compensation committee to look into past abuses, and a Senate - were not fully in place. Cabinet members ignored the requirement to declare their assets while corruption and unauthorized use of funds by senior officials went unpunished. Some of the human rights groups active during the election now were discredited or virtually defunct. Meanwhile, the army and police entered homes searching for weapons - an action necessitated and, in some Malawian eyes, legitimized by the rise in crime, so that few questioned the absence of search warrants.

Importantly, too, the media was repeatedly accused of being irresponsible by the Minister of Information, himself a journalist once jailed by Dr Banda, and by others in government. The threat of libel suits generated self-censorship, while ownership of the print media was concentrated in the hands of senior politicians. More than one MBC official complained of government interference with programming, yet there seemed to be no intention of implementing reforms to create a broadcasting authority independent of government, even though donors provided it with millions of dollars to open a second MBC radio channel and a television station.

The quest for unity in a multi-party state might also have acted to undermine the transition to democracy. A loyal opposition, new to Malawi and to many states in Africa, was vital if a government's policies were to be critically examined and evaluated, if senior politicians were to be held accountable, and if alternative opinions were to be considered. In Malawi, in the aftermath of Banda, for cultural and historical reasons, open criticism was not encouraged, and when it did take place, issues of tribal differences, personalities and political histories could be used to deflect criticism and detract from its force. In the end, an opposition that is either absorbed and silenced or discredited and weakened permits a government to trample rights, conceal corruption, avoid implementing reforms, and to silence opponents one by one. After thirty years of single-party rule, this was one lesson Malawi seemed yet to have to learn.

Unpublished and Local Sources

AFP radio report (12 December 1993), *Facts & Reports*, Amsterdam, 7 January 1994.
Article 19 (1994), 'Media Monitoring in Malawi', weekly reports, Lilongwe, April-June.
Article 19 (n.d.), 'Summary of Malawi's 1993 Referendum Result', Lilongwe.
AWEPA, Association of Western European Parliamentarians (1993), 'Report of an Observer Mission at the Malawi Referendum', Amsterdam, pp.1-13.
British House of Commons (1993), meeting with PAC, AFORD and UDF delegation, 22 February.
British House of Lords (1993), Debate on Malawi: Aid, 26 January.
Chipande, G.H.R. (1987), The Performance of the Malawian Smallholder Agricultural Subsector, 1968/69 to 1984/85, Mimeo, October.
Cuomo, K. K. (1993), Robert F. Kennedy Center for Human Rights, letter to the editor, *Malawi Democrat* (Lusaka), 30 April-13 May.
Electoral Commission (n.d.), 1994 Parliamentary and Presidential Elections Report, Blantyre.
Electoral Commission (1994a), Report to Parliament by the Electoral Commission, 5 February.
Electoral Commission (1994b), 'Procedures for media coverage of Parliamentary and Presidential Elections', 8 March.
Electoral Commission (1994c), 'Electoral Commission Concern at Intimidation', press release, 14 March.
Electoral Commission (1994d), 'Electoral Commission Report on Electoral Law Violations', 17 April.
Joint International Observer Group (JIOG) (1994), 'Report of the Joint Interactional Observer Group at the First Malawi General Election', 17 May draft.
Lawyers Committee for Human Rights (1992), 'Malawi: Ignoring Calls for Change', 13 November 1992.
National Consultative Committee, draft constitution, March 1994.
National Consultative Committee, draft constitution sent to Cabinet, May 1994.
Report of the Constitution Committee to the National Assembly on the National Constitution Conference on the Provisional Constitution held in Lilongwe, 20-24 February 1995.
Report of the Joint International Observer Group: Malawi National Referendum, n.d.
Report to Parliament by the Electoral Commission: The Number of Parliamentary Constituencies and the Boundaries of each Constituency, Blantyre, 5 February 1994.
Public Affairs Committee, 19 and 22 April 1993, in Report of the British-Malawi Association of the General Council of the Bar, the Law Society of England and Wales and the Scottish Faculty of Advocates, 21 April 1993.
Micaletti, O. (1994), 'Report of Activities', 13 February-20 May 1994, UN Centre for Human Rights and UN Electoral Assistance Secretariat, Malawi, n.d.
Snead, Ted, Joint International Observer Group, interview, 12 May 1995.

Rights in Malawi: Report of a Joint Delegation of the Scottish Faculty of Advocates, the Law Society of England and Wales and the General Council of the Bar to Malawi, 17-27 September 1992.
Nekwazi, J. (1995), 'Chihana's Book on Leadership Style', New Voice, September, pp.7-14.
UN Electoral Assistance Secretariat (UNEAS) (1994), press release, 18 April.
UN Electoral Assistance Secretariat (UNEAS) (1994), press release, 20 May.

Notes

1. In 1992 Malawi had a GNP per capita of US$210, a life expectancy of 44 years, and an under-5 mortality rate of 223/1,000. Nearly half of its under-5s were stunted due to long-term malnutrition, nearly half its population did not have access to safe water, and less than half its ten year-olds were in school (UNICEF, 1995).
2. For instance, in the UDF, were Bakili Muluzi, who had been a cabinet minister and MCP General Secretary (1977-82) before his detention; Aleke Banda, in prison from 1980 to 1992, had been head of Press Holdings, the Young Pioneers, and General Secretary of the MCP. Chakakala Chiziya was an MCP Finance Minister in the 1980s and governor of the Reserve Bank, while Brown Mpinganjira, a journalist in the Ministry of Information, had been imprisoned in the 1980s. Edward Bwanali of the UDF had been MCP Southern Region Chairman. Other reform movement leaders included Kanyama Chiume, Foreign Minister in Banda's first government, later head of the Congress of the Second Republic (CSR) in exile in Tanzania; and Harry Bwanausi, head of the United Front for Multi-party Democracy (UFMD), formerly a senior MCP politician and minister.
3. Chihana was an Amnesty International Prisoner of Conscience when imprisoned for seven years in the 1970s for advocating trade union independence from the MCP and opposing one-party rule. He became Second Vice-President in Muluzi's government in 1995.
4. MCP, AFORD, UDF, Malawi Democratic Party (MDP), Malawi Democratic Union (MDU), Malawi National Democratic Party (MNDP), United Front for Multiparty Democracy (UFMD). The Congress of the Second Republic (CSR) registered too late to join the NCC.

10 Choosing 'The Freedom to be Free': the South African general elections of 1994

ROGER SOUTHALL AND MORRIS SZEFTEL

The cycle of watershed elections that took place in Anglophone Africa from 1989 climaxed with South Africa's first ever democratic elections in April 1994. The peaceful culmination of a liberation struggle, which for years many had feared would end in a bloodbath, registered not only a triumph for the democratic ideal but the resounding defeat of racism as an organizing principle of government. The ANC's convincing victory was a triumphant realization of its historic fight for democracy and gave it an overwhelming mandate to govern.

The elections successfully legitimated the democratic transition, yet that they were held at all was itself remarkable, a 'small miracle' (Friedman and Atkinson 1994). The strength and pervasiveness of the apartheid legacy shaped the political negotiations, affected their constitutional outcome and influenced the election results. The bitterness produced by apartheid, the incompatibility and obduracy of contending interests, and the brutality and violence unleashed by the decision to negotiate an end to white rule, all made a resolution as difficult as it was imperative. In contrast, the peacefulness and friendliness exhibited by voters at the polls did seem miraculous.

Yet the 'miracle' was only possible because the protagonists ultimately compromised. In particular, the ANC made fundamental policy concessions in order to reassure opponents, end deadlock and permit a transfer of power. And where serious voting irregularities threatened both the vote count and legitimacy of the elections, the parties accepted a questionable outcome in the interest of peace and progress. So fundamental questions of social justice and political power were left unresolved, and the elections were as interesting for what they did not settle as for what they did. As Mandela put it (1994: 751) after the elections: 'the truth is that we are not yet free; we have merely achieved the freedom to be free'.

Violent Negotiations and the End of Apartheid

Virtually from the beginning of a European presence in South Africa, racial domination defined political power. The National Party (NP) government, which took office in 1948, to defend and promote white (especially Afrikaner) interests, intensified this domination through its policy of apartheid. This it did with unusual vigour and success until the late 1960s when, with the democratic, non-racial opposition broken (its leaders in prison or exile), the economy booming as a result of vast western inward investment, and legal black political activity confined entirely to the 'Bantu homelands', its hegemony seemed unchallenged. Yet, in hindsight, this triumphal moment appears ephemeral for, from the early 1970s, waves of protest and violence, coupled with economic recession, progressively undermined the ability of the racial order to survive. By 1990, the government (now led by President F.W. De Klerk) accepted the need to end apartheid and to initiate a process of constitutional reform.

De Klerk's reforms were necessitated by the failure of the 'Total Strategy' which organized government policy between 1978 and 1989. Designed as a response to the revolutions in Angola and Mozambique, the tide of indigenous working-class militancy in the early 1970s, the Soweto uprising of 1976 and ZANU's victory in Zimbabwe in 1980, it combined institutional restructuring with an unparalleled use of force in both domestic and foreign policy. Regionally, it used destabilization of neighbouring countries (through economic and military pressure and support for terrorist clients) to attack the capacity of regional states to support the ANC or act independently of Pretoria. Domestically, it combined limited reform with massive state repression. Executive power was concentrated in the presidency and security apparatus under the State Security Council. All aspects of policy were militarized and unremitting violence employed against opposition. Alongside this, a tricameral parliament sought to align 'Indian' and 'Coloured' middle-class strata with the white state; urban local councils were intended to make the small black middle class stakeholders in apartheid; trade union reform sought to incorporate black labour into the regulatory framework of industrial relations; and legal distinctions were enshrined to divide permanent urban workers from migrant workers and the rural underclass.

In the event, the strategy inflamed rather than resolved the growing crisis. In the first place, the country was confronted by enduring structural problems arising from the changing nature of capital accumulation. Industrialization, which had originally underpinned apartheid, now produced new, if ambiguous, pressures for liberalization. At the same time, apartheid imposed high costs, low growth rates and general inefficiency (Moll 1991). By the mid-1980s, it had become difficult to see how a rate of economic growth could be achieved capable of reducing black poverty and so drawing the teeth of political protest. Economic problems also highlighted a deteriorating security position signalled by the end of the Reagan administration's 'blank cheque' for destabilization of the region. The end of the Cold War and of Soviet support for revolutionary solutions in Africa weakened Pretoria's international position, while destabilization and township violence fuelled demands for sanctions and disinvestment. In addition, the mounting cost of the military solution - perhaps as much as $500 million a year in Namibia alone - produced growing internal criticism. When the South African Defence Force (SADF) became militarily bogged down in south-western Angola in 1988, the belief that military diplomacy would suffice ended. In 1989, Pretoria finally pulled out of Namibia, twelve years after accepting UN Resolutions demanding that it do so.

Most important of all was the pattern of unending protest at home, particularly in the townships. Total Strategy had sought to contain the threat from trade union radicalism, Black Consciousness and the Soweto uprising, but in practice it escalated and widened conflict, uniting non-white communities and giving rise to a proliferation of grassroots organizations which re-created the struggle from below. Investors stayed away and western governments increased their pressure on Pretoria to seek dialogue and reconciliation.

By the late 1980s it was clear even to the government that repression was compatible with neither order nor growth. In such circumstances, it became necessary to release national political leaders from prison and ask them to restore order in return for negotiating a settlement. On 2 February 1990, President De Klerk announced that Nelson Mandela and other leaders would be freed, that 33 organizations, including the ANC, Pan-Africanist Congress and the Communist Party, would be legalized and their exiled cadres permitted to return to South Africa, that normal political activity would be permitted, and that negotiations would begin to create a common political society.

However, negotiation did not mean surrender, and whilst De Klerk's famous February 1990 speech indicated that a new constitutional order would have to recognize and protect fundamental individual rights, he also insisted that it would also need to accommodate the collective rights of 'national groups'. Any constitution which failed to do so would be 'inappropriate, even harmful' (*The Independent*, 3 February 1990).

Fundamental difficulties confronting negotiations

The dynamics of the negotiations which took place between 1990 and 1994 revolved around two major concerns. The first was an attempt by the ANC and the NP, the central actors in the transition, to forge a compromise which would marry South Africa's accession to majority rule to the guaranteed protection of minority rights. The second was their determination to secure support for such a settlement from across the political spectrum. This latter ranged through: the white political establishment, dominated by the NP but also including smaller, more liberal parties such as the Democratic Party (DP); extra-parliamentary and paramilitary organizations of the white far-right; parties from the existing tricameral legislature (organized around separate representation for whites, coloureds and Indians but excluding blacks); the governments of the 10 African 'homelands' (four of which were juridically independent) and a number of movements closely associated with their regimes, most notably the Inkatha Freedom Party (IFP) led by the KwaZulu chief minister, Mangosuthu Buthelezi; and, finally, those forces associated with the anti-apartheid struggle, notably the ANC, the SACP and the PAC.

Fundamental divisions remained on virtually every issue, not least between the NP and ANC. The former wished to limit the power any future majority government could exercise, so as to prevent it from using state power to reshape South African society, while the ANC sought to ensure that negotiations would result in a new order which went beyond the question of individual political rights to embrace social justice. The NP initially sought to defend white privilege, private property and communal interests by diluting the state almost to the point of abolition (Southall, 1991). The ANC, in contrast, wanted far-reaching reform to redress the legacy of racial inequality.

Mandela (1994: 692) subsequently characterized the government's initial stance as designed not so much as to concede as to secure the survival of white privilege:

> De Klerk ... did not make any of his reforms with the intention of putting himself out of power. He made them for precisely the opposite reason: to ensure power for the Afrikaner in a new dispensation. He was not prepared to negotiate the end of white rule. His goal was to create a system of power-sharing based on group rights, which would preserve a modified form of minority power in South Africa. ... he wanted to retain a minority veto.

On the other hand, redress of the most basic African grievances required a restructuring of both state and economy. For the ANC and its allies, a negotiated outcome which circumscribed the state's capacity for intervention in social and economic issues would inevitably preserve existing injustices. For business and the white community, the problem was one of achieving political and legal justice while protecting property and ensuring the operation of market forces. Polyani's (1944) argument that the function of the separation of powers in liberal democratic constitutions serves to exclude property rights from democratic control admirably summarized the ambitions of one side and the fears of the other.

Negotiation and violence

Given the distance between the two sides it was not surprising that the transition process between 1990 and 1994 proved to be difficult, protracted and punctuated by violence and conflict. Yet in the end a transition was achieved. That it was, was because the two main protagonists, the NP and state apparatus, on the one side, and the ANC, on the other, progressively shifted their efforts from negotiating about policy goals to finding 'technical' solutions, constitutional arrangements which permitted a transfer of power and an early election. The shift was difficult for both sides. In the end, however, they settled for a rapid political transition in which the NP gave up its control of government and conceded the issue of 'group rights' while the ANC accepted a political transition which postponed questions of social transformation. Endemic political violence and continuing economic contraction made it difficult to prolong the coexistence of a state with power but no authority and an opposition with authority but no power.

These changes of strategy came in three, overlapping phases. The first, dominated by 'talks about talks' and 'wars of manoeuvre', occupied most of the 18 months following the release of Mandela in February 1990. At this stage, the ANC linked the question of democracy to the issue of social justice, while the government adamantly insisted that reform should include 'group' as well as individual rights, 'power-sharing' instead of majority rule, and local rather than central power. The government sought to consolidate an alliance of whites, 'Coloureds', Indians and conservative black interests, in particular looking to an alliance with Inkatha to provide a powerful block of votes capable of challenging the ANC (Mandela, 1994: 692). It also sought to put pressure on the ANC to abandon radical allies and policies, and violence was employed against its supporters to weaken their loyalty. The aim was to restructure the ANC before negotiations began to restructure the state (Szeftel, 1991: 69). However, the strategy was undermined by revelations in June 1991 of government dirty tricks, death squads, slush funds to support Inkatha in its conflict with the ANC in Natal and on the Rand, and covert training of Inkatha members by the SADF.

Such revelations helped bring about constitutional negotiations, and the Convention for a Democratic South Africa (Codesa), convened in December 1991, opened a second phase of the transition. However, during the months which followed it proved impossible to sustain negotiations and violence simultaneously (Meredith, 1994: 43-9). The failure of Codesa to make progress, and the continuation of state violence against popular movements, provoked ANC 'mass action' campaigns of protest as the leadership bid to retain the confidence of its constituency. These, in turn, intensified conflict with various homeland functionaries (especially with Inkatha in KwaZulu and on the Rand, and with the regimes in Ciskei and Bophuthatswana) culminating in a massacre of ANC supporters at Boipateng on the East Rand in June 1992. This resulted in the ANC withdrawing from Codesa in protest at the state's orchestration of violence, thus bringing the talks to an end. The mass action campaigns continued and in the Ciskei capital of Bisho another demonstration ended in further killings in September 1992. Once again, reports implicated not only the homeland organizations but also the state security apparatus.

The crisis which followed alarmed both the ANC and the NP. From the government's perspective, coercion had not undermined the ANC-led alliance, producing instead increasing militancy from ANC and PAC cadres and, in the Eastern Cape, attacks on whites by the PAC-aligned Azanian People's Liberation Army (APLA). The NP's own supporters were increasingly insecure about the growing turmoil and were defecting in droves to the far right and to Inkatha. Capital was fleeing the country and the economy contracting. It was evident, too, that the government's homeland clients in no way constituted a viable challenge to the ANC; even Inkatha was forced progressively to abandon pretensions of being a national alternative and to fall back on its KwaZulu-Natal redoubt and appeals to Zulu ethnic identity (Szeftel, 1994a; 1994b). The state's tactics of combining coercion with negotiation had proved a two-edged sword.

For their part, ANC leaders were faced with a mounting death toll among their supporters, disillusionment among many about the lack of change, demands that armed struggle be resumed, and growing problems of controlling militants and 'self-defence units'. These problems became even more severe after the assassination of Chris Hani, one of the leading figures in the ANC, SACP and MK, in April 1993. Key elements of the leadership became convinced that a transfer of power had to be effected quickly to avoid further turmoil and possible loss of control of the process of change. In November 1992, an ANC document (*Negotiations: A Strategic Perspective*) argued for compromises which would overcome government delaying tactics, including the possibility of a government of national unity. Correspondingly, discussions within the movement gradually shifted from issues of transformation to questions about organizing for elections and winning power (*Interviews*, May, June 1993). This generated complaints that negotiators were 'selling out' but, for those involved in negotiations, the choice was less between structural reform and 'sellout' than between a transfer of power and continuing violence. Change had to be 'sustainable'; it was better to contend with an imperfect outcome than with a lurch to 'civil war'.

The crisis thus inaugurated the third phase of the transition, convincing both sides that a settlement was the priority. In April 1993 a Multi-Party Negotiating Forum (MPNF) met to negotiate a new constitution and not even Hani's assassination stalled the talks. Despite difficulties, progress was rapid; the skills and determination of the ANC and SACP representatives (led by Cyril Ramaphosa and Joe Slovo) were now reciprocated by an NP negotiator (Roelf Meyer) interested in negotiation rather than obstruction. Between April and November 1993, the conference agreed on: 27 April 1994 as the date for the election of a Legislative Assembly and nine Provincial Assemblies; proportional representation (PR) as a basis for elections rather than the first-past-the-post system used hitherto; neutral structures to oversee the transition, notably a Transitional Executive Council (TEC) to share executive authority with the government, and an Independent Electoral Commission (IEC) to run the elections; an interim constitution, including key principles binding on the Constituent Assembly which would frame the final constitution and which provided for a five-year, multi-party Government of National Unity (GNU) after the initial elections; an interim Bill of Rights, including fundamental rights to be included in the final constitution; and a timetable for the agreement of the latter and the holding of further general elections.

The interim constitution subsequently adopted also stipulated that the Constituent Assembly (composed of the National Assembly and Senate sitting together) should frame a new constitution by a two-thirds majority by the end of 1996. If such a majority could not be obtained, an amended text would have to be referred to a new constitutional court and, if need be, thereafter to a national referendum.

The shape of the interim constitution was the product of the need to put political transition before social transformation. Government and ANC negotiators thrashed out compromises and then 'sold' them to the other delegates. Both sides made important concessions. The NP agreed to a state with strong executive authority, dropped its demands for institutionalized 'group rights', and abandoned permanent 'power sharing', accepting instead the five-year government of national unity to be followed by majority rule. But the ANC made even more fundamental concessions. Apart from agreeing to postpone a majority government for up to five years, it proposed a 'sunset clause' which served to conciliate bureaucratic interests (including civil servants and police in the homelands) by guaranteeing jobs and pensions and, by agreeing terms for amnesty for politically-motivated crimes, it proffered freedom from prosecution to those many members of the security forces who had perpetrated actions beyond the law. It also accepted a diluted federalism and agreed that whilst the interim Bill of Rights would enshrine fundamental human rights, it should nevertheless be framed broadly enough to protect many vested interests (thereby downgrading the commitment to redistribution contained in the Freedom Charter).

It is important to stress just how much was achieved by the MPNF. The apartheid state, empowered to use terror and violence against its opponents in South Africa and beyond, was wound up by mutual agreement at the negotiating table. It was replaced by a constitution extending equal citizenship to all - regardless of race, gender or status - and limiting state power in law. However, the price of this was a transition which left the distribution of wealth and the repressive apparatus of the state largely intact.

The threat to the elections

PR was adopted in the hope of achieving an inclusive settlement. This, however, proved more difficult than finding agreement between the ANC and the government, largely because three distinct groupings saw themselves as losing heavily from the introduction of democracy. First, the homeland regimes of Ciskei and Bophuthatswana insisted that legal sovereignty gave them the right to resist reincorporation into South Africa. Second, the unbanning of the ANC had shattered previous claims by Inkatha to be a truly national movement and forced it back on to its ethnicized, Zulu base, from which Buthelezi launched a campaign for regional power, demanding autonomy within a loose federal structure for the whole of KwaZulu-Natal. And third, the white extreme-right, including also the parliamentary opposition Conservative Party (CP), proclaimed the right of Afrikaners to their own self-determination.

In all, seven of the 26 organizations at the MPNF, representing the white far-right and black beneficiaries of apartheid, opposed both the fixing of an election date and the agreement on an interim constitution. They felt marginalized by the agreement and resented the speed with which ANC and NP negotiators had pushed it through. They had earlier entered into a tactical association called the Concerned South Africans Group (Cosag) and subsequently allied under the name of the Freedom Alliance. Two of them, the CP and IFP, withdrew from the MPNF in protest against the setting of the election date.

Outside the talks, a collection of neo-fascist groups, of which the Afrikaner Weerstandsbeweging (AWB) was the largest, threatened insurrection if the democratization process went ahead. The CP, one of whose leaders was convicted of Hani's murder, defended apartheid and was the main opposition in the outgoing white parliament. It was defeated, however, in a 1992 referendum when the white electorate backed De Klerk's call for 'limited' reform. The Afrikaner Volksunie wanted a separate Afrikaner *volkstaat*. This was also supported by the Afrikaner Volksfront led by General Viljoen and a group of retired generals who sought to unite the far right. But the alliance proved fractious and undisciplined, finally dissolving after a disastrous military expedition by the AWB into Bophuthatswana.

The Afrikaner dissenters sought to mobilize white farmers and workers, many of them heavily-armed ex-soldiers and territorials, to oppose constitutional change. Many farmers prevented voter education drives reaching black workers on their farms. A spate of bombs at several ANC offices, culminating in a bombing campaign and numerous deaths in the Transvaal in the last fortnight of the election campaign, underlined the nature of the threat. There were grounds for concern about the relationship between the far right and the security forces, this increased by the failure of the police to arrest those responsible for terror against the liberation movements and by their partisanship during conflict in the townships. Nor were such fears assuaged when the AWB invaded the MPNF negotiations on 25 June 1993 and the police on duty made no move to stop them. There was also concern that large sections of the police and military might join an insurrection or fail to defend the new government against it.

Most homeland leaders either sheltered within the NP or made their peace with the ANC. Three did not. The Bophuthatswana and Ciskei governments announced their determination to resist 'reincorporation' into South Africa. Both regimes were deeply unpopular, extremely brutal and notoriously corrupt, and both feared reprisals for repressive policies and the loss of homeland patronage. But an even more serious challenge was posed by Inkatha which, in contrast to the other homeland parties, had a genuine mass base, had been (covertly) heavily armed by the state and had been embroiled in a bitter war (with tens of thousands of casualties) against the democratic movement since the early eighties. In 1990, Inkatha had shared with the NP a desire for strong local autonomy, in its case to defend its domain in

KwaZulu-Natal. While the NP later changed its perception of what could be realized, the IFP did not and bitterly resented what it saw as government betrayal. The IFP was part of a Freedom Alliance delegation in December 1993 which demanded greater regional autonomy and 'the right of self-determination' as the price of participation in (suitably postponed) elections. Although the ANC sought a compromise, it was not prepared to concede the degree of autonomy demanded or the right of secession.

IFP leaders chose to depict the TEC as ANC government under another name (even though all parties were represented equally on all TEC bodies). More ominously, they determined not to permit voting in KwaZulu-Natal and denounced the IEC as an ANC proxy. In the week before polling, some young IEC agents on a voter education drive were murdered in KwaZulu-Natal. The violence continued and, with less than three weeks to go, the failure of talks on the status of the Zulu monarchy and the collapse of international mediation efforts (the ANC refused to discuss a change of election date; the IFP refused to discuss anything else) raised tensions further. Yet Mandela (1994: 740) implies that this impasse ultimately forced the IFP to end its electoral boycott:

> I had agreed to international mediation, and on 13 April a delegation arrived ... when Inkatha was informed that the election date was not subject to mediation, they refused to see the mediators, who left without talking to anyone. Now Chief Buthelezi knew the election would take place no matter what. On 19 April Chief Buthelezi accepted the offer of a constitutional role for the Zulu monarchy and agreed to participate.

The breakthrough

A series of events and late concessions allowed the elections to take place on schedule. In the run-up to polling, the governments of Ciskei and Bophuthatswana collapsed when their civil servants became worried that they would lose salaries and pensions when central funding ended after the elections. Despite government obstruction, the TEC was able to send in forces to restore order and ensure their reincorporation and the holding of elections. An abortive invasion of Bophuthatswana by the AWB (to defend the Mangope regime against the TEC) also destroyed the unity of the far right, resulting in Viljoen leaving the AVF to form the Freedom Front (FF). Subsequently, the latter entered the elections in the hope of securing enough votes to justify the case for a *volkstaat*, thus marginalizing the other segregationist parties.

The possibility of insurrection nevertheless made the ANC concerned to ensure the loyalty of state personnel. In 1992, Joe Slovo expressed concern about the capacity of the white civil service, army and police to destabilize a new democracy and suggested the 'sunset clause' to provide for power sharing for a fixed term in order to commit the state apparatus to the transition (Meredith 1994: 57). Throughout the election campaign, Mandela called on ANC supporters to support the SADF and police. The tactic worked well enough: the army commanders are said to have warned the right that they would not support rebellion against a legal government and, after an explosion at Johannesburg Airport, 31 AWB members were arrested, bringing the bombing to a halt.

Finally, as noted, Inkatha abandoned its election boycott a week before polling. On 15 April, Archbishop Tutu and a group of senior clergy persuaded the King in Ulundi to urge all Zulus to stop fighting; that weekend saw the lowest death toll in Natal for almost two years. The weekend also brought overtures from the IFP to join the electoral process in return for constitutional guarantees for the monarchy. The IEC agreed that stickers could be attached to the bottom of ballot papers to accommodate the IFP and arrangements were made for the late acceptance of its lists of candidates.

Inkatha portrayed itself as having set aside its objections to save South Africa from war. In fact, the reasons for its entry extended beyond altruism. After the elections, the KwaZulu base of the IFP would cease to exist as a political entity, salaries to IFP and KwaZulu-Natal personnel would end, and the patronage base on which the party's power rested would disappear. By entering the political process, the IFP could hope to preserve this base by capturing the new regional assembly. Had it not rejoined the process, KwaZulu-Natal would have been ruled by an ANC regional government and the IFP would have faced oblivion or the need to resort to armed insurrection.

Equally important was the hostility which Inkatha's dissenting position incurred from the business interests it had always courted. The IFP had long presented itself as the friend of capitalism and opponent of ANC 'communism', and had been heavily supported by external western interests and by domestic capital for doing so. However, by now these elements had come to prefer accommodation with an ANC government to alliance with an IFP opposition. Although they disliked ANC plans for redistribution, businessmen wanted the stability that only a settlement could bring. Business provided the secretariat for Codesa and for the MPNF, contributed heavily to voter education and the IEC, and put its planes and offices at the disposal of efforts to resolve the ANC-Inkatha dispute. When Inkatha threatened the 1994 elections, capital was furious, and the editorials of *Business Day* and much of the English press condemned it. As viewed by *The Financial Mail* (29 April 1994), the transition had brought about a relationship between the political Left and business ... not far short of a partnership. One of the common aims has been to bring democracy to SA. If there had not been this relationship, the election would almost certainly not have taken place.

The General Elections

The elections required voters to cast two ballots to elect a National Assembly (reflecting both national and regional voting strength) and nine provincial assemblies. Seats were allocated by PR. The provincial assemblies would in turn elect a Senate. The seats available in each body are shown in Table 10.1. The Government of National Unity (GNU) would be headed by a President drawn from the largest party in the National Assembly, with Deputy Presidents drawn from parties obtaining 20% of the vote. Up to 27 Cabinet positions would be distributed proportionately between parties participating in the GNU.

Candidates were elected from party lists. Because this meant that they lacked a constituency structure, the election campaign focused on the meetings and rallies of national leaders and appeals made through media and posters. Since there was no voters' roll, the IEC could only estimate numbers expected in each area and allocate ballot papers to voting stations accordingly. Fears about state interference or political intimidation resulted in the presence of large numbers of monitors and observers drawn from a variety of national and international organizations. All voting stations were to have a (thinly-spread) police and military guard. Further, to protect voters against possible reprisals, the IEC decided to use ultra-violet ink, visible only under a special light, instead of the ink dye used elsewhere to prevent double voting.

Voting was peaceful and the total poll - over 19.5 million people - far greater than expected. This led to a number of problems. For a start, because of huge, uncharted population movements since the mid-1980s, some areas experienced a much higher turnout than had been anticipated. This resulted in many voting stations not having enough ballot papers or boxes while others had too many. In the end, the IEC had to extend the elections for two more days and to hurriedly print more ballot papers. There were also difficulties about identity documents and some evidence that different presiding officers interpreted the rules about what was a valid ID in different ways. There were also isolated attempts at sabotage: the IEC's main computer began to give inaccurate results during the counting (reducing the ANC vote), but this was corrected through the two backup computer systems; and there were reports that officials seconded from the government had withheld ballot books in warehouses, preventing voters from voting on the first two days. There were also cases of ballot forms being issued without the addition of the IFP sticker.

Table 10.1   National and regional representation under the South African interim constitution

Provinces	National Assembly: National List	National Assembly: Provincial List	Provincial Assemblies	Senate
Eastern Cape		28	56	10
Western Cape		21	42	10
Northern Cape		4	30	10
KwaZulu-Natal		40	81	10
Free State		15	30	10
North West		15	30	10
Eastern Transvaal		14	30	10
Northern Transvaal		20	40	10
PWV		43	86	10
National Totals	200	200		90

Notes:
1. 400 National Assembly MPs and members of the nine Provincial Assemblies elected by PR. 200 of the 400 MPs elected from party lists according to each party's share of the national vote.
2. The other 200 MPs elected from provincial party lists according to each party's share of the national vote in each province.
3. All members of the nine Provincial Assemblies elected from provincial assembly party lists according to each party's share of the provincial (second) ballot.
4. 10 Senators from each province, elected by each provincial assembly in proportion to the seats held by each party in that assembly.

There was much criticism of the perceived inefficiency of the IEC and of its inability to prevent widespread abuses. In particular, its inability to prevent parties from turning some of their strongholds into 'no-go areas' for opponents, and the difficulties of validating the honesty of elections in certain places, provoked strong condemnation from aggrieved parties. In all, over 500 allegations of electoral irregularities and vote rigging were made, the majority being settled by negotiation between the IEC and the political parties.

Most controversial of all was the strategy the IEC adopted in dealing with disputes where irregularities were so widespread that the very fairness of the elections were put in question. This was particularly so in KwaZulu-Natal, where the IEC stopped announcing the vote count while the parties negotiated their various objections and an outcome (Johnson, 1996: 334, passim). Ultimately, however, it is difficult to believe that a legitimate election could have been held without the IEC. It is unlikely that results processed by the state, as in the past, would have been accepted by all parties; and it was useful, in any case, for disappointed groups to be able to blame the IEC rather than each other. As Johnson (1996: 348) observes:

> Although the IEC has come in for its share of criticism ... there is no doubt that it played a crucial and valuable role. ... there is a great and continuing need for a body such as the IEC and ... the main recommendation of its report - that no future election ever again be conducted without a proper voters' roll - would obviate a good deal of the abuses which did take place.

Despite numerous irregularities, there was and remains a general consensus that most people managed to vote, and for the party of their choice, and that the final outcome offered a remarkably accurate reflection of the overall wishes of the electorate.

The outcome

Opinion polls in February 1994 had indicated 69% support for the ANC, 17% for the NP and 7% for the IFP (Johnson and Schlemmer, 1996: 76-8). The election produced a smaller landslide than predicted by these figures but a landslide nonetheless. The ANC obtained an overwhelming 62.6% majority nationally (Table 10.2) and in six of the nine regions (Table 10.3). The concerns of the white right were starkly demonstrated as the ANC obtained more than 75% of the vote in the former 'Afrikaner heartland' areas of the Eastern Cape, Free State, North West, and Eastern and Northern Transvaal. Only in KwaZulu-Natal and the Western Cape did the ANC lose the provincial elections. The results confirmed the ANC's stature among all classes and ethnic groups of the African electorate and also the status of Mandela as a symbol of integrity and national unity. Not even the proliferation of homeland parties and spoilers (one even took the initials AMC) was able to confuse or reduce ANC support.

Table 10.2   1994 South African election results - National Assembly

Party	Votes (1)	% Vote	Seats
African National Congress	12,237,655	62.65	252
National Party	3,983,690	20.39	82
Inkatha Freedom Party	2,058,294	10.54	43
Freedom Front	424,555	2.17	9
Democratic Party	338,426	1.73	7
Pan Africanist Congress	243,478	1.25	5
African Christian Democratic Party	88,104	0.45	2
Other Parties (2)	159,296	0.90	0
Total			400

Notes:
1. Votes refer to 'final' figures released by IEC in May 1994.
2. Other parties contesting the national list (each unable to win the roughly 45,000 votes needed for a seat): Soccer Party; Keep It Straight and Simple Party; Women's Rights Peace Party; Workers' List Party; Ximoko Progressive Party; African Muslim Party; African Democratic Movement; African Moderates Congress Party; Dikwankwetla Party; Federal Party; Luso-South African Party; Minority Front Party.

Both the NP and Inkatha did better than opinion polls had predicted. The NP came second, as expected, and managed to obtain the 20% needed to secure a Vice-Presidency for De Klerk. It also won the Western Cape, where it obtained 53.2% of the vote compared with the ANC's 33%. Inkatha won 50.3% in KwaZulu-Natal and 10.5% of the national vote overall, but its performance outside its Zulu heartland was poor, leaving it a regional force only. In the economic centre of the country, PWV (subsequently renamed Gauteng), it obtained less than 4%, despite the significant Zulu presence in the industrial workforce. Even in KwaZulu-Natal, its power base was decidedly in the rural (especially former homeland) areas. In Durban it obtained 85,787 votes (15.64% of the city total) compared to the ANC's 255,545 (46.58%) and in Pietermaritzburg it gained 69,521 votes (20.21%) to the ANC's 182,817 (53.13%) (Johnson and Schlemmer, 1996: 383).

Other parties had even more disappointing results. The FF obtained just over 2% of the total vote, and about 12% of the white vote, less than it had wanted in order to press its case for a *volkstaat*. The DP performed even more poorly, failing to obtain even 2% of the total. The NP's conversion to free-market economics in the late 1980s had eroded the DP's role as the main political mouthpiece of business, whilst the ascent of the ANC diminished its promise as an effective influence over post-election policy. Meanwhile, on social policy, white voters clearly preferred the NP's conservatism to the DP's liberalism. Lodge (1995: 489) has suggested that its failure to attract black middle-class voters may have stemmed from the nature of its negative campaign, centred on warning the electorate about the dangers of authoritarianism if the ANC won 'too large' a mandate: they did not grasp that, for most African voters, 'this was an election about hope, not about apprehension'.

Yet the most surprising casualty of the election was the PAC, with a mere 1.2% of the national vote and only 2% in its Eastern Cape base. This negation of its claim to an historic role as a liberation movement could be ascribed, above all, to its internal divisions and the peculiarly lifeless leadership of its president, Clarence Makwetu. Otherwise, the party lacked campaign funds; many of its younger APLA cadres rejected the decision to contest the elections; and its main slogan, calling for land redistribution, said little to the urban working class and may even have been inadequate for rural voters. Even in the Western Cape, where its leadership was unusually dynamic, it did poorly. Its prospects of ever recovering from this result depend now more on the ANC failing to meet mass aspirations than on anything it might do itself.

In the end, the election confronted voters with a choice between the apartheid past and the liberation movement. Seven parties directly represented homeland or communal interests. Two more (NP and FF) were reconstructions of the white power structure that had ruled since 1948. A tenth, Inkatha, straddled the divide, appealing both to ethnic identity and to whites in Natal.

Table 10.3   1994 South African election results - regional assemblies
(seats won/percentage of votes)

	EC	WC	NC	KZN	OFS	NW	ET	NT	G
Anc	48	14	15	26	24	26	25	38	50
	84.4	33	49.7	32.2	76.6	83.3	80.7	91.6	57.6
NP	6	23	12	9	4	3	3	1	21
	9.8	53.2	40.5	11.2	12	8.8	9.0	3.4	23.9
IFP	0	0	0	41	0	0	0	0	3
	0.2	0.3	0.4	50.3	0.5	0.4	1.5	0.1	3.7
FF	0	1	2	0	2	1	2	1	5
	0.8	2.1	6.0	0.5	6.0	4.6	5.7	2.1	6.2
DP	1	3	1	2	0	0	0	0	5
	2.1	6.6	1.9	2.2	0.6	0.5	0.6	0.2	5.3
PAC	1	0	0	0	0	0	0	0	1
	2.0	1.1	0.9	0.7	1.8	1.7	1.6	1.3	1.5
Acd	0	1	0	1	0	0	0	0	1
	0.5	1.2	0.4	0.7	0.4	0.4	0.5	0.4	0.6
Oth.	0	0	0	1*	0	0	0	0	0
	0.2	2.5	0.2	2.2	1.5	0.3	0.4	1.0	1.2
Tot.	56	42	30	81	30	30	30	40	86

Notes:
1. * Seat won by Minority Front with 1.3% of vote.
2. Regions: EC - Eastern Cape; WC - Western Cape; NC - Northern Cape; KZN - KwaZulu-Natal; OFS - Orange Free State; NW - North West; ET - Eastern Transvaal; NT - Northern Transvaal; G -Pretoria-Witwatersrand-Vereeniging (now renamed Gauteng).

Table 10.4 Racial composition of ANC and NP vote 1994

Racial group	% of total votes cast	% of ANC vote	% of NP vote
Black	73	94	14
White	15	0.5	49
Indian	3	1.5	7
Coloured	9	4	30

Source: Andrew Reynolds, 'The Results' in Reynolds, ed, *Election '94 South Africa: The campaigns, results and future prospects*, London: James Currey, 1994.

In the event, relatively few voters crossed the boundaries of the traditional racial divide (Table 10.4). 94% of the ANC's vote was from blacks and only 0.5 % came from whites. The NP did slightly better, attracting strong 'Coloured' (30% of its total vote) and Indian (7%) support but only 14% of its support from black voters - not surprisingly, given its readiness to foster 'Coloured' fears of black migrants in the Western Cape.

The ones that got away

As noted, the NP and Inkatha won control of the Western Cape and KwaZulu-Natal respectively. In the provincial election in the Western Cape, the NP won 53% of the vote, despite numerous efforts by the ANC to reassure 'Coloured' voters. The result was a direct legacy of apartheid policies which had excluded blacks from the region, preserving social provision and jobs for whites and 'Coloureds'. Black migration back into the area had led to the growth of squatter settlements with high levels of political and criminal violence, whilst their inhabitants now competed for jobs so that 'affirmative action had its most determined coloured opponents amongst employed working class people, historically the beneficiaries of National Party efforts to exclude African workers from the Western Cape' (Lodge, 1995: 476). Democratization thus threatened this hierarchy of relative privilege and frightened those most immediately affected by competition for resources.

Post-election polls indicated that De Klerk was as popular among Coloureds as among whites. In any event, the legacy of apartheid delivered the region to the NP.

In the provincial contest in KwaZulu-Natal, the IFP obtained just over 50% of the vote against only 32% for the ANC, a result which surprised many observers. Opinion polls in February 1994 had indicated only 18% support for Inkatha in the province (30% excluding 'don't knows') (Johnson and Zulu, 1996: 200-2). It had been expected that the IFP would dominate KwaZulu but that the ANC would obtain a majority through its support in Durban and southern Natal. The provincial result thus depended greatly on the count in the Durban Election Centre where the ANC was expected to enjoy a huge majority. Yet the IEC stopped announcing votes for almost two days and refused to indicate votes by district or even region. Allegations of massive rigging surfaced. In general the reports centre on four types of alleged fraud: the existence of 'non-gazetted' (illegal) polling stations; widespread under-age voting with forged identity documents; pressure on voters by homeland officials in polling stations; and stuffed ballot boxes. None of these allegations was admitted or proved. Instead, the IEC met with party leaders and negotiated a result. Johnson records that much of the dispute centred on 112 ballot boxes alleged to have been stuffed, presumably by IFP. In the end, the ANC conceded their validity and thus the final result. 'Acceptance of these figures also meant accepting IFP victory in KZN as a whole' (Johnson and Schlemmer, 1996: 295).

The decision, taken at the highest leadership levels of the party, provoked outrage among many ANC cadres in the province. The difficulty for the ANC was that, in an election without a voters' roll, where voters could move around the country, it was impossible to set aside results in one area without doing so everywhere else. It was necessary to have a complete national result or none at all. Inkatha, for its part, insisted that it would reject the election results in their entirety if the disputed ballots were not counted. In the end, despite the protests of their local leaders, the national executive decided to accept the 'negotiated count' in the interests of achieving a result that was generally accepted and that permitted a transfer of power. As Mandela (1994: 743) subsequently observed, the ANC had 'underestimated Inkatha's strength in KwaZulu-Natal, and they had demonstrated it on election day'. Ultimately, an IFP dominated government in KwaZulu-Natal had to be accepted as a price to pay for a legitimate election outcome.

The IEC and the Commonwealth Observer Group hailed the election as generally free and fair. The alternative would have been to hold another election, almost certainly producing even higher levels of violence. The outcome of this negotiated election permitted reconciliation and an acceptable transfer of power. If the result slightly over-represented whites (ANC lists included many while the NP did not have black MPs) it nevertheless produced a parliament of all communities. If women were under-represented as usual, there were nevertheless more women in parliament than ever before (not least because the ANC ensured that a third of its lists were female). Overall, the elections gave the ANC an unquestionable mandate to govern. Its 63% vote brought it close to the 66% of seats in the Constituent Assembly needed to write the final constitution. It would thus have the dominant voice in constitution-making but would need to win the support of other parties. This was welcomed by Mandela (1994: 743):

> Some in the ANC were disappointed that we did not cross the two-thirds threshold but I was not one of them. In fact I was relieved; had we won two-thirds of the vote and been able to write a constitution unfettered by input from others, people would argue that we had created an ANC constitution, not a South African constitution. I wanted a true government of national unity.

How well this GNU would work, and how it would provide for the consolidation of democracy, now became the dominant political question.

The Government of National Unity

Under the interim constitution, the new cabinet was required to consist of the President, the Deputy Presidents and not more than 27 ministers who were members of parliament.[1] These latter would be drawn from parties which, having obtained at least 20 seats, would be entitled to portfolios on a proportionate basis. Any appointment of Deputy Ministers would be according to the same formula. However, although the President was required to consult with the leaders of participating parties, he alone possessed the authority to appoint ministers and to allocate the particular portfolios.

With the particular outcome of the election, this formula saw the domination of the GNU by President Mandela, Vice-President Thabo Mbeki and 18 ANC (including SACP) ministers, with the NP (led by now Vice-President De Klerk) securing six, and the IFP just three ministries. However, the allocation to the conservatively 'safe-hands' of the NP of four major ministries (Finance, Mining and Energy Affairs, Constitutional Affairs, and Agriculture) was designed to appeal to both the 'business community' and the white electorate. The appointment of Buthelezi to Home Affairs was similarly calculated to be important enough to keep the IFP on board. In all such cases, non-ANC appointments were counter-balanced by ANC junior ministers.

In the months that followed, the ANC trod relatively softly and cagily down the path to state power. It remained continuously aware that South Africa's was not so much a completed 'negotiated revolution', as a revolution still very much in the process of negotiation. Its new ministers might head their departments, but initially at least, these were still overwhelmingly staffed by white, largely male and Afrikaner, NP appointees; the integration of former Umkhonto We Sizwe guerrillas and homeland armies' personnel into the new South African National Defence Force might be proceeding remarkably smoothly (albeit with some hiccoughs), yet the security forces initially remained commanded by a hierarchy of white officers schooled in the principles of the counter-revolutionary 'total onslaught' of the 1980s; and whilst the expectations of its own mass constituency focused upon the rapid delivery of jobs, housing and improved living conditions, the ANC appreciated all too well that unless it adopted an economic policy which emphasized production and investment over consumption and service delivery it would rapidly face 'a crisis of business confidence' and a rapid outflow of capital.

In these circumstances, the GNU was inevitably very much a hybrid beast. On the one hand, its official emphasis upon consensus sought to capitalize on the mix of genuine relief and pride with which the vast majority of South Africans had greeted the outcome of the election. Importantly, the undisputed legitimacy of the transfer ensured the collaboration of the machinery of state in its own restructuring, with 'old guard' civil servants pragmatically opting for loyalty to their new masters, and/or early retirement and their guaranteed pension payouts. More particularly, the ANC and the NP both reckoned that any precipitate collapse of their joint rule would be widely viewed as undermining the constitutional settlement and any prospect for much-needed economic revival. Similarly, the NP in concert with the IFP, was bound to the GNU by the fear that to leave the ANC in sole control of events would be inherently dangerous.

Yet by far the most potent constituent element of the glue which held the GNU together was the person of Nelson Mandela, whose outstanding generosity of spirit and magnetic appeal to national reconciliation rapidly earnt him the stature amongst whites which he had only previously enjoyed amongst supporters of the ANC. Indeed, in a poll conducted in April and May 1995, Mandela scored an approval rating of nearly 20% more than the GNU itself among all four racial groups and in each and every province (*Business Day*, 23 June 1995). The lead given by Mandela provided for a remarkably smoothly working cabinet. The spirit of cooperation was undoubtedly more than just rhetoric, and day-to-day collaboration between ANC and NP ministers (particularly) was, to all appearances, collegiate. Nonetheless, precisely because the GNU represented a compromise more than it did a genuine consensus, it was inevitably subject to a host of stresses. Significantly, these were related as much to intra-party as to inter-party tensions.

By far the most high profile difficulty which the GNU encountered was the strained personal relationship between Mandela and De Klerk, itself by far the most potent symbol of the new national unity. Whilst the latter was credited by the international community with having played a key role in securing the transition (to the extent of his sharing the 1993 Nobel Peace Prize with Mandela), his duplicity during that process (notably concerning whether or not he instigated, or even just had knowledge of, 'third force' efforts to destabilize the ANC) appeared to have earnt him the open distrust of the new President. Denied a significant role other than to publicly shore up the government, and increasingly aware of Mandela's personal popularity, De Klerk was compelled to endure a series of tongue-lashings and calculated insults which did nothing for his remaining authority within his own party. But, as in February 1995, when he threatened to withdraw the NP from the government over differences with Mandela over interpretations of who was entitled to post-apartheid amnesty, he was generally reduced by the political logic of his situation to re-affirming his party's continuing commitment to the GNU 'so long as the ANC adhered to the spirit of consensus which underlies our transitional constitution' (*Citizen*, 8 February 1995).

De Klerk's dilemma was simply that of his party writ large. The post-apartheid parliamentary caucus of the NP occupied a constitutionally ambiguous position which overlaid their own acute political ambivalence. In short, were they really part of the government or not? If, in theory, their commitment to 'power-sharing' rendered them active partners in government, in practice, the experience of the overwhelming majority of NP politicians (parliamentary and provincial, save in the Western Cape) was that of subordination to the ANC. They felt reduced to a neutered secondary role inside the GNU, whereas their status as the second largest party in parliament might have given them a more telling role as a vigorous opposition.

The divide within the NP was reflected, albeit less acutely, within the ANC, where internal tensions between the new party establishment and an emergent, 'populist' wing revolved around the costs of compromise and more especially, the way in which the GNU inhibited their capacity to deliver on election promises made to the party's mass following. Whereas the main body of ministers argued for more time, the necessity of careful policy formulation, the complications of transforming both the personnel and the machinery of the state, and the determinative facts of financial restraint, its radical critics lamented its tardiness and inefficiency, the continued neglect of its agenda as a result of its unwillingness to confront the NP and old guard bureaucrats and, overall, its failure to address the racial imbalances of apartheid.

These grievances were voiced most loudly by Winnie Mandela, the estranged wife of the President. In exasperation at what was deemed to be her indiscipline, the latter fired her from her post of Deputy Minister of Arts, Culture and Technology in early April 1995.[2] In the event, despite a widespread perception that Mrs. Mandela enjoyed significant support amongst the urban poor, any immediate challenge she represented was snuffed out by her subsequent ill-health, accusations of moral turpitude and poor strategic judgement (she was found guilty of involvement in the murder of a child activist in 1992, was accused of embezzling ANC funds in the same year and, later in 1994, was at the centre of a scandal involving illicit diamond dealings, and she then proceeded to split the ANC's Women League in February 1995[3]). Nor was her radicalism unambiguous. In concert with former Transkei leader Bantu Holomisa (then Deputy Minister for Environmental Affairs and Tourism, and considered a populist) she struck up an informal alliance with the Congress of Traditional Leaders of South Africa which, although formally aligned to the ANC at the time of the election, subsequently moved steadily towards a more conservative position which was less favourable to rural local democracy and more favourable to entrenched rights and powers for chiefs (Banks and Southall, 1996; and Maloka, 1996). For the moment, at least, the populists remained committed to staying within the mainstream. The masses had put the ANC into government, averred Mrs Mandela; the struggle now was to put them into power (*Sowetan*, 28 March 1995).

Fortunately for the GNU, without any concerted or independently weighty leadership the populist critique remained little more than an inchoate tendency, with minimal organizational basis within the party. Its cry that the government had failed the people was echoed by the PAC, which spurned an invitation by Mandela to join the government in mid-1995 (*City Press*, 25 June 1995). But, again fortunately for the GNU, that party and its fringe associates in AZAPO remained stridently committed to sloganizing and devoid of the leadership and imagination to cope with the new politics of the post-apartheid era.

Nor, in policy terms, did the IFP constitute a threat to the ANC's domination of the national agenda. Indeed, although holding an important ministry, Buthelezi remained an isolated figure within the cabinet, prompting occasional rumours that he was on the verge of quitting to assume the premiership of KwaZulu-Natal. Yet the IFP remained central to the longer term prospects for the new democracy, as its energies were directed to retaining control over its provincial base and continuing the constitutional battle to entrench its regional hegemony.

Provincialism and the making of a new constitution

The negotiation of powers between different levels of government constituted one of the most contentious issues of the transitional pact. The resultant decision to divide the country into nine new provinces, each with their elected government, was widely viewed as a retreat by the ANC from its previously trenchantly articulated centralism, and as having laid the seeds of an emergent federalism. Against this, the agreement embodied in the interim constitution left to the post-election political process and the courts considerable discretion as to how much autonomy the regions would come to have. More important, however, was how such developments would articulate with the making of the final constitution, which had to be completed within two years, and responsibility for which lay with the CA. At its inaugural meeting in May 1994, Cyril Ramaphosa (who had led the ANC negotiations in the MPNF) was elected to its chair.

A new feature of this constitutional landscape was the development of a regional politics which began to assume its own dynamic. This was composed of a conflicting mix of three major elements. The first was the sheer fact of diversity, imposed upon a manifest inequality of inheritance. Not only were two provinces (Western Cape and PWV, latterly renamed Gauteng) far wealthier than the rest, but they also shared with Northern Cape (the third best off) the advantage of not having to face the enormous structural and organizational problems imposed by the need to incorporate former bantustans. So acute were these latter in the Eastern Cape (which absorbed both Ciskei and Transkei), that Mandela's own intervention became required to quash both calls for the excision of the former Transkei as a separate province, and conversely, for central government to assume direct control of the area so as to reverse a collapse of public administration, service delivery and political order (Southall, 1996).

The second element was that the new regionalism imported a proto-federal politics into the heart of the ANC. Not only did ANC provincial governments begin to compete for resources,[4] but provincial legislatures provided a power base for ambitious politicians. The most notable example was Tokyo Sexwale, whose performance as Premier of Gauteng rapidly brought him a prominence unmatched by any but the most senior of the ANC's national ministers. Against this, the party hierarchy subsequently sought, in 1996, to resolve a bitter struggle within the Free State party between Premier 'Terror' Lekota and members of his Executive by removing the former to the Senate and replacing him by Dr Ivy Matsepe-Cassaburi, the chair of the South African Broadcasting Corporation.

The third, and final, factor was that the provinces' efforts to assume effective powers inevitably became entangled with the re-writing of the constitution and with battles within and between the three component parties of the GNU. Roelf Meyer, the Minister for Constitutional and Provincial Affairs, complained in June 1995 that an increasingly strained relationship between central and provincial governments was threatening good governance and undoing the potential virtues of a decentralized and responsive administration. Governments should temper their ambitions and work towards a more cooperative relationship between the first and second tiers (*Business Day*, 21 June 1995).

Meyer was taken as referring in particular to the belligerent postures adopted by the regional administrations of Western Cape and KwaZulu-Natal. Both governments sought to maximize their autonomy from the ANC-dominated central government. However, in the case of the Western Cape, this was complicated by a shifting balance of forces within the NP. De Klerk might be Vice-President and the national leader of the party, but Hernus Kriel, as Premier of this one province which the NP controlled, wielded more immediate power, patronage and influence. With no likely electoral prospect of securing control of other provinces, the dilemma facing the NP was the extent to which the regionalist aspirations of its Western Cape element should be allowed to trespass upon the potential for continued 'power-sharing' at the centre.

In contrast, the ambitions of the IFP were more naked. It inevitably interpreted the outcome of the 1994 election as confirming the need to shore up its ethnic defences against a now hostile central government. Buthelezi's participation in the cabinet consequently constituted more a strategic concern for his presence at the centre during the continued process of constitutional negotiation than any determined commitment to the GNU's non-racial, pan-South African, 'nation-building' project. As a result, inter-governmental relations between the central government and KwaZulu-Natal were conducted through a prism of intense ANC/IFP rivalry, charged by radically opposed visions of what the new South African state should be.

Two issues defined the outlines of what became an increasingly bitter conflict. The first was how far and on what terms the ANC might be able to gain access to the regional fortress. The second was the determination of the leadership of the IFP to wrest a virtual confederal status for KwaZulu-Natal out of the negotiations for a new constitution.

The electoral deal which had handed majority control of KwaZulu-Natal to the IFP did not entail the abandonment of its provincial wing by the ANC. This in any case was scarcely possible, for the truce imposed by the election soon collapsed amidst a resumption of political violence, as rural and peri-urban African communities again polarized into 'no-go' areas along party lines. The ANC therefore embarked upon what it considered to be a long-term strategy to weaken the IFP, initially by (successfully) encouraging King Goodwill Zwelethini to declare the monarchy above party politics, then by seeking to strike at the heart of Inkatha patronage by insisting that chiefs should be paid by central government, and not by the provinces. The Remuneration of Traditional Leaders Bill, passed in the face of IFP opposition, did not prevent the provinces from also paying chiefs out of their own resources, but made it clear that such expense would not be recoverable from the central budget (*Sunday Times*, 18 June 1995). The prospect of such an extra cost was not welcome to Premier Frank Mdlalose and certain IFP colleagues in the provincial executive who were rather more inclined to work cooperatively with central government than was Buthelezi and the cabal of advisers around him. But against this, the large body of the *amakhosi* (chiefs) viewed the ANC's move as no less repellent than its determination to bring democracy to rural local government which, by relegating them to the role of advisors to elected authorities, would strike at the base of the IFP's power (*Weekly Mail & Guardian*, 7-12 April 1995).

The defence of the *amakhosi* was basic to the IFP's effort to wrest from the central state constitutional autonomy over its fiefdom. The last minute deal which had brought it into the election included what the IFP considered to be a firm commitment by the ANC to post-electoral international mediation concerning outstanding constitutional issues. According to the IFP, these were the form of state (including the extent of provincial powers and fiscal autonomy, the right of provinces to make their own constitutions, and the definition of citizenship) and the status of the Zulu monarchy (*Business Day*, 23 February 1995). However, the ANC denied that it had agreed to such terms, and declined to refer these matters to international mediation, not least because that would circumvent the CA, which was committed to a participatory and transparent procedure for making the new constitution.

The immediate problem for the IFP was that with only 48 out of a total membership of 490 in the CA, its input could easily be swept aside. In contrast, international mediation promised a surer means of having its key demands dealt with, for in this way the IFP would become one of two equal parties to a dispute. When the ANC refused to go to mediation, therefore, the IFP walked out of Parliament and suspended its involvement in the CA, just as it had pulled out of the multiparty negotiations process at Kempton Park two years previously (*Sowetan*, 23 February 1995). Although it returned to parliament two weeks later, it gave notice that unless the ANC acceded to international mediation by early April, it would withdraw from the CA completely (*Sowetan*, 24 March 1995).

Even without an IFP presence, the debate within the CA assumed largely predictable lines. The NP argued both for an extension of enforced coalition rule and a federalism which would give greater powers to the provinces. On the other hand, the ANC argued for the right of a majority party to govern on its own, and for a framework that would prevent provincial and ethnic balkanization. By this it meant that whilst the central parliament should acquire greater capacity to lay down policy requirements and minimum standards, the provinces might be enabled to enjoy greater powers to implement laws that were currently administered nationally. A second chamber, moreover, might be more directly 'owned' by the provincial governments, and might be given greater powers to veto legislation emanating from the National Assembly.

Protest by the ANC's regions, notably Gauteng (*Business Day*, 28 March 1995), as well as the by the NP, DP and FF, that the proposals of the national ANC would weaken existing provincial competencies resulted in an eventual compromise to the effect that the legislative powers of the provinces would not be diminished under the new constitution. Furthermore, the ANC national executive subsequently came out in favour of a proposal to replace the Senate by a Council of Provinces which would have increased influence over national legislation (*Business Day*, 5 September 1995). However, not least because of forthcoming local elections, the different parties were not then ready to indicate the full extent of any major concessions they might be prepared to make.

In the meantime, the IFP had staked out its claim to what the ANC was to term a 'secessionist' provincial constitution (*Mail & Guardian*, 27 October - 2 November 1995). Proposing to rename the province the 'Kingdom' of KwaZulu-Natal, which it described as a 'sovereign member state of the Republic of South Africa', this called for the creation of a provincial army, exclusive provincial policing powers, and the right to refuse intervention by the SANDF. Furthermore, whilst providing for a major shift of legislative, financial and judicial competence towards the province, it proposed that neither the premier nor other members of the provincial cabinet need come from the elected legislature. Instead, the king would be mandated, albeit in 'consultation' with the leaders of the major parties, to choose a premier, who would then be empowered to exercise discretion in the choice of ministers. The legislature would be restricted to approving or disapproving a cabinet put before it. However, now that King Zwelethini had broken with the IFP, it now proposed that the regional parliament would possess the authority to withdraw the powers of or, *in extremis*, depose the king (*Mail & Guardian*, 15-21 September 1995; *Business Day*, 20 October 1995).

The IFP's proposals appeared to set the scene for a dangerous impasse, one that might be resolved by appeal to the Constitutional Court but, in the view of Steven Friedman, one which more urgently required a political solution (*Business Day*, 20 November 1995). However, whether this could be on terms acceptable to the IFP was made less likely by a resounding victory for the ANC in the local elections which took place throughout most of the country on 1 November 1995.

The structure of the local elections

Local government elections constituted a key second aspect of the transition, deepening the democratization process inaugurated with the general election. The promulgation of the Local Government Transition Act in early 1994 was followed by negotiations, throughout the country, between 'statutory' (largely white) and 'non-statutory' (largely black) interests, leading to the establishment of nominated non-racial transitional local councils (TLCs). These were charged, *inter alia*, with preparing to have themselves replaced by elected bodies after local government elections, which, under the interim constitution, were required to take place all over the country on the same day (subsequently fixed for 1 November 1995). However, these new councils would continue to be labelled 'transitional', not least because the voting system adopted would perpetuate power-sharing at local level until local government reform was completed under the terms of the final constitution.

There were three main categories of transitional structure: (i) transitional metropolitan councils (TMCs) established to govern six metropolitan areas (Greater Pretoria, Greater Johannesburg, Vaal, North East Rand, Greater Durban and Cape Town), each of which was to be sub-divided into metropolitan substructures, each with their own elected council; (ii) transitional local councils (TLCs), governing urban areas outside metropolitan areas; and (iii) rural district councils (RDCs) which would include both directly elected councillors and TLC delegates, as well as representatives of rural interest groups such as chiefs, farm workers and landowners. Elections for TLCs would elect 60% of seats from wards and 40% by PR. The Act further prescribed that black community areas should be allocated half the number of wards, with the other half split among historically white, Indian and coloured community areas. In TMC areas, meanwhile, voters would also exercise a third vote, for 40% of seats on the TMC, the other 60% of their seats being nominated by their substructures from their elected members on a pro rata basis. The system for RDCs was similar to that for TLCs, with some variation by province.

Unlike the general election, this highly complex set of arrangements required the demarcation of electoral areas and the registration of voters (a provincial responsibility). The latter process, particularly, caused much anxiety in the months leading up to the elections, as much popular confusion about why people were being asked to vote again within the space of eighteen months led to an initial very low rate of registration (necessitating an extension of the deadline of 28 April to 5 June, 1995). Ultimately, 73% of potential voters were estimated to have registered, although this varied considerably by province, ranging from an estimated high of 86% in Western Cape to a low of 63% in KwaZulu-Natal (*Citizen*, 16 June 1995).

Registration apart, the local elections ran into two major difficulties. The first revolved around demarcation disputes, notably concerning TMCs, as political parties sought to either include or exclude black areas within metropolitan substructure areas. By far the most significant of these concerned Cape Town, where the Provincial Demarcation Board's recommendations were rejected by the NP, which came up with alternative proposals. The essential differences were that the Board recommended six substructures, and the NP four; and whereas the Board proposed that the debt-ridden former black local authorities and squatter camps would be divided between the central and Tygerberg substructures, the NP insisted that they all be included in the former. Tygerberg would thereby be preserved as a white, NP homeland and spared the pain of paying for the upgrading of black areas. When the central government then stepped in to quash this gerrymandering by passing amendments to the Local Government Transition Act, the provincial government opted to contest the overruling in the courts, thereby rendering it impossible to hold elections in Cape Town on 1 November (*Business Day*, 15 June 1995).

The second problem concerned KwaZulu-Natal, where the resistance of IFP chiefs to the threat of local democracy also forced the postponement of the poll. Their collective weight had been tirelessly mobilized by Buthelezi in rallies staged throughout the province, in rural and urban areas, following the general election (*Weekly Mail*, 3-9 February 1995). This strategy denied territorial access to a demoralized regional ANC and was designed to win concessions for the IFP in the CA; in February 1995, IFP chiefs threatened to wreck local elections unless the ANC agreed to international mediation of the dispute over the status of the Zulu Kingdom (*Sunday Times*, 5 February 1995).

Such were the difficulties confronting the ANC in the region after a decade of violence and the seeming shift of white and Indian voters to the NP that, had the election been held, some observers felt it probably would have faced widespread defeat (*Business Day*, 18 May 1995). It therefore probably welcomed the decision that elections would be postponed because the Demarcation Board was unable to resolve the issue of whether tribal land adjacent to Greater Durban should be incorporated into the TMC, and the provincial government was unwilling to have staggered elections (*Sowetan*, 24 August 1995). Were it to gain time, the ANC seems to have reckoned, it might gain opportunity to further encircle the IFP constitutionally, to stiffen its regional party organizationally, and to exert maximum pressure upon the chiefs to force a free election.

The outcome of the local government elections

Predictions that the ANC would suffer a setback, with disillusioned voters taking revenge upon it for perceived failure to deliver the goods after its eighteen months in government, were confounded when it secured roughly 69% of the vote and outright majorities in 231 of 510 councils. Winning virtually everywhere it was expected to, the ANC was also encouraged by its support in the Western Cape (exclusive, of course, of Cape Town) where it won 34% of the vote and 306 council seats compared to 33% and 292 seats won by the NP (independents and non-party groups securing the balance).

Although it performed poorly in the Western Cape, the NP otherwise maintained its support, securing some 20.5% of the vote overall. It was disappointed, though, not to outflank the FF, which increased its vote to 5% (compared to 2.2% in 1994), apparently by capturing ground from the CP which, having opted to contest the elections, won only a handful of seats. With the DP (up from 1.7% in 1994 to 2.5%) similarly reclaiming lost territory among its English-speaking middle class voters in Gauteng, the biggest loser was the PAC, which registered another dismal performance (1.7%), losing even in its supposed strongholds in the Eastern Cape. Meanwhile, with no election taking place in KwaZulu-Natal, the IFP was a virtual absentee, and its regional status was confirmed by its inability to secure more than just 0.5% of the vote. (*Sunday Independent*, 5 November 1995; *Sunday Times*, 5 November 1995; *Business Day*, 8 November 1995).

Comparison between the 1994 poll and the local elections is dangerous. However, the overall conclusions were easy to draw. The dominance of the ANC, so forcefully expressed in 1994 was assured in the local elections; the NP, despite its troubles, managed to hang on to its white support but appeared unable to mark out a political terrain beyond it; and whilst the FF emerged as the pragmatic champion of a small Afrikaner right, the DP demonstrated little ability to expand beyond its traditional base in affluent, white suburbia. Any progress the minority parties might make in the future would require a major realignment of forces to construct a non-racial, centre-right alternative to the ANC.

Conclusion

As we noted at the outset of this essay, the general elections of 1994 brought South Africa what Mandela described not as freedom but as 'the freedom to be free' (1994: 751). For all the problems they encountered, there was little doubt that the overwhelming majority of South Africans voted for liberation and democracy. History may even judge that the irregularities of the elections, by forcing the parties to negotiate an outcome, bound their leaders together in a commitment to this political transition. Certainly, for all that the crisis in KwaZulu-Natal continued, the developments which took place after the election indicated a remarkable degree of settling down to 'normal politics'. This was subsequently to be confirmed by the negotiated conclusion of the final constitution in late 1996, and the related decision by the NP to withdraw from the GNU and unambiguously assume the tasks of opposition.

Yet it cannot be stated with any certainty that democracy inaugurated can be consolidated easily. A daunting agenda remains to be confronted. Issues of economic and social justice must inevitably outlive the euphoria of 'negotiated liberation'. The ability of the government to satisfy popular demands whilst promoting economic growth has so far been limited by inherited economic structures and negotiated political compromises. It remains necessary to develop electoral procedures and political arrangements that can withstand the organized irregularities and threats of violence of 1994 and to build state institutions that mirror the democratic moment of the elections of 1994 and 1995 rather than the apartheid state and its functionaries. As Lodge (1994) has observed, the challenge to South Africa is whether such institutions can be evolved from 'the formulaic prescriptions of liberal constitution-making' which have so far dominated the transition.

Notes

1. Subsequently, following the surprise resignation of Finance Minister Derek Keys, a fourth amendment to the constitution in September 1994 allowed for the addition of one further minister who was not a member of parliament. This enabled Mr Chris Liebenberg, who was deemed to enjoy the trust of the business community, to replace Keys in the Finance portfolio on a non-party basis.

2. Apart from the personal cost, this move involved Mandela in a political embarrassment, as his wife successfully challenged a first dismissal (in late March) on the grounds that it had failed to observe certain constitutional technicalities. She therefore had to be rehired, so that she could be legally (re-)fired.

3. Led by Adelaide Tambo, 11 senior members of the Women's League resigned from its Executive in February 1995 in protest against the allegedly autocratic and unaccountable behaviour of Mrs Mandela, who had been elected the organization's President in 1993 (*Sunday Times*, 12.02.95).

4. For instance, Northern Cape premier Manne Dipico, described the allocation of 1.6% of national revenue to his province for the 1995/96 financial year as 'laughable', and as perpetuating the skewed allocation of resources to the richer parts of the country (*Business Day*, 14.09.95). He was protesting against a provincial funding formula, presented by the Financial and Fiscal Commission, which would increase Gauteng's share from the national fiscus whilst giving all three Cape provinces proportionately less (*Business Day*, 06.09.95).

11 Conclusion: false dawn or democratic opening?

JOHN DANIEL AND ROGER SOUTHALL

These pages have reviewed mixed experiences in the recent electoral history of Anglophone Africa. On the one hand, the round of elections which began in 1989 in Namibia and inaugurated regime changes in central and southern Africa, culminating in the demise of apartheid and the democratic transition in South Africa, represented a definitive shift away from authoritarianism (whether in the form of military junta, single-party state or racial autocracy) towards some form of pluralist democracy as the normative basis for political rule in Africa. Set against the alternative political scenarios which Szeftel noted in the first chapter - predatory elites using the coercive force of crumbling states to repress and plunder and/or the actual collapse of such states into warlordism or communal violence - the democratic impulse which the elections examined in this volume represent is an impressive achievement indeed.

Yet, against that, the medium-term results have not been wholly auspicious. In Nigeria, the result of the 1993 presidential election was overturned and democratic transition blocked. The Abacha regime which followed the aborted 1993 elections introduced not only high levels of repression and state coercion but also the progressive destruction of a whole range of institutions and organizations (parties, intellectual currents, voluntary associations, state structures) which might later support a restoration of democracy. With Abacha's death, Nigeria enters a dangerous period of uncertainty, its new rulers caught between the growing certainty that, on the one hand, military repression cannot be sustained indefinitely and, on the other, that the basis of democratic society is not readily available to take over. In Kenya, an authoritarian regime survived a return to electoral competition, buoyed by the inability of opposition elements to combine; in the years that have followed, the old order has entrenched itself further and increasingly plundered both state and economy. In Zambia, a successive election in 1996 seems to have called into question most of the democratic advances celebrated in 1991. In Lesotho, new-born democracy has been imperilled by the

238

continuing power of the military in a fragile state. And in Malawi, despite a constitution which formally prevents the derogation of civil liberties and human rights, democratically-elected regimes have shown an ambiguous commitment to democratic values and to the rules of the game. Only in Namibia and South Africa did it seem that democracy remained firmly on track,[1] albeit even there under the aegis of emergent party systems wherein the dominance of post-liberation ruling parties seems unlikely to be challenged in the foreseeable future.

After the initial flush of optimism that the 'third wave of democracy' had reached Africa's shores, there is now a growing sense of resignation in many quarters that the tide has ebbed and that, throughout the continent, the problems of post-colonial instability are reasserting themselves. From a broader perspective, such doubts stem from a growing belief that this third wave of democracy (preceded, according to Huntington, by first and second waves from 1828 to 1926 and from 1943 to 1964 respectively), which was inaugurated by the overthrow of the Portuguese dictatorship in 1974, is over. Liberal democracy, and political freedom more generally, argues Diamond (1996: 31), is no longer expanding, and its quality in many third-wave countries has begun to deteriorate. Nor, for the moment, is there any prospect of the world's most powerful and influential authoritarian states (China, Indonesia, Iran, and Saudi Arabia) themselves undergoing a fundamental democratization that might give renewed impetus to the process elsewhere.

From a narrower perspective, doubts about democratic prospects in Africa stem from a certain boredom with the continent's problems (coups, corruption and economic crises) in influential Western policy circles, and from a profound 'Afro-pessimism', which views the continent as increasingly marginal to world developments. Africa, it is said, no longer plays a substantial role in the international division of labour, whilst the end of the Cold War has seen a precipitate decline in its politico-strategic importance. 'Economic crisis and marginalization on the one hand, and political weakness on the other - are magnified by interrelated social, health, ecological, and infrastructural crises' (Callaghy 1994: 134). In such a context, it will be difficult for democracy to survive and, even though it is likely that there will be cycles of regime change, the 'bedrock political form will remain weak, authoritarian, clientelist, and inefficient', heralding the spectre of anarchy (ibid.: 143).

In such a situation, it is likely that Western governments will worry less about how democratic African regimes are and more about whether or not they are committed to economic reform. Better for Africa to follow East Asia, they will reason, where economic development has laid the groundwork for subsequent democratization; where, since 1945, 'major transformations have most frequently taken place under authoritarian regimes'.

For all the difficulties associated with democratization in Africa, we do not endorse this outright pessimism. A careful reading of the case studies in this book indicates that considerable gains were made during the recent era, and that these will not be easily negated. We number amongst them the following.

First, the recent round of elections re-affirmed the right and desire of ordinary Africans to choose their own rulers. No-one who witnessed the steely determination of voters in countries like Lesotho and South Africa to sit for hours in extremes of temperature to cast their ballot, or their excitement and satisfaction at the moment of choice, can doubt the importance which they attached to this act. There was not always a depth of attachment to, or understanding of, the niceties of liberal political culture, yet there appeared to be a more solid, popular basis for anti-authoritarianism. Reversions to dictatorship cannot be discounted, but it seems (at the very least) that today's rulers will find it that much more difficult than did their post-independence predecessors to abandon the outward forms of multi-party democracy. In recently democratized African countries, a demographically younger population has learnt anew the importance of the franchise. Civil society remains weak, yet groups such as trade unions, professional associations and non-governmental organizations (NGOs) played an important role in dislodging authoritarianism.

Second, associated with these elections (even in Nigeria, where there was a deliberate effort to craft a two-party system spanning North and South), there is a renewed appreciation of the importance of institutions for engineering and maintaining domestic political peace. The attempted or actual displacement of dictatorial regimes saw concerted constitutional negotiation and debate, with a new emphasis on the importance of the rule of law and constitutional protections. If President Moi continued to manipulate the remains of the inherited Westminster system to his advantage in Kenya, the counterpoint was the adoption of a final constitution in South Africa (in 1996), which is generally reckoned to be amongst the most democratic in the world and to impose significant checks upon the executive. For all that there will be backsliding, constitutionalism in South Africa appeared to be based on reasonably firm bedrock, in particular with regard to the subordination of the military to civilian power, a differentiated and relatively advanced economy, a degree of decentralization of power from the central state to the provinces, an independent media and, not least, a relatively developed and varied civil society.

Third, with the collapse of African marxisms and socialisms, there was a shift away from utopianism amongst intellectuals towards a more pragmatic assessment of the purposes of politics. From this perspective, there was a growing recognition that democracy is a process rather than an end state. There was, in short, a greater awareness that democracy must be deepened; in Diamond's terms (1996), that it must go beyond a minimalist notion of electoral democracy (implying uncertain electoral outcomes, whereby victory cannot be assured to one party in perpetuity), to the more expansive realization of liberal democracy (entailing extensive protections for individual and group freedoms, pluralism and space for the organs of civil society, accountability of the executive to the legislative and judicial powers, and the subordination of the military to civilian control).

For a whole host of historical reasons that do not need to be elaborated, the recognition of the distinction between electoral and liberal democracy ran deepest in South Africa, where individual liberties were previously so grievously abused and where, as in no place else throughout the continent, there were potentially solid counterweights to government. Indeed, not just because of South Africa's enormous economic importance regionally but also because of the symbol of aspiration which it holds out to a continent historically held in thrall to foreign power, the deepening of democracy in that country seems likely to be critical to the strength of democracy elsewhere. If the model fails there, so may efforts to emulate it. The prestige of democracy in Africa is tied to its success in South Africa where, fortunately, the prospects for consolidation are for the present underpinned by modest economic growth and continuing commitment by all key elites to democratic rules.

Fourth, contrary to Afro-pessimists who (seeing themselves make a virtue out of necessity) incline to argue that Africa must ape East Asian authoritarianism, we argue a likely positive association between democracy and development. Each in turn enhances the possibilities of the other. Based on a review of the survival and death of political regimes in 135 countries since 1950 (or their year of independence), Przeworksi et al. (1996: 41) conclude that there is 'no income level at which democracies become more fragile than they were when they were poorer'. The fragility of democracy at low levels of economic development flows from vulnerability to economic crisis. 'Conversely, economic growth is conducive to the survival of democracy' - especially where income inequality is declining over time (ibid.: 42-3). In short, whereas in post-independence years even well-intentioned rulers such as Nyerere credibly subordinated liberal freedoms to development, no such justification can be accepted now. Authoritarianism has lost any developmental legitimation.

Finally, for all the many arguments that democracy is unlikely to survive in Africa because of the fragmented nature of so many states, we follow Diamond[2] in suggesting that what is basic is the commitment to democracy by elites as their least-worst option. South Africa constitutes by far the most advanced case of an 'elite pact' in Africa, but Cammack describes a not dissimilar situation in Malawi. In contrast, democratization in Nigeria was cut short by the failure of a potential elite pact, which would have institutionalized a bargain between the North and the South of that country. Yet the possibility, and opportunity, were there for the taking, indicating that democratization is more than the outcome of ineluctable historical forces. More usually it is brought about by conscious historical agency. This suggests the need for an activist approach to democracy in Africa.

The Case for Activism

There is widespread agreement that the return to electoralism in Africa was greatly influenced by the end of the Cold War and by a renewed emphasis on the part of Western diplomatic and financial powers on the need for human rights and 'good governance'. The changing international climate compelled internal rivals for power to re-assess their options and for authoritarian regimes to risk their survival at the polls. The preceding essays demonstrate conclusively that these external pressures were not definitive for, in all the cases examined, internal pressures shaped the momentum and dynamic of change. Moreover, in countries such as Nigeria and Kenya, blatantly authoritarian regimes survived despite all the pressures directed from abroad. Nonetheless, the shift towards democracy globally, and the imposition of pressures for democratic reform by external governments and institutions, proved critical in assisting internal democratic struggles. Equally, they may also prove vital for the survival of democracy, since 'international conditions predict regime survival better than does the level of development' (Przeworski et al.: 43). For some considerable time, it is likely that the maintenance of a democratic trajectory in Africa will depend on external support and pressure to ensure that reforms do not founder in the face of economic difficulties, internal conflicts and the temptation to resolve problems by coercion.

Yet this is worrisome, for there are clear indications that the contemporary global impulse towards democracy is weakening, that it may even be possible that 'the third wave of democratic expansion has come to a halt' (Diamond 1996: 31). In Africa, where much of the excitement which accompanied the election cycle in the early 1990s has evaporated, the international community s less united and less supportive of democratic struggles and reforms. States like Uganda and Ghana, which have earned accolades from the international financial institutions for economic reform, feel less pressure to democratize. Talk about 'good governance' moves away from political to economic indicators, increasingly confined to the institutional requisites for sound 'macroeconomic management' and an 'enabling environment' for freer markets (Young, 1996: 62).

Even more significantly, the fragile process described in this volume may well be threatened by the crisis unfolding in central Africa in the latter part of the nineties. The countries considered in this book lie, for the most part, in eastern and southern Africa. To their north and west, rather different scenarios have been unfolding. In countries like Sudan and Somalia, the institutional decay of authoritarian states was succeeded not by democratization but by warlordism and predation. In the Horn of Africa, the end of the Ethiopian empire was followed by conflict over borders and territory. In east and central Africa, the collapse of the state in Rwanda and Burundi, in the aftermath of communal mass murder, was followed by the displacement of large populations and continuing violence. This in turn contributed to the destabilization of the corrupt Mobutu regime in Zaire and the armed conflict which saw its replacement by the Kabila government. The latter quickly demonstrated that it preferred to concentrate on consolidating its military hold on the country and meeting the patronage demands of its leaders rather than on negotiating with its opponents to initiate institutional reform and democratic structures. Not surprisingly, this stance resulted in renewed fighting as contending factions fought over the distribution of spoils. More alarmingly, the military forces of Angola, Zimbabwe, Namibia, Uganda and Rwanda were drawn into the Zaire crisis during 1998.

Political and military turmoil throughout the region, a worsening refugee crisis, and continuing state crises in Sudan, Somalia, Rwanda, Zaire and Congo-Brazzaville, as well as a continuing insurgency in northern Uganda, place the emphasis on security rather than democracy. Western governments, anxious to avoid expensive and politically risky peacekeeping operations, are likely to opt for stability and 'strong men' where they can find them. In the process, policies to promote democracy (themselves not easily defined or prioritized) may fall prey to the 'imperatives' of *realpolitik*. From the Western perspective, Order may be All.

In this context, the consolidation of democracy in those countries in Africa which undertook transitions assumed greater importance. Five of the seven cases reviewed in this book, the most successful ones, are located in southern Africa. In addition to the countries dealt with here, multi-party democracy seemed well established in Botswana, while both Mozambique (after a relatively successful election at the end of a long civil war) and Angola were somewhat reluctantly edging towards peace, and with it the possibilities of democratic renewal, at the end of the decade. Moreover, at the time of writing, there were periodic popular pressures upon royal absolutism to concede democratic elections in Swaziland and upon the Zimbabwe government to allow a greater democratic voice. Despite the crisis in central Africa, there was some basis for hope that southern Africa might constitute an area in which democratic progress could be sustained.

Yet dangerous contra-indications were also evident. The southern sub-continent remained awash with small arms as a legacy of previous struggles in the region and war and disorder to its north created the possibility of an inflow of yet more, the result of arms smuggling across porous borders. Such turmoil might generally strengthen forces hostile to democracy, whether in the form of mercenary groups flown in to prop up local dictators or local mafias profiting from arms trading. Disorder and upheaval might also increase the political weight within democracies of local militaries, and within South Africa particularly, of a largely unreconstructed arms industry, already versed in the mechanics of breaching sanctions and flouting international law. The involvement of the South African security apparatus in illegal activities, as part of its counter-insurgency and destabilization strategy during the last decade of apartheid, left it with a capacity for extra-constitutional intervention against political forces it opposed. Whether that capacity is matched by an inclination to undermine democratic change has yet to be tested.

At this difficult conjuncture, the democratic achievements in southern Africa are coming under strain. Diamond (1996: 35) has warned that the 'overriding imperative for the long-term global advance of democracy is to prevent its near-term recession into a new reverse wave'. Democracies must be consolidated and deepened, but consolidation will only likely take place if major crises can be avoided and overcome and effective governance be provided. Consequently, he stresses the greater importance of the established industrialized democracies not only demonstrating the moral and practical superiority of their political systems, but of 'their increasing use of pressure and conditional assistance to promote democratic development around the world'. Diamond's concerns are echoed also by Munslow and Ekoko (1995: 172) who argue that

> Democracy costs money, not least at the initial stage of its implementation. Inevitably without the necessary means no sustainable genuine participatory democracy is possible. Thus the call for democracy made by the North,

without providing adequate support to help create a viable civil society, the seedbed for democracy's growth, is simply to acquiesce to nominalism and promoting the fad of the moment. The dilemma is that without some form of participatory democracy, there is little hope of alleviating poverty or achieving sustainable development. Without development, political instability is more likely and this in turn increases the risk of the re-emergence of authoritarian regimes.

This is in line with our argument in chapter 3 that - for all its ambiguities - the international monitoring of elections should remain an important prop to the democratization process, even if it is inevitable and praiseworthy that the big international organizations should hand over (yet not abdicate) many of their monitoring responsibilities to local bodies. But Munslow and Ekoko stress, too, the need for strengthening civil society, for 'people's empowerment'.

Viewing it as 'a set of organizations, associations and communities that are not directly involved in the exercise of power and who can provide a balance to power elites', Munslow and Ekoko stress the heterogeneity of civil society. Relationships between such groups and political elites may be cooperative or conflictual, depending upon their interest. Contrary to some contemporary views of 'civil society' as representing a general interest, or as embodying participatory democracy, it is made up of contending, special interests. Nonetheless, the complex of such organizations can serve to counterbalance the state machinery and ruling elites, thereby promoting representative democracy (ibid.: 174).

The viability of this civil society in contemporary Africa is particularly fragile and uncertain. A post-apartheid funding crisis in South Africa, for instance, affected NGOs when foreign donors withdrew their support and funnelled their aid through the new government's Reconstruction and Development Programme. This threatened the very survival of many of these organizations. The problem was later alleviated, to some extent, by the government itself establishing a machinery for its own, foreign and private-sector assistance to be channelled to NGOs (James and Caliguire, 1996). Such a development demonstrated the problem in the starkest terms. On the one hand, government assistance to NGOs, whilst welcome in the short term, raised questions about the autonomy of much of civil society from the state. On the other hand, a civil society dependent on western donors for handouts raises very different questions about autonomy. The autonomy - and hence future as a democratic force - of 'civil society' thus rests heavily on the financial resources it can command. Worryingly, the financial condition of most NGOs has deteriorated under the pressures of structural adjustment

(Gyimah-Boadi, 1996). It indicates to Western powers who preach democracy and African democrats alike, that African democracy cannot be purchased on the cheap, nor can it succeed in international isolation. The case for extensive external support is compelling. The problem of how it is to be provided without undermining the development of an autonomous democratic society is equally compelling - and more difficult to solve.

False Dawn or Democratic Opening?

For Afro-pessimists, the recent democratic awakening in Africa constitutes a false dawn. For them, apart from a few exceptional cases, the pre-conditions for democracy do not exist. The determination by democratically-elected governments, to hang on to power in subsequent elections, harkens back to the post-independence collapse of constitutionalism and presages a reverse wave. Democracy in Africa, if it arrives at all, will only follow a long process of development fostered or accompanied by authoritarian rule.

A more nuanced, scarcely Afro-optimist, but certainly more measured view, suggests that the reality is likely to prove more complex and contradictory. Young (1996: 67) pronounces the interim balance sheet on democratization in Africa as mixed yet mildly positive. There are likely to be backward steps, yet in most countries which recently experienced competitive multi-party elections, there has been change for the better which is likely to persist: the press tends to be freer, there is greater respect for human rights, and there is more concern for the rule of law. This is undoubtedly the case in all the countries examined in this volume, save Nigeria. Even in Kenya, those opposed to the government enjoyed a greater democratic space in the nineties than they had done a decade earlier. If, in Africa, the consolidation of democracy fell significantly below the level attained by some new democracies elsewhere, there was nonetheless 'slow, halting, uneven, yet continuing movement' towards polyarchy.

We adopt Young's conclusion here. Civilian and military autocracy has failed. Democracy has yet to prove that it can succeed. Yet, as the century drew to a close, there seemed no alternative, no other credible way forward. For many African countries, the fragility of the post-colonial order was such that the alternative to democracy was (and remains) not authoritarianism but the collapse of the state itself. As the case studies in this volume show, wherever they were given the right to choose, African citizens voted for democracy.

Notes

1. Recent moves in Namibia to amend the constitution to allow President Nujoma to serve a third term indicated that serious problems of succession had yet to be resolved. In South Africa, democratic institutions had yet to negotiate Mandela's retirement in 1999. Moreover, violence continued in Kwazulu-Natal in 1998, crime was seemingly beyond the capacity of the police to control, and a number of corruption scandals pointed to pressures to use the state for personal accumulation as elsewhere in post-colonial Africa.
2. 'Democratic consolidation', paper given to the Human Sciences Research Council, South Africa, 10 March 1997.

Bibliography

A Local Observer (1988) 'The Rigged 1980 Uganda General Elections', in Karugire, S. R. (ed.) *The Roots of Instability in Uganda*, New Vision Printing, Kampala, pp.84-100.

ACR, *Africa Contemporary Record* (various years). Edited by Colin Legum, Africana Publishing House, New York and London.

Africa Watch (1990) *Where Silence Rules: The Suppression of Dissent in Malawi*.

Africa Watch (1991) *Kenya: Taking Liberties*, Human Rights Watch, London.

Africa Watch (1993) *Divide and Rule: State Sponsored Ethnic Violence in Kenya*, Human Rights Watch, London.

Aitchison, J. (1989) 'The Civil War in Natal', *South African Review*, Ravan Press, Johannesburg, pp.457-73.

Ajulu, R. (1992) 'Kenya: The Road to Democracy', *Review of African Political Economy*, 53, pp.79-87.

Ajulu, R. (1993) 'The 1992 Kenya General Elections: A Preliminary Survey', *Review of African Political Economy*, 56, pp.98-102.

Ajulu, R. (1995) 'An Historical Background to Lesotho's Election of 1993', in Southall and Petlane (eds) pp.3-17.

Ajulu, R. and Fox, R. (1995) 'The Transition to Multi-partyism in Kenya: the December 1992 Presidential, Parliamentary and Municipal Elections', Centre for Democratisation Studies, Working Paper, Department of Politics, Leeds University.

Ake, C. (1985) 'The Nigerian State: Antinomies of a Periphery Formation', in Ake C. (ed.) *Political Economy of Nigeria*, Longmans, New York.

Ake, C. (1995) 'The Democratisation of Disempowerment in Africa', in Hippler (ed.) pp.70-89.

Akinola, A. (1989) 'Manufacturing the Two-party System in Nigeria', *The Journal of Modern African Studies*, 27, 1, pp.109-24.

Allen, C. (1992) 'Restructuring An Authoritarian State: Democratic Renewal in Benin', *Review of African Political Economy*, 54, pp.43-58.

Allen, C. (1995) 'Understanding African Politics', *Review of African Political Economy*, 65, pp.301-20.

Allen, C. (1997) 'Who Needs Civil Society?', *Review of African Political Economy*, 73, pp.329-37.

Allen, C., Baylies, C. and Szeftel, M. (1992) 'Surviving Democracy?', *Review of African Political Economy*, 54, pp.3-10.

Amnesty International (1987) *Kenya: Torture, Political Detention and Unfair Trial*, London.

Amnesty International (1992) *Malawi: Prison conditions, cruel punishment and detention without trial*, 6 March, London.

Amnesty International (1993) *Malawi: Preserving the one-party state - human rights violations and the referendum*, 18 May, London.

Anglin, D. (1994) 'International Monitoring of the South African Elections', paper presented to the Annual Meeting of the African Studies Association, Toronto, November, pp. 1-34.

Anyang 'Nyong'o, P. (1989) 'State and Society in Kenya: The Disintegration of the Nationalist Coalition and the Rise of Presidential Authoritarianism', *African Affairs*, 88, pp.241-66.

Anyang 'Nyong'o, P. (1992) 'Democratization Processes in Africa', *Review of African Political Economy*, 54, pp. 97-102.

Article 19, International Centre Against Censorship (1993) 'The Referendum in Malawi: Free Expression Denied', *Censorship News*, 22 April.

Article 19 (1994a) 'Freedom of Expression in Malawi: More Change Needed', *Censorship News*, 32, 3 February.

Article 19 (1994b) 'Malawi's Elections: Media Monitoring, Freedom of Expression and Intimidation', *Censorship News*, 34, 29 April.

Article 19 (1994c) 'Freedom of Expression in Malawi: The Elections and the New Media Reform', *Censorship News*, 35, 21 July.

Atieno-Odhiambo, E. (1993) 'The Agrarian Question, Ethnicity and Politics in Kenya, 1955 - 1993', Conference on Ethnicity, Identity, and Nationalism in South Africa, Rhodes University.

Austin, D. (1970) *Politics in Ghana 1946-1960*, Oxford University Press, Oxford.

Awolowo, O. (1968) *The People's Republic*, Oxford University Press, Ibadan.

Awolowo, O. (1970) *The Strategy and Tactics of the People's Republic of Nigeria*, Macmillan Press, London and Basingstoke.

Azikiwe, N. (1961) *Zik: A selection from the speeches of Nnamdi Azikiwe*, Cambridge University Press, London.

Azikiwe, N. (1974) *Democracy with Military Vigilance*, Africa Book Co., Nsukka.

Banks, L. and Southall, R. (1996) 'Traditional Leaders in South Africa's New Democracy', *Journal of Legal Pluralism and Unofficial Law*, 37/38, pp.407-29.

Bardill, J. and Cobbe, J. (1985) *Lesotho: Dilemmas of Dependence in Southern Africa*, Westview Press, Boulder, Colorado.

Barkan, J.D. (1993) 'Kenya: Lessons from A Flawed Election', *Journal of Democracy*, 4, 3, pp.87-94.

Bates, R. H. and Collier, P. (1993) 'The Politics and Economics of Policy Reform in Zambia', in Bates, R.H. and Krueger, A.O. (eds) *Political and Economic Interactions in Economic Policy Reform: Evidence from Eight Countries*, Blackwell, Cambridge, pp.387-443.

Bavu, I. K. (1989) 'Policy Issues on the Democraticness of One-Party Elections in Tanzania - An Empirical Analysis', in Meyns, P. and Nabudere, D.W. (eds)

Democracy and the One-Party-State in Africa, Institut fur Afrika-Kunde, Hamburg, pp.91-110.

Bayart, J-F. (1993) *The State in Africa: The Politics of the Belly*, Longmans, London.

Baylies, C. (1995) '"Political Conditionality" and Democratisation', *Review of African Political Economy*, 65, pp.321-37.

Baylies, C. and Szeftel, M. (1992) 'The Fall and Rise of Multi-party Politics in Zambia', *Review of African Political Economy*, 54, pp.75-91.

Baylies, C. and Szeftel, M. (1997) 'The 1996 Zambian Elections: Still Awaiting Democratic Consolidation', *Review of African Political Economy*, 71, pp.113-28.

Beckett, P.A. (1985) 'Elections and Democracy in Nigeria', in Hayward, F.M. (ed.) *Elections in Independent Africa*, Westview Press, Boulder, Colorado.

Beetham, D. (1994) 'Conditions for Democratic Consolidation', *Review of African Political Economy*, 60, pp.157-72.

Bennett, G. and Rosberg, C.G. (1961) *The Kenyatta Election: Kenya 1960-61*, Oxford University Press, Oxford.

Bjornlund, E., Bratton, M. and Gibson, C. (1992) 'Observing Multiparty Elections in Africa: Lessons from Zambia', *African Affairs*, 91, pp.405-31.

Boahen, A. (1995) 'A Note on the Ghanaian Elections', *African Affairs*, 94, pp. 277-80.

Bratton, M. and van de Walle, N. (1997) *Democratic Experiments in Africa: Regime Transitions in Comparative Perspective*, Cambridge University Press, Cambridge.

Bromley, S. (1995) 'Making Sense of Structural Adjustment', *Review of African Political Economy*, 65, pp.339-48.

Bush, R. and Szeftel, M. (1994) 'Commentary: States, Markets and Africa's Crisis', *Review of African Political Economy*, 60, pp.147-56.

Callaghy, T. M. (1990) 'Lost Between State and Market: the Politics of Economic Adjustment in Ghana, Zambia and Nigeria', in Nelson, J. (ed.) *Economic Crisis and Policy Choice: the Politics of Adjustment in the Third World*, Princeton University Press, Princeton, pp.257-319.

Callaghy, T. M. (1994) 'Africa: Back to the Future?', *Journal of Democracy*, 5, 4, pp.133-45.

Cammack, P. (1997) *Capitalism and Democracy in the Third World: The Doctrine of Political Development*, Leicester University Press, London.

Campbell, B. and Parfitt, T. (1995) 'Virtual Reality: Whose Adjustment?', *Review of African Political Economy*, 63, pp.3-8.

Campbell, I. (1994) 'Nigeria's Failed Transition: The 1993 Presidential Election', *Journal of Contemporary African Studies*, 12, 4, pp.179-99.

Chazan, N. (1979) 'African Voters at the Polls: A Re-examination of the Role of Elections in African Politics', *The Journal of Commonwealth and Comparative Politics*, 17, 1, pp.136-58.

Cheche Kenya (1982) *(In)dependent Kenya*, Zed Press, London.

Chikulo, B.C. (1981) 'Elections in a One-Party Participatory Democracy' in Turok, B. (ed.) *Development in Zambia*, Zed Press, London, pp.201-13.

Chiluba, F. J. T. (1995) *Democracy, the Challenge of Change*, Lusaka, Multimedia Publications.

Cliffe, L. (ed.) (1967) *One Party Democracy: the 1965 Tanzanian General Elections*, East African Publishing House, Nairobi.

Cliffe, L., Bush, R., Lindsay, J., Mokopakgosi, B., Pankhurst, D. and Tsie, B. (1994) *The Transition to Independence in Namibia*, Lynne Rienner Publishers, Boulder and London.

Coleman, J. (1958) *Nigeria: Background to Nationalism*, University of California Press.

Cowen, M. (1981) 'Commodity Production in Kenya's Central Province', in Heyer, J. (ed.) *Rural Development in Tropical Africa*, London, pp.121-42.

Cowen, M. (1982) 'The British State and Agrarian Accumulation in Kenya', in Fransman, M. (ed.) *Industry and Accumulation in Africa*, London, pp.142-69.

Cowen, M. K. and Kinyanjui, K. (1977) 'Some Problems of Class Formation in Kenya', Institute of Development Studies, University of Nairobi.

Cullen, T. (1994) *Malawi: A Turning Point*, The Pentland Press, Edinburgh.

Daniel, J. (1995) '"You United Nations have delivered us": Monitoring the 1993 Election in Lesotho', in Southall and Petlane (eds), pp.93-104.

Daniel, J. and Vilane, J. (1985) 'The Crisis of Political Legitimacy in Swaziland', *Review of African Political Economy*, 35, pp.54-67.

Davies, R. and O'Meara, D. (1985) 'Total Strategy in Southern Africa: An Analysis of South Africa's Regional Policy since 1978', *Journal of Southern African Studies*, 11, 2, pp.183-211.

Diamond, L. (1992) 'Economic Development and Democracy Reconsidered', *American Behavioral Scientist*, 35, pp.450-99.

Diamond, L. (1996) 'Is the Third Wave Over?', *Journal of Democracy*, 7, 3, pp.20-37.

Diamond, L. (1996a) 'Toward Democratic Consolidation', in Diamond and Plattner (eds), pp.227-40.

Diamond, L. and Plattner M.F. (eds) (1996) *The Global Resurgence of Democracy*, Johns Hopkins University Press, Baltimore and London.

Diouf, M. (1992) 'State Formation and Legitimation Crisis in Senegal', *Review of African Political Economy*, 54, pp. 116-25.

Dollie, N. (ed.) (1989) *A Political Review of Namibia - Nationalism in Namibia*, Windhoek, private publication.

Dos Santos, T. (1970) 'The Structure of Dependence', in Wilber, C.K. (ed) (1973) *The Political Economy of Development and Underdevelopment*, Random House, New York, pp.109-123.

Dudley, B.J. (1966) 'Federalism and the Balance of Power in Nigeria', *Journal of Commonwealth and Comparative Politics*, 4, 1966, pp.16-29.

Dudley, B.J. (1973) *Instability and Political Order: Politics and Crisis in Nigeria*, University Press, Ibadan.

Economist Intelligence Unit (EIU) (1989) *Country Report: Nigeria*, 3rd Quarter.

EIU (1990) *Country Report: Nigeria*, 1st Quarter.

EIU (1991) *Country Report: Nigeria*, 4th Quarter.

Eldridge, M. and Seekings, J. (1996) 'Mandela's Lost Province: The African National Congress and the Western Cape Electorate in the 1994 South African Elections', *Journal of Southern African Studies*, 22, 4, pp.517-40.

Epelle, S. (ed.) (1964) *Nigeria Speaks: Speeches of Alhaji Tafawa Balewa*, Longmans, London.

Falola, T. and Ihonvbere, J. (1985) *The Rise and Fall of Nigeria's Second Republic 1979-84*, Zed Books, London.

Forrest, T. (1986) 'The Political Economy of Civil Rule and the Economic Crisis in Nigeria (1979-84)', *Review of African Political Economy*, 35, pp.4-26.

Fox, R. (1991) *Ethnic Distribution in Colonial and Post-colonial Kenya*, Human Sciences Research Council, Pretoria.

Fox, R. (1995a) 'Kenya: The Politics of Place', in T. Unwin (ed.) *Atlas of World Development*, Institute of British Geographers, London.

Friedman, S. (1993) *The Long Journey: South Africa's Quest for a Negotiated Settlement*, Ravan Press, Johannesburg.

Friedman, S. and Atkinson, D. (eds) (1994) *The Small Miracle: South Africa's Negotiated Settlement*, Ravan Press, Johannesburg.

Fukuyama, F. (1989) 'The End of History', *The National Interest*, 16, pp.3-18.

Furedi, F. (1974) 'The Social Composition of the Mau Mau Movements in the White Highlands', *The Journal of Peasant Studies*, XIV, 2, pp.486-505.

Garber, L. (1990) 'Guidelines for International Election Observing', International Human Rights Law Group, Washington DC.

Geisler, G. (1993) 'Fair? What has fairness got to do with it? Vagaries of Election Observations and Democratic Standards', *The Journal of Modern African Studies*, 31, 4, pp. 613-37.

Geisler, G. (1994) 'Observing the Elation of Liberation: Being a UN Observer in Lebowa, Northern Transvaal' in Elling N. Tjonneland (ed.) *South Africa's 1994 Election*, Norwegian Institute of Human Rights, Oslo, pp.69-74.

Gertzel, C.J., Goldsmith, M. and Rothchild, D. (1964) *Government and Politics in Kenya*, East African Publishing House, Nairobi.

Gibbon, P., Bangura, Y. and Ofstad, A. (1992) (eds) *Authoritarianism, Democracy and Adjustment*, Uppsala, Scandinavian Institute of African Studies.

Goldsworthy, D. (1982) *Tom Mboya: The Man Kenya Wanted to Forget*, Heinemann, Nairobi.

Good, K. (1995) 'Authoritarian Liberalism and Democracy: Botswana and its Neighbours', *Journal of Contemporary African Studies*, 14, 1, pp.29-52.

Green, R., Kiljunen, K. and Kiljunen, M-L. (1981) *Namibia: The Last Colony*, Longman, Harlow.

Gyimah-Boadi, E. (1996) 'Civil Society in Africa', *Journal of Democracy*, 7, 2, pp.118-32.

Ham, M. (1992) 'Defying the Dictator', *Africa Report*, May-June, 21-24.

Hamalengwa, M. (1992) *Class Struggles in Zambia 1889-1989 and the Fall of Kenneth Kaunda 1990-1991*, University Press of America, Lanham, Md.

Harris, B. (1967) 'The Electoral System', in Cliffe, L. (ed.) *One Party Democracy: The 1965 Tanzania General Elections*, East African Publishing House, Nairobi, pp. 21-52.

Hawkins, J. J. (1991) 'Understanding the Failure of IMF Reform: the Zambian Case', *World Development*, 19, 7, pp.839-49.

Hayward, F. (ed.) (1987) *Elections in Independent Africa*, Westview Press, Boulder and London.

Hayward, F.M. and Kandeh, J.D. (1987) 'Perspectives on Twenty-Five Years of Elections in Sierra Leone', in Hayward F.M. (ed.) pp.25-59.

Healey, J. and Robinson, M. (1992) *Democracy, Governance and Economic Policy: Sub-Saharan Africa in Comparative Perspective*, London, Overseas Development Institute.

Hippler, J. (ed.) (1995) *The Democratisation of Disempowerment: The Problem of Democracy in the Third World*, Pluto Press, London.

Horowitz, D. (1993) 'Democracy in Divided Societies', *Journal of Democracy*, 4, 4, pp.13-38.

Hyden, G. and Leys, C. (1972) 'Elections and Politics in single-party systems: the case of Kenya and Tanzania', *British Journal of Political Science*, 2, 4, pp.389-420.

Huntington, S.P. (1996) 'Democracy's Third Wave', in Diamond and Plattner (eds) pp.3-25.

Imam, A. (1992) 'Democratization Processes in Africa: Problems and Prospects', *Review of African Political Economy*, 54, pp. 102-105.

International Forum for Democratic Studies (1995) 'Nigeria's Political Crisis: Which way forward?', Conference Report.

Iroh, E. (1993) 'The best way forward', *Newswatch*, 18 October.

James, W. and Caliguire, D. (1996) 'Renewing Civil Society', *Journal of Democracy*, 7, 1, pp. 56-66.

Jaster, R. (1990) *The 1988 Peace Accords and the Future of South-western Africa*, Adelphi Papers 253, International Institute for Strategic Studies, London.

Johnson, R.W. and Schlemmer, L. (eds) (1996) *Launching Democracy in South Africa: The First Open Election, April 1994*, Yale University Press, New Haven.

Jowitt, K. (1996) 'The New World Disorder', in Diamond and Plattner (eds) pp. 26-35.

Kaggia, B. (1975) *Roots of Freedom, 1921-1963*, East African Publishing House, Nairobi.

Kamwambe, N. (1991) *Frederick Chiluba: Is He Riding a Tide to Fortune?*, Ngubola Kamwambe and Shelley Printers, Lusaka.

Kaplinsky, R. (1980) 'Capitalist Accumulation in the Periphery - The Kenyan Case Re-examined', *Review of African Political Economy*, 17, pp.83-105.

Kasfir, N. (1991) 'The Ugandan elections of 1989: Power, Populism and Democratisation', in Hansen, H.B. and Twaddle, M. (eds) *Changing Uganda*, James Currey, London, pp.247-78.

Khaketla, B.M. (1971) *Lesotho 1970: An African Coup Under the Microscope*, C. Hurst & Co, London.

Kintu-Nyago, C. (1996) *Realising Good Governance in Uganda*, MA Thesis, Rhodes University, Grahamstown (unpublished).

Kitching, G. (1980) *Class and Economic Change in Kenya: the making of an African Petty-Bourgeoisie*, Yale University Press, New Haven.

Leakey, L.S.B. (1954) *Defeating Mau Mau*, Methuen, London.

Leeman, B. (1985) *Lesotho and the Struggle for Azania*, Vols. 1 and 2, University of Azania, PAC Education Office, London.

Leftwich, A. (1996) 'On the primacy of politics in development' in A. Leftwich (ed.) *Democracy and Development*, Polity, London, pp.3-24.

Lemon, A. (1987) *Apartheid in Transition*, Gower, London.

LeVine, V.T. (1993) 'Administrative corruption and democratization in Africa', *Corruption and Reform*, 7, 3, pp. 271-8.

Lewis, Sir A. (1965) *Politics in West Africa*, Oxford University Press, London.

Leys, C. (1975) *Underdevelopment in Kenya: The Political Economy of Neo-Colonialism*, Heinemann Educational Books, London.

Leys, C. (1978) 'Capital Accumulation, Class Formation, and Dependency: The Significance of the Kenyan Case', *The Socialist Register*, Merlin Press, London, pp.241-66.

Leys, C. (1994) 'Confronting the African Tragedy', *New Left Review*, 204, pp.33-47.

Leys, C. and Saul, J. (eds) (1995) *Namibia's Liberation Struggle: the Two-edged Sword*, James Currey, London.

Lijphart, A. (1984) *Democracies*, Yale University Press, New Haven.

Lindeke, W., Wanzala, W. and Tonchi, V. (1992) 'Namibia's Election Revisited', *Politikon*, 18, 2, pp.121-37.

Lodge, T. (1994) 'SA '94: Election of a Special Kind', *Southern African Review of Books*, 6, 2, pp.3-5.

Lodge, T. (1995) 'The South African General Election, April 1994: Results, Analysis and Implications', *African Affairs*, 94, pp.471-500.

Lonsdale, J. (1964) 'The Politics of Conquest: The British in Western Kenya', *The Historical Journal*, XX, 4.

Loxley, J. and Seddon, D. (1994) 'Stranglehold on Africa', *Review of African Political Economy*, 62, pp.485-93.

Macartney, W.J.A. (1973) 'The Lesotho General Election of 1970', *Government and Opposition*, 8, 4, pp.473-94.

Mackenzie, W.J.M. (1958) *Free Elections: An Elementary Textbook*, George Allen and Unwin, London.

Mackenzie, W.J.M. and Robinson, K. (eds) (1960) *Five Elections in Africa*, Clarendon Press, Oxford.

Mackintosh, J.P. et al. (1966) *Nigerian Government and Politics*, Allen and Unwin, London.

Madunagu, E. (1992) 'Humiliating Would-be Successor', *The Guardian* (Lagos), 12 November.

Maja-Pearse, A. (1987) *In My Father's Country: A Nigerian Journey*, Heinemann, London.

Maloka, T. (1996) 'Populism and the Politics of Chieftaincy and Nation-Building in the New South Africa', *Journal of Contemporary African Studies*, 14, 2, pp.173-96.

Mamdani, M. (1996) *Citizen and Subject: Contemporary Africa and the Legacy of Late Colonialism*, James Currey, London.

Mandela, N. (1994) *Long Walk to Freedom*, Little, Brown, London.

Mare, G. (1989) 'Inkatha and regional control: policing liberation politics', *Review of African Political Economy*, 45/46, pp.179-89.

Matlosa, K. (1995) 'The Military after the Election: Confronting the New Democracy', in Southall and Petlane (eds), pp.118-39.

Mbikusita-Lewanika, A. (1990) *Milk in a Basket: The Political-Economic Malaise in Zambia*, Zambia Research Foundation, Lusaka.

Mboya, T. (1963) *Freedom and After*, Andre Deutsch, London.

Meredith, M. (1994) *South Africa's New Era: The 1994 Election*, Mandarin, London.

Mhone, G. (1992) 'The Political Economy of Malawi: An Overview', in Mhone, G. (ed.) *Malawi at the Crossroads: The Post-Colonial Political Economy*, SAPES Books, Harare, pp.1-33.

Moll, T. (1991) 'Did the Apartheid Economy Fail?', *Journal of Southern African Studies*, 17, 2, pp.271-91.

Moore, M. (1993) 'The Emergence of the Good Governance Agenda: Some Milestones', *IDS Bulletin*, 24, 1.

Moyo, J. (1992) *Voting for Democracy: Electoral Politics in Zimbabwe*, University of Zimbabwe Press, Harare.

Munslow, B. and Ekoko, F. E. (1995) 'Is Democracy Necessary for Sustainable Development?', *Democratization*, 2, 2, pp.158-78.

Murray-Brown, J. (1972) *Kenyatta*, George Allen and Unwin, London.

Mutibwa, P. (1992) *Uganda since Independence: A Story of Unfulfilled Hopes*, Hurst and Company, London.

Mwanakatwe, J. (1994) *End of Kaunda Era*, Multimedia Publications, Lusaka.

Ngunyi, M. (1993) 'Interpreting Political Liberalism in Kenya', Scandinavian Institute of African Studies and Centre for Development Research, Copenhagen.

Njonjo, A. L. (1977) *The Africanization of the 'White Highlands': A Study of Agrarian Class Struggles in Kenya, 1950-1975*, PhD thesis, Princeton University.

Nnoli, O. (1981) 'A Short History of Nigerian Underdevelopment', in Nnoli, O. (ed.) *Path to Nigerian Development*, Codesria, Dakar.

Nwabueze, B.O. (1974) *Presidentialism in Commonwealth Africa*, C. Hurst & Company, London.

O'Donnell, G. (1996) 'Do Economists Know Best?', in Diamond and Plattner (eds) pp. 336-41.

Odinga, O. (1966) *Not Yet Uhuru*, Heinemann, Nairobi.

Odugbemi, S. (1993) 'A Revolution Postponed?', *The African Guardian*, Lagos, 19 July.

Okeke, O. (1993) *Hausa-Fulani Hegemony: The Dominance of the Muslim North in Contemporary Nigerian Politics*, Acena Publishers, Enugu.

Ollawa, P. (1979) *Participatory Democracy in Zambia: The Political Economy of National Development*, Arthur H. Stockwell, Ilfracombe.

Onimode, B. (1981) 'Imperialism and Nigerian development' in Nnoli, O. (ed.) *Path to Nigerian Development*, Codesria, Dakar, pp.76-93.

Oquaye, M. (1995) 'The Ghanaian Elections of 1992 - A Dissenting View', *African Affairs*, 94, pp.259-75.

Orkin, M. (1995) 'Building Democracy in the New South Africa: Civil Society, Citizenship and Political Ideology', *Review of African Political Economy*, 22, pp.525-37.

Osoba, S. (1977) 'The Nigerian Power Elite, 1952-65', in Gutkind, P. and Waterman, P. (eds) *African Social Studies: A Radical Reader*, Heinemann, London.

Osoba, S. (1978) 'The Deepening Crisis of the Nigerian National Bourgeoisie', *Review of African Political Economy*, 13, pp.63-77.

Othman, S. (1989) 'Nigeria: Power for Profit - Class, Corporatism and Factionalism in the Military', in Cruise O'Brien, D. (ed.) *Contemporary West African States*, Cambridge, pp.113-44.

Oyediran, O. and Agbaje, A. (1991) 'Two-partyism and the Democratic Transition in Nigeria', *The Journal of Modern African Studies*, 29, 2, pp.213-35.

Oyovbaire, S.E. (1983) 'Structural Change and Political Process in Nigeria', *African Affairs*, 82, 326, pp.14-15.

Pankhurst, D. (1995) 'Towards Reconciliation of the Land Issue in Namibia: Identifying the Possible, Assessing the Probable', *Development and Change*, 26, 3, pp.551-85.

Parson, J. (1984) *Botswana: Liberal Democracy and the Labour Reserve in Southern Africa*, Westview Press, Boulder, Colorado.

Parson, J. (1986) *The 1984 Botswana General Elections and Results: A Macro-Analysis*, Mimeo, unpublished.

Plattner, M.F. (1996) 'The Democratic Moment', in Diamond and Plattner (eds) pp.36-48.

Posner, D. N. (1995) 'Malawi's New Dawn', *Journal of Democracy*, 6, 1, pp.131-45.

Post, K.W.J. and Vickers, M. (1973) *Structure and Conflict in Nigeria 1960-66*, Heinemann, London.

Potgieter, P.J.J.S. (1991) 'The Resolution 435 Election in Namibia', *Politikon*, 18, 2, pp.26-48.

Pryor, F. L. (1990) *Malawi and Madagascar: The Political Economy of Poverty, Equity and Growth*, World Bank and Oxford University Press, Oxford.

Przeworski, A., Alvarez, M., Cheibub, J. and Limongi, L. (1996) 'What Makes Democracies Endure?', *Journal of Democracy*, 7, 1, pp.39-55.

Quinlan, T. (1995) 'Sentiments of Unity, Sentiments of Marginality: Election Politics in the Khubelu Constituency, Mokhotlong District', in Southall and Petlane (eds) pp.78-92.

Reynolds, A. (1993) *Voting for a New South Africa*, Maskew Miller Longman, Cape Town.

Reynolds, A. (ed.) (1994) *Election '94 South Africa: the Campaigns, Results and Future Prospects*, David Philip, Cape Town.

Reynolds, A. (1995) 'Constitutional Engineering in Southern Africa', *Journal of Democracy*, 6, 1, pp.88-99.

Rueschemeyer, D., Stephens, E.H. and Stephens, J.D. (1992) *Capitalist Development and Democracy*, London, Polity.

Rwelamira, M. and Abiola, D. (1993) 'International Monitoring of Free and Fair Elections', in Steytler et al., *Free and Fair Elections*, Juta and Co, Cape Town, pp.209-39.

Sekatle, P. (1994) 'King or Country: The Lesotho Crisis of August 1994', *Indicator SA*, 12, 1, pp.67-72.

Sekatle, P. (1995) 'Disputing Electoral Legitimacy: The BNP's Challenge to the Result', in Southall and Petlane (eds) pp.105-18.

Shafer, D. M. (1990) 'Sectors, States, and Social Forces: Korea and Zambia Confront Economic Restructuring', *Comparative Politics*, 22, 2, pp.127-50.

Shields, T. (1988) 'The Queuing Controversy', *Africa Report*, May, pp.47-9.

Sidaway, J. and Simon, D. (1993) 'Geopolitical Transition and State Formation: the Changing Political Geographies of Angola, Mozambique and Namibia', *Journal of Southern African Studies*, 19, 1, 1993, pp.6-28.

Simon, D. (1995) 'Namibia's First Post-Independence Election', *Review of African Political Economy*, 63, pp.107-14.

Sklar, R.L. (1963) *Nigerian Political Parties*, Princeton University Press, Princeton, 1963.

Sklar, R. L. (1965) 'Contradictions in the Nigerian political system', *The Journal of Modern African Studies*, 3, 2, pp.201-14.

Sorrenson, M.P.K. (1967) *Land Reform in the Kikuyu Country*, Oxford University Press, Nairobi.

Southall, R. (1984) 'Trade Unions and the Internal Working Class in Lesotho', *South African Labour Bulletin*, 10, 3, pp.85-113.

Southall, R. (1991) 'The Contradictory State! Comments on the Proposals of the National Party for a New Constitution', *Monitor*, October, pp.90-92.

Southall, R. (1994) 'The South African Election in Comparative African Perspective', *Africa Insight*, 24, 2, pp.86-98.

Southall, R. (1994) 'The South African Elections of 1994: the Remaking of a Dominant-Party State', *Journal of Modern African Studies*, 32, 4, pp.629-55.

Southall, R. (1995a) 'Lesotho's Transition and the 1993 Election', in Southall, R. and Petlane, T. (eds) pp.18-44.

Southall, R. (1995b) 'The Candidates in the 1993 Election', in Southall, R. and Petlane, T. (eds) pp.58-77.

Southall, R. (1996) 'Regionalisation and Differentiation in South Africa: Some Policy Implications for Canadian Aid', in Swatuk, L. and Black, D. (eds) *Canada and South Africa after Apartheid: Foreign Aid and Civil Society*, Centre for Foreign Policy Studies, Dalhousie University, Halifax, pp.61-84.

Southall, R. and Petlane, T. (eds) (1995) *Democratisation and Demilitarisation in Lesotho: the General Election of 1993 and Its Aftermath*, Africa Institute, Pretoria.

Spencer, J. (1985) *The Kenya African Union*, Routledge and Kegan Paul, London.

Stepan, A. and Skach, C. (1993) 'Constitutional Frameworks and Democratic Consolidation: Parliamentarianism versus Presidentialism', *World Politics*, 46, 1, pp.2-22.

Swainson, N. (1980) *The Development of Corporate Capital in Kenya*, Heinemann, Nairobi.

SWAPO (1981) *To Be Born a Nation: The Liberation Struggle for Namibia*, Zed Press, London.

Szeftel, M. (1982) 'Corruption and the Spoils System in Zambia', in M. Clarke (ed.) *Corruption: Causes, Consequences, Control*, London, Pinter.

Szeftel, M. (1987) 'The Crisis in the Third World', in Bush, R. et al. (eds) *The World Order*, London, Polity, pp.87-140.

Szeftel, M. (1991) 'Manoeuvres of War in South Africa', *Review of African Political Economy*, 51, pp.63-76.

Szeftel, M. (1994a) 'Ethnicity and Democratisation in South Africa', *Review of African Political Economy*, 60, pp.185-99.

Szeftel, M. (1994b) ' "Negotiated elections" in South Africa, 1994', *Review of African Political Economy*, 61, pp.457-70.

Takaya, B.J. and Toyden, S.G. (eds) (1987) *The Kaduna Mafia: A Study of the Rise, Development and Consolidation of a Nigerian Power Elite*, Jos University Press, Jos.

Tangri, R. (1993) 'Foreign Business and Political Unrest in Lesotho', *African Affairs*, 92, pp.223-38.

Tignor, R.L. (1976) *The Colonial Transformation of Kenya: The Kamba, Kikuyu and Masai from 1900 to 1939*, Princeton University Press, New Jersey.

UNICEF (1995) *The State of the World's Children*, Oxford University Press, Oxford.

UNIN, United Nations Institute for Namibia (1986) *Namibia: Perspectives for National Reconstruction and Development*, UN Institute for Namibia, Lusaka.

Van Donge, J.K. (1995) 'Kamuzu's Legacy: The Democratization of Malawi', *African Affairs*, 94, pp.227-57.

Williams, G. (ed.) (1976) *Nigeria: Economy and Society*, Zed Books, London.

Wood, B. (1992) 'Preventing the Vacuum: Determinants of the Namibian Settlement',

Journal of Southern African Studies, 17,4, pp.742-69.

Woods, T. (1992) 'The High Costs of Obstinacy: Banda Hangs On', *South African Report*, November 1.

Young, C. (1996) 'Africa: an Interim Balance Sheet', *Journal of Democracy*, 7, 3, pp.53-68.

Zolberg, A.E. (1966) *Creating Political Order: The Party States of West Africa*, Rand McNally, Chicago.

Index